THE POODLE

POPULAR DOGS' BREED SERIES

THE
POODLE

CLARA BOWRING
and
ALIDA MONRO

Revised by
Shirley Walne

POPULAR DOGS
London

Popular Dogs Publishing Co Ltd
3 Fitzroy Square, London W I P 6JD

An imprint of the Hutchinson Publishing Group

Hutchinson Group (Australia) Pty Ltd
30–32 Cremorne Street, Richmond South, Victoria 3121
PO Box 151, Broadway, New South Wales 2007

Hutchinson Group (NZ) Ltd
32–34 View Road, PO Box 40–086, Glenfield, Auckland 10

Hutchinson Group (SA) (Pty) Ltd
PO Box 337, Bergvlei 2012, South Africa

First published (as *The Popular Poodle*) 1953
Second edition 1955
Third edition 1957
Fourth edition, revised 1958
Fifth edition, revised 1960
Sixth edition, revised 1962
Seventh edition 1962
Eighth edition, revised (as *The Poodle*) 1965
Ninth edition, revised 1968
Tenth edition, revised 1973
Eleventh edition, revised 1976
Twelfth edition, revised 1980

Set in Monotype Baskerville

Printed in Great Britain by The Anchor Press Ltd
and bound by Wm Brendon & Son Ltd
both of Tiptree, Essex

ISBN 0 09 140440 1

PUBLISHERS' NOTE

Chapters I and III to IX, and Chapter XVI are by Clara Bowring. Introduction, Chapter II and Chapters X to XV and Chapter XVII are by Alida Monro. Chapter XVIII has been added to the twelfth edition by Shirley Walne.

CONTENTS

ILLUSTRATIONS

In the Text

*The line illustrations were designed by Alida Monro and
executed by Anne Hudson*

1 July, 1973

(Reproduced by permission of the Kennel Club, 1–4 Clarges Street, London, W1Y 8AB)

POODLE (STANDARD)

CHARACTERISTICS AND GENERAL APPEARANCE.—That of a very active, intelligent, well balanced and elegant looking dog with good temperament, carrying himself very proudly.

Gait.—Sound, free movement and light gait are essential.

Head and Skull.—Long and fine with slight peak at the back. The skull not broad and with a moderate stop. Foreface strong and well chiselled, not falling away under the eyes; bones and muscle flat. Lips tight fitting. Chin well defined, but not protruding. The whole head must be in proportion to the size of the dog.

Eyes.—Almond shaped, dark, not set too close together, full of fire and intelligence.

Ears.—The leather long and wide, low set on, hanging close to the face.

Mouth.—Teeth—white, strong, even, with scissor bite. A full set of 42 teeth is desirable.

Neck.—Well proportioned, of good length and strong to admit of the head being carried high and with dignity. Skin fitting tightly at the throat.

Forequarters.—Shoulders—strong and muscular, sloping well to the back, legs set straight from the shoulders, well muscled.

Body.—Chest—deep and moderately wide. Ribs—well sprung and rounded. Back—short, strong, slightly hollowed, loins broad and muscular.

Hindquarters.—Thighs well developed and muscular, well bent stifles, well let down hocks, hind legs turning neither in nor out.

Feet.—Pasterns strong, tight feet proportionately small, oval in shape, turning neither in nor out, toes arched, pads thick and hard, well cushioned.

Tail.—Set on rather high, well carried at a slight angle away from the body, never curled or carried over the back, thick at the root.

Coat.—Very profuse and dense of good harsh texture without knots or tangles. All short hair close, thick and curly. It is strongly recommended that the traditional lion clip be adhered to.

Colour.—All solid colours. White and cream poodles to have black

13

nose, lips and eyerims, black toenails desirable, brown poodles to have dark amber eyes, dark liver nose, lips, eyerims and toenails. Apricot poodles to have dark eyes with black points or deep amber eyes with liver points. Black, silver and blue poodles to have black nose, lips, eyerims and toenails. Cream, apricot, brown, silver and blue poodles may show varying shades of the same colour up to 18 months. Clear colours preferred.

Size.—15 inches and over.

Faults.—Heavy build, clumsiness, long back, snipy in foreface, light or round or prominent eyes, lippiness, bad carriage, heavy gait, coarse head, over or under-shot or pincer mouth, flesh coloured nose, coarse legs and feet, long flat toes, open soft coats with no curl, parti-colours—white markings on black or coloured poodles, lemon or other markings on white poodles, vicious temperament.

Note.—Male animals should have two apparently normal testicles fully descended into the scrotum.

POODLE (MINIATURE)

The Poodle (Miniature) should be in every respect a replica, in miniature, of the Poodle (Standard). Height at shoulder should be under 15 inches but not under 11 inches.

POODLE (TOY)

The standard of the Poodle (Toy) is the same as that of the Poodle (Standard) and Poodle (Miniature) except that the height at shoulder should be under 11 inches.

(*See also Addendum, page 171*)

INTRODUCTION

by Alida Monro

Dog is the friend of man . . . with what assurance we make this statement! And yet, if we pause to think, we may well ask ourselves: how did he come to forsake his position in the pack to become the guardian of the hearth and property, and companion and well loved and trusted friend? How was the bond established? Did Man observe Dog lurking in the forest, tracking and bringing down his prey, and then decide to break him and bend him to his will? Or did Dog, cunning and clever as he is, observe Man also tracking and killing, and attach himself in the first place for the advantage gained? For the easy meal from Man's unconsidered trifles? Having forsaken his own kind, did he feel the need to belong outside his world and so for ever unite his own interests with Man's? However that came about, through the years he has established himself so well in Man's affections, that today a complete stranger to an individual dog will cheerfully hazard his life to rescue him from mine-shaft, burning house, or drowning. In this century most civilized communities the world over have thousands of people who bind themselves together in diverse societies and clubs to see that he is never ill-treated, and to protect him from those who do not respect the dynasty of breed and would allow the ill-bred cur to dominate his kind.

If we look briefly back through the ages we see him in the dawn of time seeking the warmth of the cave with Man his god, and the comfort of the dead beast's still warm body in the darkness of the caves in which mankind sheltered from icy winter. And again we see him trekking across the desert, herding the cattle as other members of human society fled to the warmth of the Orient. We can see him fanning out across the Continents to far Peru, to the jungles of Brazil, to Africa, to Asia, to the wastes of Australia, characteristically the same, yet different. The astonishing fact is that Man has descended in a common type that can be easily recognized as the same whatever the colour of his skin, and indeed in type, feature and character Men are brothers, but Dog in his journey with mankind across the world, derived as we are told from one single type, has developed such diverse appearances that it is difficult to believe that the hirsute Chow and the hairless Mexican dog stem from the same root. Think of Greyhound and Pekingese, Bulldog and Borzoi, and think again and remember that legend says Dog comes to resemble his companion, Man. By these bare facts we dimly recognize how Man, as is his way, began to interfere and to practise selection by putting certain dogs together to get certain results. He must have discovered, for instance, that one kind of dog always followed him out hunting, and always found the stricken quarry. He must then have found ways to gain that animal's confidence, and eventually to domesticate him and to make him the companion of the home as well as the field. Once having made this discovery the rest was easy, as we well know today.

The Poodle is the dog, *par excellence*, for the discerning owner. In appearance he has come down almost unchanged through the centuries. He appears on statues in Ancient Rome; he can be seen woven into the tapestries of the fifteenth century. He has been, and is, the companion of Kings, Soldiers and Statesmen. He has distinguished himself on the battlefield; he has had statues raised in his honour. He has delighted millions through the ages with his antics in the Circus, where he walks proudly upon the stage in appearance the replica, in miniature, of the King of Beasts. Woodcutters of mediaeval times have reproduced him in their pictures, and in the last century he has graced thousands of homes in the guise of a Lord Chancellor upon the Woolsack, gazing at humanity with all the wisdom and dignity that is inherent in the true Poodle.

To see him in his home, leaping, prancing, feinting, turns the mind at once to the Renaissance, and to the heraldic beasts of ancient coats of arms.

His ability as a sportsman is unsurpassed, as many a keeper can testify. He has beaten the Alsatian in his own field of obedience. He is bold, and he is tender. He is full of the wisdom of the ages, as his expression shows. He partakes of the gaiety of his native France whence he came in the dim past. One Poodle is known to have died on the battlefield. He is courteous to visiting dogs, but he will allow no liberties. He will not fight, but if he is attacked he will defend himself to the death.

He will herd sheep, retrieve game, protect his owner's life and property. He will play the clown, he will grace the Show Ring, he will add gaiety to life with his zest. He will learn any tricks with apparently no effort. He has fire and intelligence in his bearing. He is unique in the Show Ring in that he is the only dog who may have his coat clipped to suit himself, with Kennel Club sanction, whereas his brother canines are forbidden to interfere with their natural endowments except in trifling details. He dances with ease, he leaps gracefully to your arms, he surmounts walls, he tracks, he retrieves, he dies for his country—in fact he does everything but speak. In the words of the late Miss Brunker: "He has but one fault—he cannot live for ever."

Following the death in 1969 of my collaborator and friend of many years, Mrs. Alida Monro, I have endeavoured to keep this book up to date from edition to edition. In this task I have been greatly aided by Miss Shirley Walne, and I am most grate-ful to her for her help.

C.B.

1975

REVISER'S NOTE TO TWELFTH EDITION

by Shirley Walne

FOLLOWING the death of Miss Clara Bowring in 1978 the task of keeping this book up to date has been given to me.

How fortunate today's Poodle breeders are that two such dedicated people took the trouble to research into early Poodles: Miss Clara Bowring and Mrs. Alida Munro, both of whom I had the privilege of knowing. It is to them we owe so much.

Looking and reading through this book, many of today's breeders must smile when they see the photographs, such as Nunsoe Dandy Jim, one of the first of the long-legged white miniatures to be bred, and numerous others who, in their day, did so much for the breed.

When this book was first written we had hardly recovered from World War Two, during which time it was a case of feeding to keep a dog alive with no other thoughts in one's mind, certainly not of the show dog, whereas today every conceivable type of food is prepared for dogs and easily obtainable. It is, therefore, up to the breeder to feed the Poodle to the best of his ability. In this book the diets consist of bare necessities. I am leaving them mostly as they are, as to try and add to them or alter them, in many ways would need a whole new book; so too it would mean a much bigger addition to include all the new equipment one can obtain for the preparation of the show dog as we know him today.

Trimming, like most things, becomes a fashion and alters from time to time, but basically the drawings in this book give one guidance as to where the hair should be removed, although today the mane is left further down the body than it was; so too are the bracelets left longer.

Before the 1950s the traditional trim was adhered to and it would have shocked many a judge had they been presented as they are today, minus the patterns on their quarters etc. All the same I think it would have gladdened the hearts of many of the foregone breeders to see today's Poodles in their splendid coats and being presented as they are. Handling too has changed; one would have been thought very odd not to have steadied the heads and tails of the standards. To have been seen squatting on the ground with a miniature would have been an insult. The judge concentrated on the make and shape of the Poodle rather than the presentation.

Critiques given in the dog papers differ in that words such as "stacked", "packs" etc were never heard of.

How interesting it is to see, by the three photographs the publishers have allowed me to include in this revised edition, the obvious improvement in presentation of today's Poodles. I feel sure the devotees of the early Poodles would have appreciated the dedication of today's breeders in interpreting their original standard, as we hope they intended.

As you will have read elsewhere, The Poodle Club was founded in 1876, so it was in 1976 that the club held its centenary show. The 1970s have seen many changes particularly in new Exhibitors entering into the breed; so too have we lost a number of our great breeders.

It would be quite impossible to include all affixes and winning dogs in this revised edition. I have included a number taken at random; a lot more could be written to bring this edition even more up to date. I have altered as little as possible as, after all, this book is Clara Bowring's and Alida Monro's book, not mine.

1980   S.W.

Chapter I

THE ORIGIN OF THE POODLE

*Au commencement Dieu crea l'homme et le
voyant si faible, il lui donna le chien.*

COSMOPOLITAN as the Poodle is—he is found in all parts of the Continent and even farther afield—there is a good deal of difference of opinion as to the true origin of the breed. That the Poodle is a very ancient breed is well established; indeed, a writer in Le Chenil stated that the Poodle was sculptured in bas-relief as early as the year A.D. 29, but as he gives no details to substantiate this claim it cannot strictly speaking be depended on. Gesner mentioned the Poodle in 1524, and there is also the well-known picture of Tobias by De Vos which shows a Poodle as his companion. A well-trimmed Poodle is also depicted in a series of paintings by Pinturicchio in which Griselda appears with a small Lion-clipped dog.

By the kindness of the Hon. Mrs. Ionides I have been able to go through the valuable collection of paintings, engravings, books and china, all concerned with Poodles, made by herself and her husband, the late Mr. Basil Ionides, over many years. It is a fascinating and unique record of the Poodle for a period of over four hundred years. In many countries it shows the Poodle as the faithful companion and happy friend of those in high places as well as of humbler folk. For the Poodle is a true aristocrat and is at his ease and at home wherever he may be. It is most important to note that in every one of these pictures the Poodle is depicted with the Lion-clip, thus showing that this was always the traditional way of cutting the hair of these dogs. The prevalence of the grotesque Dutch-clip is much to be deplored.

A very old and charming print of 1529 in this collection shows Ceres by the side of a lake, accompanied by a white-clipped Poodle, with the sun ripening the fruit in her basket. In 1636 Stern painted *The Dancing Boy*, a white Poodle. *The Dog Barbers*, a print published by Bretherton in 1771, shows the professional clippers in France, cutting Poodles, whilst several dogs await their turn to be barbered. Another later print of 1819 shows the same scene with two Frenchwomen energetically clipping Poodles with the most enormous scissors on the Pont Neuf in Paris. Kitchingman painted *The Beggar and his Poodle* in 1774. In another particularly happy picture we see a Poodle being guided on his path by a dove which is flying above the dog and is inscribed *Je suis toujours guidé par la fidelité*. In 1777 John Collet published an engraving of an actress at her toilet with a white Lion-clipped Poodle lying at her feet. These latter were all French publications, but we also have Fores, of Piccadilly, publishing a print of a milliner's shop in London, with a very small white Poodle in the foreground. In Germany, Wolf and Son of Munich printed a broadsheet narrating the adventures of a white Poodle named Nero. *Le Debarquement de John Bull et son famille à Boulogne* amusingly shows the arrival of an English family in France where they are welcomed by a very motley collection of dogs, including a very aggressive Poodle. And there is an exceedingly funny print published by Gillray, depicting a lady of fashion putting on her cap, whilst in the background a Poodle is busily employed tearing up her unwound turban. Ulysses is portrayed in a French print with a Poodle. Maison Marbout published a print of a Poodle and a horror-struck family with the caption—*Qui vient d'apprendre qu'il est encore question d'etablir un impot sur chiens.*

Historically, we have Les Hautes Allies, *partant pour la Guerre*, Poland, Italy, Saxe and Mayence, the latter accompanied by a clipped Poodle prancing at his side. The Emperor Napoleon is shown returning from the wars and being greeted by his queen and her Poodle in 1812, whilst in 1811 the Prince Regent, afterwards George IV, sits with a Poodle at his feet, showing that the Poodle had his honoured place at the English Court.

In another print of the same period, Mrs. Fitzherbert is depicted sitting under a tree. Doves fly round her whilst a devoted white Poodle lies by her side. The print, entitled *Bond Street Loungers*, shows in 1820 the Earl of Sefton, the Duke of Devonshire, the Duke of Beaufort and Lord Manners, the last-named leading his favourite Poodle, Byng, in Bond Street. Another print of a Poodle called Sancho is especially interesting. This dog belonged to the Marchioness of Worcester to whom it had been given by her husband. He had found this Poodle exhausted and starving, lying on the grave of his master, a French officer, after the Battle of Salamanca. He was rescued with difficulty, for the dog resisted being taken from his beloved master's grave. This print was produced from a picture which had been painted for the Princess Charlotte of Wales, who had known and greatly admired this faithful Poodle. Sancho is a white Poodle with brown ears. Indeed, it is interesting to see how often these parti-coloured Poodles are depicted in the old prints, and very charming they appear.

The frontispiece of *The Book of Animals*, by Chalons, published in 1823, shows a French Pointer, a parti-coloured Terrier, a Setter and a Water-Dog or Poodle. The dedication of this book is to the then Duchess of York, whose great love of dogs is well known. She was always surrounded by them at her home at Weybridge. The Poodle in this engraving is brown in colour with a large white collar, white feet, and a white mark on the head. One of the most charming of all the engravings owned by Mrs. Ionides is one showing the Duchesse d'Angoulême walking in the snow with Louis XVIII. They are accompanied by a clipped Poodle. This print was engraved by le Conte de Paroy.

The very old tradition of clipping the Poodle in the Lion-clip is well shown in an old French print entitled *Bichon, privé de son poil á visage, aux jambes et au trou de derrière*. In the early part of the last century, Poodles were largely used for sport. Meyrick, writing in 1861, says that in France the Poodle accompanies the village sportsmen. He describes a Poodle as being 15 to 18 inches high, the hair very thick in twisted curls, the colour, pure white or pure black. Stonehenge lamented that there were so few Poodles in England, for, said he, they had been long established as a British dog. The *Sportsman's Calendar*, published in 1802, had an illustration of a Water-Dog as distinct from the Water-Spaniel, which appears to be a curly-coated Poodle. Perhaps the most interesting book on the subject is that entitled *Hunger's Prevention, or the Art of Fowling*, by Gervase Markham, published in 1654. The frontispiece is the picture of a clipped Poodle carrying a bird in his mouth. Markham states:

"Dogges are ever most laden with hair on the hinder parts, nature as it were labouring to defend that part most and because the hinder parts are ever deeper in the water than the foreparts, therefore nature hath given the greatest amount of hair to defend the wet and coldnesss, yet this difference in summer time by the violence of the heate is very noysome and troublesome, and not only makes him sooner to faint and give over his sport, but more subject to take the mange. So, likewise in matter of water it makes a very heavy burthen to the dogge and maketh him to swim lesse nimbly. Now for the cutting or shaving from the navell downwards and backwards it is two ways well to be allowed that it is for the Summer hunting. But for the shaving of a dogge all quite over from Foot to Nostrill, that I utterly dislike, for it brings such a tendernesse and Chillnesse over all his body that the water will grow irksome to him. If anyone should keep his Water Dogge only for his use of Fowling, then not to shave his dogge at all, for he shall find in sharpe frost and snow when the ayre shall freeze the drops of water faster as the ayre, then the dogge can cast them offe."

Mrs. Ionides possesses a most delightful painting of 1701 which shows a party out fowling, with their falcons, a clipped black Poodle following the horses. *Cockney Sportsmen*, published by Cleary, is a print showing a clipped Poodle accompanying his master with his gun, near Hornsey Woods. Hornsey, as we know it now, seems very remote from those days. Robert Leighton, one of the greatest authorities on dogs, was of the opinion that the breed of Poodle originated in Germany where it was known as, and classified as, *Canis Familiaris Aquaticus*. This might well be, for in structure and coat the Poodle seems closely allied to the old Water-dogge. Indeed, the resemblance of a brown Poodle to the Irish Water-Spaniel is most marked. The head study made by Cecil Aldin of the latter breed could easily be mistaken for that of a Poodle. Caius also describes the Poodle as a Water-Spaniel, and it is an established fact that the Poodle has been, and is, widely used in various countries for retrieving water-fowl.

Doctor Fitzinger, the great German expert on all breeds of dogs, stated that there were six varieties of Poodles, namely the Gros Pudel, the Mittlere Pudel, the Kleine Pudel, Kleine Pinsch, the Schnur Pudel and the Schaf Pudel. The word 'schnur' means 'Corded' and 'schaf' means 'Curly'. There also used to be some tiny Poodles in Germany called Zwerg Pudel. Mr. Lewis Clements elaborates this arrangement by Fitzinger, saying that the Gros Pudel, or Great Poodle, originated in Morocco. Specimens of these were in colouring white, light liver, light and dark grey with black patches occurring. He states that when liver colour there were often black markings on breasts, bellies and tails. The Italians called these dogs Can Barbone; the French designated them Grands Barbets. The Mittlere Pudel, or Middle Poodles, Mr. Clements says, are only a variety of the Great Poodle. They were two-thirds the size. In Italy, France and England no difference is made between this variety and the Great Poodle. This medium-sized Poodle was also known to the Romans; on certain pictures painted at the time of the Emperor Augustus, in the last century before Christ, the Poodle's portrait is found. The Kleine Pudel, or Little Poodle, was half the size of the Middle Poodle, his muzzle longer and his body more slender. Italians called them Barbinos and the French, Le Petit Barbet. The Schnur Pudel is a pure breed, being a variation of the Large Poodle from which he differs only in coat. In size it is the same as the Large Poodle. These dogs were usually white, and some say that they came from Spain or Greece. This Poodle is rarely met with now. The Schaf Pudel is the same in size as the Middle Poodle, but shorter in ear than the Great Poodle and higher on the leg. Some of these Poodles were ticked and had patches of brown on their black coat. They were sometimes found in the Campagna of Rome.

The Poodle has of course always been considered to be of French origin, and French Poodle is a term commonly used to describe the breed. The French absolutely reject the German claim to be the country of origin, asserting that the Poodle is the direct descendant of the Barbet. Formerly the male Poodles in France were known as Canes and the females as Caniches, but later this was altered and the word Caniche now embraces both sexes. The Corded Poodles were known as Poil Cordés and the Curly Poodles as Poil Bouclés, the latter more fully described as *resembler à la toison d'une brebis* (resembling the fleece of a sheep). The Lion-clip was seen everywhere, especially during the reign of Louis Quinze, and so popular were these dogs, in spite of their aristocratic appearance, that many well-known personages at the time of the Third Republic were the owners of Poodles. The old saying in France, *fidele comme une caniche*, showed the high esteem in which the Poodle was held for his trustworthiness and devotion to his owner. Sir Walter Scott was not so complimentary to the Poodle, for he wrote: "The *garçon perruquier* and his bare-bottomed, red-eyed poodle, though they are both amusing animals and play ten thousand tricks, which are diverting enough; yet there is more of human and dog-like sympathy in the wag of old Trusty's tail than if his rival Toutou had stood on his head for a twelve-month."

There used at one time to be small Poodles in France called Caniches Nain, whose hair was said to be softer than that of their larger brethren, they being under 12 inches in height. In the current French publications all Miniature Poodles in France are described as 'Nain' and Poodles as 'Grand'.

There were also very small Poodles in Holland—as, indeed, there still are—called Dwergpoedel. On the other hand, the Russian Poodle was a very large dog, much heavier in build than the other Continental types. Some of the best of the English Poodles descend from dogs originally bred in Switzerland, Germany and Holland.

But in whatever country he may dwell, or have dwelt, the Poodle has always been accepted as the wisest and most intelligent of all dogs. His acute reasoning powers, his qualities of affection and devotion to his owner, make him one of the most charming and interesting companions of the canine race. The dignified carriage of his head, the beautiful eye, full of fire and intelligence, his elegant, graceful movement and glossy coat, combine to make him, to the discerning dog-lover, the acme of all that a perfect dog should be. Added to all his charm and beauty, the Poodle is one of the best of companions. He has a great sense of fun, and even when old, most Poodles love a game. They are the friends of all the world, treating acquaintances with a dignified friendly reserve. But they have eyes only for their owner whom they love with the most touching devotion. Mrs. Douglas Beith (Miss Florence Brunker) so aptly describes this as—"the proud and haughty look, with the loving glance for their owner alone." Can one wonder that the greatest of living Englishmen, Sir Winston Churchill, chose a Poodle, Rufus, to be his devoted associate and maybe confidante?

Chapter II

POODLE PERSONALITIES

SCIENTISTS tell us that the Poodle has a much larger brain cavity than any other dog and that the general contours and formation of the skull give every sign of extraordinary intelligence. No wonder that he of all breeds is the only one to have had a monument erected to him, and that he has been the supreme performer in Circuses and the Show Ring for many hundreds of years. Poodles, because of their intelligence, have always been able to distinguish themselves in every kind of way. When they were first introduced into England as pet dogs, or, rather, as house dogs, in the middle of the last century, unthinking observers labelled them as fops, and the term 'only a poodle' was used in a derogatory sense in comparing them with other breeds. A very short acquaintance with Poodles very quickly disposes of such a superficial generalization.

In France in the last century they used to perform in the streets as pendants to performing bears. The Poodle would jump through hoops, turn somersaults, dance and do all kinds of tricks. As long ago as the early eighteenth century there was a showman in London who performed all over England with a troupe of Poodles. He called his act 'The Ball of Little Dogs'. The dogs were said to have come from Belgium, and they danced before Queen Anne, greatly to Her Majesty's delight. Two of the dogs carried very grand titles, the Marquis of Gaillerdain and Madame de Poncette. They danced, so it is said, in perfect time to the cadence of the music. A little later on, in the eighteenth century other Poodles performed a unique act in which they sat at a banqueting table and were waited upon by dogs of lesser breed. There were said to be about eighty in the troupe and most of them were Miniature Poodles. They all performed horrible and astonishing acts, such as walking on a tight-rope on their hind legs, or with monkeys on their backs and running races with their monkey riders. Of course, in the eighteenth century, no one thought anything of cruelty to animals. In these days doubts assail us, and many people will not sit through acts of performing dogs. However, we are not concerned with the morals of the eighteenth century. From then on to the end of the nineteenth century Poodles, because of their high-grade intelligence, were used almost exclusively in the performing dog acts. There is a very interesting colour print of a Paris street in the eighteenth century. It shows a Poodle being shaved and turned-out very smartly almost in the manner of today, while others sit round waiting their turns. Owners of puppies are there, holding their dogs, waiting to have their tails docked, and other ladies, evidently going shopping, are handing over their Poodles to be looked after until they have made their purchases.

There are many stories about Poodles that show them in an heroic light or a comic one. Also, their great intelligence has been used to their owner's advantage in performing actions that might be frowned upon by the police. I think present-day owners of Poodles would like to hear the story of the great Moustache. Moustache has been celebrated many times for his unique bravery. We all know that any dog will defend his home and master without a thought of any danger to himself, but this dog Moustache fought for his country.

History relates that he was born in Normandy about 1800. At a very early age he joined a regiment of French Grenadiers entirely on his own, and went through several campaigns with them and fought at the battles of Marengo and Austerlitz. On one occasion when the regiment was surprised by the Austrians he gave the alarm so quickly that the regiment was able to beat the enemy and save itself. For this he was given a decorated collar and put on the strength with a Grenadier's ration daily. During the Battle of Austerlitz the soldier who carried the colours of the regiment was cut off from his comrades and was surrounded by the enemy. Moustache flew to the attack and attempted to rescue the soldier who, though wounded, had managed to keep a hold on the colours. A sudden burst of shot killed the soldier and scattered the enemy. With great skill Moustache managed to pick up the colours and dash back with them to his regiment. Later on he fought again in Spain and was killed at the Battle of Badajoz in 1811. He was buried on the battlefield with his collar and his medal. A stone was erected over his grave and on it was written *Ci git le brave Moustache*. When the war was over the Spaniards broke the stone and burned his body.

This story is worth recording at length because it does away with the idea that a Poodle is merely a lady's pet and lap-dog. A very interesting woodcut of the period 1811 shows Moustache in what we know as the Continental-clip, perfect in every detail and identical with those we see in the Ring today except that his tail is much longer. However, it carries a very full pompon in the correct style.

Here is another story of the Poodle in the Army. In America during the Spanish War a regiment was ordered aboard ship and the troops were forbidden to take their dogs with them. Several of them actually decided that this order could not be obeyed and a number of pets were secreted in their owners' drums. Before leaving, however, the band was ordered to sound a parting fanfare. When the drummers hit their drums quite suddenly and with great effect, a number of dogs burst forth from the instruments. One, however, kept his head and remained quiet and went on board with his owner. This was a Poodle. He fought with his master and came safely home.

There is rather an amusing story of an Englishman travelling in France during the eighteenth century. Somehow or another he lost a Golden Louis, which was worth quite a lot of money in those days. He was very disconsolate as he did not know where he had lost it—in the house or out. He spent a whole day out of doors trying in vain to find it and returned home tired and hungry. On arrival he was met by his family and staff very upset because their Poodle had been behaving so strangely all day. He was curled up in the sitting-room and, quite contrary to his usual behaviour, snapped and snarled at anyone who approached. Completely mystified by such behaviour, and fearing for his favourite's health, the master went into the room where the Poodle lay. No sooner had he opened the door than the dog jumped to his feet, leapt at his master and dashed backwards and forwards from his bed to his master. Still more perplexed, his owner went to the bed, only to see that the dog had vomited his dinner. Further inspection showed that in the vomited meal was the missing Golden Louis!

A friend once told me that his Poodle, who was always dispirited on Sunday mornings when the family went off to church without him, was found on one occasion burying the prayer books under the hall rug, hoping that if they were missing he might get his usual walk.

Someone else told me that he introduced a new Poodle pup to the home and the one already there was extremely jealous of the newcomer. He was sternly admonished when he attempted to eat the puppy's dinner. What was the owner's surprise when he saw his pet advance towards the puppy's bowl and proceed to blow sawdust all over the unfortunate animal's food!

Lastly, as is abundantly demonstrated, the Poodle is an extra-ordinarily intelligent dog. Was it for this reason that Goethe made Mephistopheles visit Faust in the guise of a Poodle?

Poodles have had their uses in the business world, too. In the days when there was a heavy duty on Brussels lace it was a common practice to shave the Poodle to the skin, from head to foot. Lace was then wound round his body, a false skin sewn on, and the dog sent off on his journey. So clever were the dogs that they were adepts at crossing frontiers and avoiding encounters with gendarmes or Customs officers.

Everyone knows the story of the Parisian bootblack whose Poodle used to rush up to passers-by, greet them with enthusiasm, and in doing so tread all over their boots with muddy feet so that the wearers were forced to go to his master and have them cleaned.

From Spain comes the story that Poodles there used to have their coats cut right off twice a year, the hair thus obtained being made into felt for hats.

Everyone who has neglected his Poodle's coat will know into what felty mats it goes if it is neglected for any length of time. If a handful of hair is squashed between the hands and then pressed heavily on a table it will quickly make a hard felt pad that is unbeatable as a polisher for furniture and for giving the final shine to boots and shoes.

Poodles make excellent gun-dogs, both Large and Miniature. People who have used them for duck shooting say they are superior to Spaniels or Retrievers. Their coats are so dense that they can dive in and out of water for hours on end and never get soaked through to the skin.

Chapter III

THE CORDED POODLE

THE Poodle has long been known in England. In 1635 Prince Rupert came to England to help King Charles the First in his struggle with the forces of the Roundheads. He brought with him his Poodle, Boye. This dog has passed into history, and there can be few real Poodle lovers who have not heard his story. A pamphlet entitled *Observations upon Prince Rupert's White Dogge called Boye* was published in 1642. A copy of this pamphlet is in the possession of the Kennel Club and another copy is owned by Mrs. Ionides. This pamphlet was produced as a dialogue between Boye and another Dogge called Pepper. The two dogges argue the case between the Cavaliers and the Roundheads and Boye states that he is of 'a high German breed'. The frontispiece of this production shows Prince Rupert with Boye at his side accompanied by a band of Cavaliers. They are confronted by a number of Roundheads. The Prince is urging Boye to attack the Roundheads, saying 'To him, Pudel.' One wonders if perhaps in some roundabout way the modern expression 'Atta Boy' has descended from this old picture. Boye accompanied his master wherever he went and was killed at the Battle of Marston Moor in 1643.

The English Kennel Club had not long been founded before Poodles came on the scene. The first mention of the breed in the *Kennel Club Stud Book* is in 1874, when the following dogs were registered as Poodles: Don, Elmer, Flo, Frank and Lion. At Nottingham Show that same year Elmer was placed first, Flo second and Frank third. Later in the same year Lion took a first prize at the Birmingham Show. In 1875 Captain Allen registered what he called a Russian Poodle. This dog was whelped in Riga in August, 1870; the sire was stated to be Moscow and the dam Zulie. He was described as dark grey in colour with a light grey eye. In the same year a Mr. Jepson registered Billy Ayshford's Bob, which was whelped in France, and at the time of registration was three years of age.

It was in 1876 that the Poodle Club was founded by some Poodle enthusiasts, though application to the Kennel Club for formal recognition was not made until 1896, when the Club was placed on the Kennel Club Register. In the early days there was no obligation for Breed Clubs to be registered. This was a later development.

In 1877 four more Poodles appear in the *Kennel Club Stud Book*—Charlie, Fecken, Michael Angelo and Touche. Fecken was whelped in 1872 and belonged to a Mr. Rutan of New York. Michael Angelo was also owned by an American, Mr. Felder of Brooklyn, and was whelped in 1874. This last-named dog was imported from England and took a first prize at the New York Show. It is most interesting to see how closely Poodles have always been linked in a number of ways with England and the United States. From the earliest days there has been a two-way traffic of Poodles between the two countries and several of the greatest English breeders have had close ties with America.

In 1878 Mrs. Compton's Grafin and Kaiser, both whelped in 1876, were stated in the *Kennel Club Stud Book* to have been imported. Judging by their names, they most probably came from Germany. Their pedigrees were said to be 'unknown'. In 1879 eight dogs were registered, among them being Miss Bell's Bismark, evidently another German Poodle. The succeeding year, 1880, saw the number of Poodle registrations increased to thirteen. Out of eleven Poodles mentioned in 1881 three of them were white, namely Duchess, Doll and Fairy Queen. In this same year Captain Hart's Satanella was placed first at a Show held at Alexandra Palace, but was afterwards disqualified for having been tampered with by some foreign substance rubbed into the coat. Was this the first of the 'Poodle fakers'?

In 1883 the sexes were first divided in the *Kennel Club Stud Book*, there being eleven dogs and five bitches. Mr. Murray's Sifrit is mentioned as being 'black all over'. First mention of a French dog, after Billy Ayshford's Bob, seems to be Jacques, the first typically French name to appear, which was owned by Mr. Loggins. In the two succeeding years ten dogs were registered and six bitches, and eighteen dogs and one bitch in the second year. Mr. Callaghan showed a Poodle called Pom Pom at the Ryde Show, with which he took a second prize. It was described as 'white with black pompons on the back and tail'. Here we have the first description of a parti-coloured Poodle, which, as mentioned elsewhere, were often to be seen in former days.

A small Poodle owned by Mr. Tronghea of Leeds, called The

Fairy Queen, was so covered with long hair that it was impossible to tell her head from her tail, and she created much amusement when shown.

The Reverend G. Bolt's Styx presumably was imported from France, his breeder being given as Monsieur Duchateau. This dog afterwards went to America, where he made Poodle history.

An interesting fact is that nearly all the Poodles being shown at this time were stated as 'pedigree unknown'. The Corded Poodles were most popular and were always to the fore, and 1886, with eleven dogs and twelve bitches registered at the Kennel Club, saw the first appearance of the famous Champion Achilles, who became a truly legendary figure. He was bred and owned at this time by Mr. Chance. His sire was Champion Lyris, imported and owned by Mr. Kemp. Lyris stood 21 inches in height, his cords measuring 23 inches. He won the first prize at the Kennel Club Show in Jubilee year 1886. Mated by Mr. Chance to his bitch Begum, the foundation was laid of a strain which produced most of the prize winners of that time. The most famous of the resulting litter was the Champion Achilles, a far better dog than his sire Lyris. He was the first Poodle to gain the title of Champion in this country. This was in the year 1890. He proceeded to carry off three more Challenges in the following year.

In those days the title of Champion was gained in a different manner from the present time. The title could be won only by entry in what was called a Championship Class and these were scheduled at only three Shows, the Kennel Club Show, Birmingham Show and the Scottish Kennel Club Show, Birmingham being the oldest established Dog Show in England. But to be eligible to compete in a Championship Class a dog had already to have won in certain other classes. Champion Achilles stood 23 inches high at the shoulder and his cords hung down for 30 inches. He was a magnificent Poodle, carrying his huge coat with much dignity, with a proudly held head. The Corded Poodles were very popular, and most of the winning dogs at this time were coated. The hair was allowed to grow and was never combed out but continually rolled and twisted with paraffin and vaseline to cause longer and ever longer cords to be added to the coat.

One of the greatest difficulties attached to the ownership and showing of these Poodles was that, apart from the bother of keeping them always tied up in linen bags, no trace of oil was permitted to remain in the coat when the dog was in the Show Ring. This was a hard task, and the almost superhuman work of washing a Corded Poodle was not often undertaken. The cords fell in cascades to the ground, the tip of the tail carrying smaller hanging cords instead of the pompon of the Curly Poodle.

It was in 1890 that Monsieur Dagois first showed the well-known Champion The Model, and the Reverend R. V. O. Graves carried off four Firsts with Champion The Sorceress at four successive Shows. By 1891 Champion Achilles had passed into the possession of Mr. Graves and won three more Challenges. Mr. Graves also won four Challenges with his Champion The Witch, another Corded, whilst his The Woman in White started her winning career at three Shows at all of which she carried off a first prize. In the same year Mr. Graves also showed The Ghost, a white of which no details are given, and his Sorceress won four Firsts at four Shows and was an unbeaten bitch. In the following year Mr. Ogden Mills of New York showed Black Nigger, another dog with pedigree unknown. In 1892 Champion Achilles took four more Challenges whilst Champion The Witch carried off two, one of them being at Cruft's Show. Champion The Model was a medium-sized black Corded Poodle with the most lovely head and expression. Indeed, all these famous Corded Poodles excelled in fineness of head and sweet expression.

Champion The Joker, owned by Monsieur Dagois, was the sire of Mrs. Leonard Crouch's beautiful Champion Orchard Admiral. The Joker was sired by Champion The Model. Though these dogs were Corded Poodles, Champion Orchard Admiral was a Curly Poodle. After Champion Achilles they held pride of place in the Show Ring. The Model lived to a great age and many present-day winning Standards can trace their descent from him. Monsieur Dagois was now one of the most famous Poodle breeders in England; his Tissie beat The Witch at the Kennel Club Show in 1888. There was a tremendous division of opinion at that time regarding Corded and Curly Poodles. It was not until 1904 that the breed was divided by the Kennel Club into Corded Poodles over 15 inches and Non-Corded over 15 inches. Previous to this Poodles were classified at the Kennel Club under the simple registration of Poodles. This included both Corded and Curly Poodles and the height could range from 12 to 24 inches. Included among these were certain medium-sized Poodles which might be said to be in the middle-size group.

Ch. Firebrave Gaulois
(*Miniature black*)

Ch. Vulcan Champagne Tiger
(*Standard brown*)

An English sportsman with falcons, poodle and spaniels in the early nineteenth century

Corded Poodles. *From the drawing by Arthur Wardle*

Ch. Flashlight of Mannerhead
(*Miniature blue*)

Whippendell Abricotinette
(*Miniature apricot*)

Ch. Chieveley Chopstick, Ch. Chieveley Chivy and
Ch. Chieveley Chenile (*Miniature blacks*)

All this was very unsatisfactory. The new division by the Kennel Club considerably eased the situation as it was becoming manifestly impossible to judge the Corded and Curly Poodles in the came classes and give a fair deal to both. The definition of over 15 inches also simplified the position. In 1901 the only Curly Poodles to have won Championship status were both owned by Mrs. Leonard Crouch, Champion The Pilot and Champion The Black Coquette. It was in the previous year that Mrs. Crouch's name appears as the exhibitor of Champion The Pilot, winning with him at Cruft's Show, the Kennel Club Show, and Richmond Show in 1903; the position having been cleared, Champion Cannon Hill Beauty, owned by Miss Netty Levy, won the Certificate for Corded Dogs at Cruft's Show, whilst in the Non-Corded section Mrs. Leonard Crouch's white Champion L'Enfant Prodigue took the same honour. In 1904 at the same Show, Champion Cannon Hill Beauty and Champion The Joker took the Certificates for Corded Dogs, whilst Mrs. Crouch's Champion Orchard Admiral and the same owner's Champion L'Enfant Prodigue took those offered for Non-Cordeds.

The following description of Mrs. Crouch's famous Champion L'Enfant Prodigue, born in 1899, sire Ivan, dam Flossie, is of interest:

"He stood 21 inches in height, at the shoulder, with tail carried high and he is a most graceful mover. Head long and fine, ears long and wide hanging close to his head. Eyes have coal-black rims and his lovely white teeth are set off by his black lips. He has a dense long, snow-white coat."

Mrs. Crouch's prefix Orchard now came strongly to the fore, and for some years dominated the scene in Non-Corded Poodles. Her Orchard Wildflower, Orchard Whitefrock and Orchard Sally were all in the money during the year 1904, to be succeeded by the lovely Champion Orchard Whiteboy. The competition was getting exceedingly hot, with Miss Brunker's famous Whippen-dells coming forward, and Miss May Hawley (Mrs. Cyril Pacey) beginning to show and win with her Wolveys. The Whippendells, Orchards and Wolveys were all Curly Poodles.

It was decided to form the Curly Poodle Club, with Miss M. Brunker as secretary, and in the rules of this newly formed association there is a statement:

C

"No dog exhibited by a member as a Corded Poodle shall ever be exhibited as a Curly Poodle and *vice versa*, and after April, 1900, no Curly Poodle bred from Corded parents shall be eligible for the trophies of the Curly Poodle Club."

Here we have a real schism in Poodle circles, some insisting on a difference which other breeders firmly refused to recognize. It certainly was a remarkable fact that the famous Champion The Pilot, a Corded dog, was the sire of the equally famous Champion Orchard Admiral, the dog owned by Mrs. Crouch, of whom Mr. Croxton Smith said that he would like him taken out of the Ring as he was such a super Poodle that he put his eye out for judging the other Poodles. Now Mrs. Crouch says:

"Some people say there are two kinds of Poodles, but this is not so; only one, the Corded Poodle. The Curly Coat is obtained by constant brushing and combing and a Poodle left to nature will cord rapidly. My dog Champion The Pilot when I first owned him was shown as a Corded Poodle, his coat touching the ground. I untwisted his cords and combed him out and now he is shown as a Curly Poodle. Any Poodle which is true-bred and has no cross in his strain will be corded if not brushed and combed, and this I assert after long years of experience."

On the other hand, Mrs. Robert Long says that Curly Poodles require careful breeding to eliminate any strain of Corded blood. Both Miss Millie and Miss Florence Brunker were most insistent that the Cordeds and Curlies were of different strains. Indeed, it was through their exertions that the Curly Poodle Club was formed. Miss Florence Brunker writes:

"With regard to the Curly Poodle as it exists today, there is an inclination amongst some breeders to get the head too long and narrow and so lose the distinction that undeniably exists between the Russian and the French Poodles. The original French Curly Poodle possessed a head altogether broader and shorter in muzzle than the Russian or Corded Poodle, and it is a pity to alter the type by mixing the two strains."

Mr. R. W. Furness, in *The American Book of the Dog*, states:

"So decided is the tendency of the German Poodle to cord that even if you should comb it out, it divides up again into separate locks and in a few days is so felted as almost to defy the comb again."

So here we have all the best authorities differing. It seems that the only thing to do is to assume that the Corded Russians and Germans were the same dog as the French Curlies, but a different variety. The Rev. R. V. O. Graves, who was the owner of, and one of the most spectacular breeders of Corded Poodles ever seen in the Show Ring, writes: "We want better bodies and shorter backs to retain the noble carriage of the head which is in danger of being lost." Mrs. Robert Long's pronouncement is of interest because it was she who brought out the first brown Poodle, Rufus, the sire of a long line of splendid browns. His sire was Black Prince, his dam Maiwa. He was whelped in 1891.

Mr. Theo Marples narrates that two Corded Poodles which were very noted were put back at one of the Kennel Club Championship Shows because the Judge said that their coats were too long, having been cultivated to an unreasonable extent in length, so that it impeded their locomotion.

Poodle wool was sometimes spun and when told of this an old shepherd remarked: "Nae wonder sheep is sae cheap when these new-fangled dogs can grow four pound o'wool apiece." The yarn is silky, though of hard texture, and is difficult to tease.

Marples states his views on the ideal Poodle thus:

"A long, clean-cut head, dark eye, short body and beautifully straight forelegs, and cat-like feet. Full eye or thick head, flat sides or long back, straight stifles and thin or open feet are faults to be avoided in any Poodle whether large or small."

Meanwhile the Poodle Club was carefully considering the matter. In 1899 the Kennel Club Committee received a deputation consisting of Mr. Robert Long, the Rev. R. V. O. Graves, Mr. Charles Tryon and Mr. and Mrs. Albert Dagois. Mr. Long presented a memorial from Poodle owners and breeders requesting that the classification of Poodles might be divided and a separate classification given for the Curly-Coated and Corded varieties. The discussion was a lengthy one. Mr. Long, in his address, referred to various authorities in support of his contention, whilst

Mr. Graves spoke very ably in opposition to Mr. Long's contentions, quoting the opinions of both British and Continental breeders to prove that there was only one breed and one variety of Poodle. This Committee were unable to accede to the request of those who wished for a separate classification. In 1903 it was decided by the Committee to ask the Kennel Club to insert a provision in its Rules "as to the preparation of dogs for competition" permitting Corded Poodles to be shown with oil in the coat. In 1905 the Poodle Club recommended that the coats of Corded Poodles should be short enough to clear the ground. Throughout the passing year the Poodle Club was continually reviewing the changing conditions in the world of Poodles, and it is gratifying to observe the happy relations which existed between Poodle breeders in England and those in the United States. In 1900 a letter was received by the Poodle Club from the Philadelphia Dog Show, offering two medals for competition amongst the members of the Poodle Club, and this was reciprocated by the Club offering two medals to the Philadelphia Show. It was also in 1900 that the then Kennel Club Council of Representatives sent round a circular suggesting that Poodles should be classified at the Kennel Club as a non-sporting breed, not being generally used for sporting purposes. In 1910 it was decided that the Poodle Club and the Curly Poodle Club should meet to discuss the possibility of agreeing to a Standard of Points.

The question of size has for long been a moot point amongst Poodle breeders. As has been said, Poodles of all sizes were originally registered simply as Poodles. Then we had the division of Corded and Non-Cordeds and the immensely important Registration of Miniatures in 1910. In the *Kennel Club Stud Book* for 1913 there is a record that in March, 1912, it was agreed that Miniature Poodles could not be re-registered as Poodles. At the present time a mating between a Poodle and a Poodle Miniature is recognized as a cross-breeding and the resulting progeny require the necessary three generations before they can be regarded as either pure Poodles or pure Poodles Miniature.

Lady Stanier has for some time been specializing in the breeding of very small Poodles, her aim being to produce a tiny Poodle in all respects as good in the Show Ring as his larger brother. With this end in view she bought a small white Miniature bitch from the Swanhill Kennels and a Miniature dog of Miss Statter's strain, Seahorses Powder Puff, and Seahorses Rettats Frisk.

One of a resulting litter was Seahorses Snow Queen, which is less than 9 inches high and the same length in back. Snow Queen was the foundress of Lady Stanier's little Poodles; mated to Drift of Piperscroft she produced three very small white Poodles. The dog in the litter was Seahorses Snow Marquess, the sire of all Lady Stanier's little Poodles. Lady Stanier has found that the way to get these tinies is by line breeding back to her Snow Queen. Whites are the easiest to breed; blacks and silvers the most difficult. They are tough little dogs with great intelligence and will follow a horse for miles cross-country.

The Toy Poodle was recognized as a separate Breed by the Kennel Club in 1957, the height being fixed at 11 inches and under. At first the Kennel Club gave a time limit for Registrations so that any Poodle born within that limit and conforming to the height limit could be registered as a Toy Poodle, though born of Miniature parents. An enormous number of Toy Poodles were immediately registered as such. But after nogotiations with various Poodle Clubs the Kennel Club finally issued the following Regulation: "A dog bred from parents of the same Breed, but of different Varieties, must be registered as an Interbred, except that such a dog bred from Dachshunds, Collies, Fox Terriers and Poodles must be entered in the Register of the Variety it most closely resembles. In all cases the name of the Varieties making the interbreeding must be stated."*

Thus largely through the perseverance of Lady Stanier the Toy Poodle was recognized. The British Toy Poodle Club came into being early in 1957 with Miss Bowring as President, Mrs. Boyd as Vice President and Lady Stanier as Chairman, Miss Joan Eddy being the Secretary. They were supported by many of the best-known breeders on the Committee. By the kindness of Mrs. Hall, the Treasurer, a very successful Toy Poodle Party was held at Ewelem in June, 1957, where there was a large attendance of Members and their dogs. This was followed by a Club Show held at Ascot in September, 1957. The first Challenge Certificates for Toy Poodles were offered by the Kennel Club at Crufts Show, 1958, to be followed by Certificates at West of England Show, the Scottish Kennel Club Show and Birmingham National.

* For latest Kennel Club regulations regarding Miniatures and Toys see Addendum, page 171.

Chapter IV

THE CURLY POODLE

PREVIOUS to the First World War the large Poodles practically held the stage, with the Cordeds dominating the scene. After the death of the Rev. R. V. O. Graves his widow, Mrs. Graves, continued to breed the Cordeds, and it was rare indeed to attend a Championship where Mrs. Graves in her invalid chair was not present to watch the continued triumphs of her outstanding Kennel. As we have seen, it was in 1903 that the Standard was divided into Cordeds and Non-Cordeds. This gave a tremendous impetus to the breeding of the Curlies, and the advent on the scene of Miss Millie Brunker and her sister, Miss Florence Brunker, saw the beginning of great progress, not only in the larger Poodles but also in what were eventually classified as Miniatures, though this last classification came much later. Miss Brunker founded the Curly Poodle Club to advance their interests and remained its secretary until the day of her death. All the records of this Club were lost during the Second World War— Miss Millie Brunker died in 1943 and there was no provision for the preservation of these records.

The Poodles were also fortunate in having the backing and interest of Mr. Will Hally, most accomplished and knowledgeable of all dog journalists. It is largely owing to him that Poodles were placed on the map, and his great knowledge of the breed is still unfailingly placed at the disposal of enquirers. He indeed knows all about Poodles.

Miss Millie Brunker's name will always stand out in Poodle annals as she was without doubt or question the greatest authority and breeder of Poodles, both large and small, in this country. She imported many very famous dogs, and it is largely due to her work and great skill in breeding that we now have the various winning strains in England. Miss Brunker was American by birth. When she started her Kennels she owned the large variety as well as smaller Poodles. At that time Poodles of all sizes were being shown in the same classes, and many of the medium-size dogs were winning, Champion Harcourt Jack and Champion Chieveley Grumps being examples. In what are known as Standards at the present time, perhaps Miss Millie Brunker's Champion Whippendell Carillon and Champion Whippendell Negrillon were amongst the best she bred. These were black dogs, but one of Miss Brunker's greatest interests was the breeding of coloured Poodles.

Mrs. Lee French's Silver Belle appeared at the Ladies' Kennel Association Show in 1899, the sire being a dog called London Pride, the dam an unregistered bitch named Bijou. She was a blue-grey and the first of this colour to be exhibited in this country. In 1901 Miss M. Brunker brought out Nanette Grise, a blue, sired by London Pride, which was an imported grey, the dam being the celebrated Pierrette Jackson. Now Pierrette Jackson's sire Moustache and her dam Toupet were both coal black. She was whelped in 1895. The entire litter were born black but three of them changed to grey at the age of three months, being the first grey Poodles to be born in England. Moustache's sire was Peter Jackson and his dam was unknown. Toupet was also sired by Peter Jackson, again the dam being unknown. So we are left to speculate as to how the blue and grey colouring came into being. Miss Brunker continued her efforts to establish blue Poodles and in 1902 brought out another of this colour, namely, Moufflon Bleu. This dog, whose name appears in most of the pedigrees of blue Poodles, was sired by Sowden Bijou, the dam being named Fidolette. Sowden Bijou was sired by Little Boy Blue, whose pedigree is stated to be unknown, his dam being Sowden Bluette. Fidolette's sire was Kiddye and her dam Sowden Bluette. Bluette's sire was called Bluejacket and her dam Spider. Neither of these Poodles has a pedigree given. In 1906 Lavender Blue, owned by Mrs. Robert Long, was shown by her; the sire was stated to be Little Tommy Tucker, the dam Sowden Tweedledum. The last-named bitch was sired by The Bluejacket, the dam being aptly named Speculation, with no pedigree.

These blues, together with the browns and apricots, were great colour novelties and aroused the keenest interest. Among the wisest of the colour breeders were Miss Brunker and her sister, who were already making that great name for their Whippendell Poodles. Their Nanette Grise had been the first grey Miniature shown after Mrs. Lee French's Silver Belle had excited so much comment in 1899. In 1905 Miss Florence Brunker showed a tiny Poodle named Le Roi Café. His sire was Loubet and dam Babette Brune. Loubet was sired by Jarnara out of Valmar, and Babette Brune was sired by Rufus, the original and first brown to be exhibited in England, owned by Mrs. Robert Long, his dam being Daphne of Thradeston. Miss Florence Brunker also imported from France a very small white, Le Roi Blanc, which had a great influence on the Miniature whites in this country.

Whippendell Abricotinette was a true apricot and Miss Millie Brunker always considered her one of the best Miniature Poodles she had bred, and also the only real apricot. Her sire was Whippendell Mouche, her dam Whippendell Midinette. Whippendell Midinette was sired by Whippendell Moufflon Bleu out of a brown bitch called Whippendell Toto. Most unfortunately the beautiful Abricotinette was run over and killed by a car just outside Miss Brunker's gate at her home near King's Langley. Whether her lovely apricot colouring would have lasted is a matter for speculation. Before her early demise Whippendell Abricotinette had been mated to Whippendell Mouchoir Blanc, the result being Whippendell Boule de Neige, which dog is found at the back of nearly all the winning Miniature white pedigrees.

Whippendell Azor was another lovely blue first shown in 1916, sired by Whippendell Grison, the dam being Whippendell Marionette. After the marriage of Miss Florence Brunker to Major Douglas Beith, Miss Millie Brunker carried on the Whippendell Kennel by herself, although her sister continued to take the greatest interest in Poodles until she died shortly before Miss Millie Brunker's own death. The craze for colour breeding was now well under way. Some of the new colours were very beautiful. But the trouble began when later progeny were mated, and a great confusion of colours became apparent in many instances. The blues now ranged from smoke grey and pure silver to a most beautiful forget-me-not blue. Mixing colours in breeding without proper knowledge of what the results may be is a sheer gamble, and later litters may well prove to be mis-colours. It was found that white blood should not be introduced into any colour. Miss Moorhouse, of the famous Chieveleys, used occasionally to introduce blue blood into her blacks and *vice versa* with many excellent results. But this is not as easy as it may appear to be; it requires great skill, and knowledge of how the stock you use has been bred. Indeed, this mating of different colours should only rarely be done and only if the breeder has the experience and knowledge to carry it through. Colour in Poodles should be sound all through, or 'solid', as many people define it. The earlier breeders always aimed at getting this clear colour. Any shading in the colour of Poodles is incorrect, though it may be mentioned here that in the 1600s, before Shows were thought of, most of the Poodles depicted in paintings and engravings were parti-coloured. It must be confessed that some of them were very handsome, attractive dogs.

Certain strains in the earlier days carried the blue colour more successfully than others, notably Miss Fletcher's Kennel of Campdens and Miss Nunn's Watercrofts. Most of the blue Poodles shown before the war carried one or other of these strains.

We have a good example of excellent colour breeding in Mrs. Ionides' Vulcan Champagne Silvo, by Vendas Blue Masterpiece out of Harpendale Trixie. Masterpiece carried a strong strain of the best blue. His sire was Vendas Arrow of Silver, his dam Leila. Vendas Arrow of Silver was sired by Hunningham Silver out of the great Champion Angel of Mine. Leila had been sired by Champion Whippendell Crepon out of Babette Grise and was registered as a Poodle. Hunningham Silver's father was the unbeaten Champion Silver Gnome, and in Champion Angel of Mine we go back to the Watercrofts, Chic of Watercroft being her sire and her dam the lovely Champion Arcangel. With Babette Grise we get right back to the beginnings of the blue Poodles, The Midshipmite mated to The Blue Bird. Thus Silvo's ancestry is a direct line of descent through some of our best blues; he amply shows this in his clear, beautiful colour.

Although Miss Brunker was so interested in the coloured Poodles, her blacks were always well to the fore. The great Champion Whippendell Carillon was a magnificent black dog. One of his principal assets was his lovely deportment and carriage. He was a most elegant and graceful Poodle and stood out in the Show Ring whenever he appeared. His sire was Whippendell André, his dam Lola being an unregistered bitch. Whippendell André was by Champion Chieveley Grumps, his dam Biffey Girl of Locklands. Grumps was a medium-sized dog, being sired by Champion Harcourt Jack out of Desdemona de Monte Cristo. Whippendell Drapeau, by Whippendell Gasparde out of Qui Qui, was another much-used sire belonging to Miss Brunker. In 1901 Mrs. Leonard Crouch began showing Poodles and her Orchard prefix became famous. Her first dog Orchard Toby was bred by Mr. Molineux by Jon Jones out of Judy of Wilmslow. Her large white Poodles were very beautiful. It was in 1907 that she brought out the great Champion Orchard Admiral, a black dog of outstanding merit.

This Chapter concerning the early days of the Poodle in the Show Ring may aptly close with the following quotation from Miss Florence Brunker's description of her ideal Poodle:

"He may be a dense jet black with no sign of rustiness however strong the light. He may be a rich red with eyes and nose to match exactly, or a shimmering silver grey that glistens in the sun, or white as the driven snow with a coal-black nose and eyes put in with smutty fingers. But whatever his colour, his style, which belongs par excellence to the Poodle, must be supreme. He is 'chic' from top to toe. His expression is usually supercilious and haughty—at least to the world in general. The tender speaking glance, which I know so well, is reserved for his mistress alone. His coat is long and so crisply curly that, when combed out, his head and shoulders are grotesquely large in proportion to his slender shaven flanks, garnished with rosettes to accentuate their grace. His straight, elegant legs are encircled with the neatest of frills round wrists and ankles, and the Poodle de luxe is never without his pretty bangle. His ears are long and wide and give him a strangely dignified and judge-like aspect, and when he opens his long and narrow jaw, strong white teeth shine like ivory set in coral. His perky tail is short and ends in a pompon that spells defiance to his enemies. As a rule, he is gentleness itself and polite to all men, if indifferent to those outside his own circle. But he allows no liberties and can hold his own with any dog. His proportions are just right, short in the back but not on the leg and he moves as freely as a greyhound. His intelligence is a proverb. He is game, too, and many keepers confess that a Poodle may put trained gun-dogs to shame."

Can anyone equal this so charmingly written description of the Poodle?

Chapter V

THE EARLY POODLES

MISS THOROWGOOD, who was becoming known in the Show Ring, brought out the Champion Ambrette in 1923. She was sired by Whippendell Cordon Bleu out of Whippendell Mascotterina and, mated to Whippendell Drapeau, she produced the great Champion Tom, an outstanding black dog. This splendid Poodle so much beloved by his owner, Mrs. Lowry, made an immense impression on the breed. He was a beautiful dog with dark amber eyes. It can be seen that it was the Whippendells and their descendants who laid the foundation of most of the well-known strains of the present time. Thus we have the grand Kennel of Rathnallys owned and bred by the late Mrs. D'Arcy Thompson. One of the earliest bitches in this Kennel was Champion Sheila of Rathnally. She was sired by U.S.A. Champion Whippendell Poli of Carillon out of an Irish Champion Lady Nanette. Whippendell Poli was a son of Champion Whippendell Carillon out of Whippendell Lolita. Pompey of Rathnally, the son of Champion The Vagabond King (Corded) out of Banshee of Rathnally, was mated to Sheila of Rathnally, producing the Champion Princess Sheila of Rathnally. The Rathnallys have continued to breed good dogs to the present time, their latest Champion Peter of Rathnally being a worthy descendant of his forebears. The recent death of Mrs. D'Arcy Thompson is a great loss to the breed.

The Wivelsfields owned by Mrs. Della Gana were now coming into the Show Ring. Again Miss Brunker's Whippendell Drapeau, mated to a bitch named Trifle, had produced a winning dog in Wivelsfield Bogie, the founder of Mrs. Della Gana's Kennel.

Mrs. Hutchinson and her daughter started their famous Nymphaea Kennel with stock imported from Belgium. Nymphaea Alice, their first Show winner, was sired by Sieger Gunter out of Lennep which was not registered, her dam was Nymphaea Fee von Moseland, whose sire was Siege Rigo von Konigstuhl, her dam Nymphaea Flora von Gropen Belchen. This was in 1925, and in the following year the Hutchinsons produced

43

Champion Nymphaea Cheetah. Their Kennel owed little to Whippendell stock, being continually reinforced by new stock from Germany. It is lamentable that during the Second World War the Konigstuhl Kennels and their owners were all liquidated by Hitler in his stupid, insensate fury against everything of Jewish origin.

The year 1927 is an important one in Poodle history. It was in this year that Miss Jane Lane showed Champion Nunsoe Chivalrous, bred by Mrs. Wainwright, his sire being Ambroise of Summerleaze, the dam Whippendell Riquette. This grand dog did a great deal of winning for his new owner. Miss Lane also invested in Nymphaea stock, procuring from Mrs. Hutchinson her fine dog Nymphaea Swift. This dog was entirely of German breeding, the sire being Nymphaea Rigoletto von Schopplatz out of Nymphaea Grisette. Miss Lane has had a remarkable success in dog breeding for she has bred and owned Champions in eight different breeds.

Miss Millie Brunker was showing four winning dogs in 1928, all with the Whippendell prefix—namely Chantecler, Marron Deux, Peridot and Sonneur.

In 1930 Champion Tom took four of the six Certificates offered for dogs. Champion Tom in the following year sired Nunsoe Lady Mary out of Nunsoe Hazel, which was sired by Champion Nunsoe Chivalrous out of Derian Dinah. Nunsoe Lady Mary became a Champion after being shown at four Shows. Another noteworthy bitch owned by Miss Lane was Aunt Chloe, another sired by Whippendell Drapeau out of Trifle. She was bred by Mrs. Levett and was originally sold as a pet. She was the dam of Champion Nunsoe Clever and many other winners, and was a most beautiful black bitch.

Nymphaea Swift had now passed into the possession of Miss Graham Weall, who took the prefix of Phidgity. It was in 1931 that Mrs. G. L. Boyd, whose Piperscrofts were to become so famous, won with her King Leo of Piperscroft, a dog bred by Mrs. Thomson by Jolicoeur out of Champion Scarlett Nanette.

Miss Jane Lane was now working hard to establish her Nunsoes, which have so strongly influenced the breed. She was sure that temperament had much to do with the breeding of good stock, and in this she followed the example of the breeders of Arab horses. She looked abroad for new stock for her Kennels, and in 1932 she made Poodle history by importing from Switzerland that great dog, International Champion Nunsoe Duc de la Terrasse, International Champion de Beaute Chevalier Labory, International Champion de Beaute Nellie von Lirridenquai, and two years later International Champion Dolly von Bremerwald. The Duc's sire was Prinz Alexander von Rodelheim, his dam Leonore von der Seestadt. The Prinz had been sired by the International Champion Prinz von Bereslingen out of Carmen von Lennep. Another dog of the same breeding was International Champion Piperscroft Pippo de la Terrasse. The Duke, as he was familiarly spoken of by Poodle folk, was a truly magnificent Poodle. He excelled in all the points asked of a Poodle, a large dog, but infinitely graceful, moving like the Royal Duke that he was. He did not stay very long in this country, but in the short time he was in England he won the Dog Challenge Certificate at every Show at which he was shown, with three exceptions. The Judges who placed him Best of Breed at one Show after another were Mrs. Arthur Hudson, Mr. Holland Buckley, Mrs. Pacey, Miss Bowring and Miss Hutchinson. Mr. Upton Robins placed him as Reserve to Champion Polichinelle owned by Mrs. D'Arcy Thompson, and he was twice beaten for the Certificate by Champion Nunsoe Nickola's Christopher Robbin.

After annexing all these honours in England, and being universally admired by all Poodle lovers, he was bought by Mrs. Sherman Hoyt and sailed for America, where he quickly became an American Champion and a Triple International Champion. This wonderful dog joined the famous Blakeen Kennel and became the constant, greatly loved companion of Mrs. Sherman Hoyt and her husband. In a recently published book[1] Mrs. Hoyt speaks of the gentleness and nobility of the Duke, and anyone who saw him during his brief stay in England can well believe this. He might well be called a Royal Duke.

By this time many more breeders of Poodles were establishing Kennels in England. Mrs. Murray Wilson's Stillington dogs were winning, her first in the Ring being Stillington Pippa Passes, whose sire and dam were both unregistered dogs. Champions Stillington Clausekins and Stillington Jeremie were especially well known.

In 1933 Miss Jane Lane had again made history with her lovely Champion Nunsoe Nickola's Christopher Robbin. This dog, born in 1928, won over twenty Challenge Certificates and was

[1] *Your Poodle.* (Popular Dogs Publishing Co. Ltd., 1952.)

made Best in Show at seven successive Shows in the space of one month. He was bred by Mr. Harper. Miss Lane then imported Nunsoe Nellie von Lirridenquai, and the Nunsoes became continuous winners at all the Shows.

Mrs. D'Arcy Thompson's Champion Polichinelle won five of the nine Dog Certificates offered in 1934. He was a great dog. Mrs. G. L. Boyd's Champion Pippo de la Terrasse took four Certificates in 1935, and Mrs. Murray Wilson's Champion Stillington Jeremie carried off the same number. Miss Rochford (Doctor Leach) started her winning career with Berkham Apollo sired by Nunsoe Nickola's Christopher Robbin out of Nunsoe Em'ly Brown, whose sire was Champion Tom. Champion Amour Labory of Piperscroft, another of Mrs. Boyd's importations, was bred by Madame Reichenbach by her Petit Poucy Labory out of Mira Labory.

These imported dogs from the Continent added much strength to the Whippendell and other older strains. They were judiciously purchased and wisely bred from. Poodles have been fortunate in that they have always had certain clever and skilful breeders whose whole activities were for the improvement of the breed.

In 1936 Mrs. Ionides won four Certificates with her Vulcan Champagne Pommery. Mated to Nunsoe Damsel he produced Vulcan Jean, the dam of the well-known Champion Vulcan Champagne Darcy. The Vulcan Champagnes soon established an excellent strain, now with a world-wide reputation. Baik de Pladjoe, which came from Holland, was the founder of the black Vulcan Champagnes. He was a beautiful dog and made a great impression on succeeding generations. He was sired by Warsawas Joeb out of Sarina de Pladjoe. Champion Vulcan Champagne Titan was another great dog, sired by Vulcan Champagne Dragonfly out of Judy. Dragonfly was by an imported dog named Tommy, whilst Judy was sired by Nunsoe Tawny out of the imported Sheila. The dam of Tommy was Questing Kiki, which was by Brin of Rathnally out of Nunsoe Athene, whose dam was Nunsoe Em'ly Brown. It was most unfortunate for the Vulcan Champagnes that the Second World War came so soon after their establishment.

Miss Lane continued to bring out winners, with Champion Nunsoe The Florin quickly taking his three Certificates. Pompey and Banshee, both of Rathnally, were prominent in 1937 and Miss Statter, who became so sound and practical a breeder, was winning with her Rettats Spanker, which was by Maréchal of Piperscroft out of Phidgity Swallow. In 1937 Blakeen Durante of Gilltown was imported from the United States by Lady Furness. His sire was a Nunsoe Darling David, a lovely silver dog, his dam being Blakeen Vigee Le Brun. The year which saw the outbreak of the Second World War was a great one for Mrs. D'Arcy Thompson, who was winning with four of her Rathnallys— Pompey, Thomond, Romulus, and Amber. The Nunsoes were also busy with Nunsoe Driver and Champion Nunsoe Brown Bess. This last bitch was by Nunsoe Chevalier Labory out of Nunsoe Em'ly Brown, again sired by Champion Tom. Most of the principal strains of Standard Poodles were now established. The Whippendells and Summerleazes owned by Mrs. Wainwright had fanned out to start the Nunsoes which, with the wise importations of Miss Lane, had quickly established themselves in a prominent position in the Poodle world. They also had a say in the Rathnallys, which has been a consistently winning Kennel ever since.

The Nymphaeas, mostly imported from Germany by Mrs. Hutchinson, were a very distinct strain, and many Kennels, including some in America, owed their winning lines to Nymphaea stock.

During the years of the Second World War little was heard of the Poodles. This applies only to the showing and registration of dogs. But unfortunately for the breed the Poodle had suddenly become popular in England, as indeed most dogs had. There seemed to be some feeling amongst English people that dogs were essential to their happiness. Maybe it was because dogs knew nothing of the war itself, although they were in the midst of the air-raids and suffered much therefrom. It seemed to be a form of escapism among human beings. The fidelity and devotion of the Poodle made an appeal to a people ravaged by war and its consequences. But this led to the dogs being commercialized. Poodles had to be produced, and were produced for money-making. A few irresponsible breeders who cared little or nothing for the Poodle as a breed seized the opportunity to coin money out of them. Pedigrees were just made up and the abuse of this commercialization continued for two or three years after the war had ended. It was owing to the action taken at last by the Kennel Club that the abuse was finally stamped out, though there remained the sad fact that many of the pedigrees of those war years cannot be relied on as it is difficult to say whether a pedigree is genuine or not.

In 1945 one large Poodle was registered in the *Kennel Club Stud Book*—Vulcan Champagne Amazement, sired by Vulcan Champagne Pommery out of Champion Nunsoe Brown Bess. It was fortunate for the breed that the Vulcan Champagnes had been carefully preserved, also the Nunsoes, the Rathnallys, the Piperscrofts and the Hockfords, amongst the Standard Poodles.

The first Miniature and Toy C.C. winners were:

Miniature dog—Alresford Powder Puff, owned by Miss Levy, Pet Dog Show, 9 December 1910

Miniature bitch—Jeanette of Ellingham, owned by Miss Newall, Kennel Club Show, 7 February 1910

Toy dog—Poupou of Braxted, owned by Mrs Spencer, Cruft's Show, 7 February 1958

Toy bitch—Wendoley Annette, owned by Mr and Mrs Andrews, Cruft's Show 7 February 1958

Chapter VI

THE MINIATURE POODLE

THE BLUES AND WHITES

PREVIOUS to the establishment of the Miniature Poodle at the Kennel Club there had been many small Poodles which won in hot competition with their larger brothers. All sizes competed in the same ring as just Poodles. The writer's first Poodle, Mowgli, would at the present time have to be counted as a Poodle for he stood about 17 inches in height. He came to her as a puppy in 1904, being bred by Colonel Chapman, the sire being Piccolo, the dam Frou Frou. Mowgli did a lot of winning at West Country Shows in Variety Classes and was her constant companion until his death at the age of fourteen years. His gravestone has the following inscription:

Mowgli, a Poodle who loved greatly and was greatly loved.

"Who loved to see the constant ball a-throw, to fetch it scampering gaily to and fro, Content in every change of mood, if one dear voice, one only, called him good, Such was my dog who, couched before the Heavenly gate, Waits for my step as here he used to wait."—Rudolph Lehman.

In 1910 the Secretary of the Kennel Club wrote to the Poodle Club asking its opinion on various points connected with the breed. The Club replied that in the opinion of its Committee Miniature Poodles should be measured on a table in the Show Ring by a standard measure, either by one of the Ring stewards or by a veterinary surgeon. And that no Miniature should be shown under the age of twelve months. They did not consider that certificates given by a Specialist Club concerning the height of a dog would be satisfactory. Finally, the Committee stated that in their opinion puppies born before January 1st, 1912, the progeny of a Poodle and a Poodle Miniature, should be allowed to be registered in accordance with their height in the register of either breed. In 1911 the Poodle Club and the Curly Poodle Club agreed to meet to discuss the possibility of formulating a Standard of Points. This registration according to height without reference to breeding has for some years been abandoned, and a true Miniature Poodle must now be born of Miniature parents and grandparents whilst conforming to the height limit of 'under 15 inches'.

In 1911 a statement was made in the *Kennel Club Stud Book* that sixteen Poodles had been registered as Miniatures during the preceding year. These were: Miss Millie Brunker's Whippendell Cachet, Whippendell Cabillat and Whippendell Turqu; Miss Newall's Manikin of Ellingham and Mrs. Cobbold's white Alresford Powder Puff in dogs, whilst in bitches there were Mrs. Knowles's Barbette of Hook, a silver grey, Miss Newall's brown Cadbury Cocoa of Ellingham, Chaseley Lamb, a silver grey, Wendette of Hook, another grey, Ilona and Jeanette of Ellingham, both black, and Mrs. Leonard Crouch's Orchard Blossom. In the following year twenty Miniatures were registered and the size was definitely established. Miss Brunker, though still showing and winning with her large Poodles, was enthusiastically breeding and showing Miniatures.

The large white Poodles were always very popular in England, and in the earlier days before the Miniatures were recognized as such there were quite a number of beautiful whites. The larger white Poodles were far better in head properties than the smaller ones; the tinies, lovely though they were, were usually rather thick in skull and it was not until recently that we have seen a marked improvement in this respect. Mrs. Leonard Crouch had showed several good large whites, such as Champion Orchard Whiteboy, which could have held his own with any of the present-day white Standards, Orchard Whitefrock being another good one. In 1907 Miss Rose Armitage was having considerable success with her small whites under the prefix of Chaseley. Miss Florence Brunker's small white Le Roi Blanc was beginning to make his mark on the breed. Mated to Blanchette Blondie she produced Perrito which, mated to an unregistered bitch called Chiffon, bred the well-known Champion—Champion Alresford Powder Puff. At this same time Miss May Hawley (Mrs. Pacey) began showing Chaseley Leo, sired by Kleine Wilhelm, the dam being Chaseley Jose. Kleiner Wilhelm had been sired by another unregistered dog—Fido out of Chaseley Camille. Miss Hawley did a lot of winning with Chaseley Leo.

It is interesting to read that in an Open Class at the Ladies'
Kennel Association Show a small white named Lady Betty won
the first prize in an Open Class confined to dogs measuring under
12 inches. Mrs. Walpole Harvey was another continuous breeder
and winner of small whites. Her dogs were very small and of a
dazzling whiteness with coal-black points, and they were always
full of life and zest. I think Mrs. Harvey would have been amazed
to see the silver skin in Poodles about which we hear so much
nowadays. At that time all the white Poodles, whether large or
small, had pink skins sometimes with slight brownish markings.
La Culotte Blanche was one of the first winners shown by Mrs.
Walpole Harvey, but her Champion Kasha was the biggest
winner of all her Kennel and was almost a legend. This little
bitch had an enormous coat of the correct texture, snow white,
beautiful small feet, and she was a wonderful showman. If there
was ever a dog who enjoyed a Show it was Champion Kasha. She
had, however, the rather thick skull which all the whites of that
day possessed and this sometimes made her the loser to the black
and blue Miniatures. The all-round Judges could rarely resist
Champion Kasha swaggering in the Ring and she also made a
great appeal to the ringsiders. She was sired by Mon Cheri Blanc
out of L'Aigrette Blanche. Miss Lane also had a hand in the
breeding of the small whites. Her Nunsoe Dandy Jim is at the
back of all the winning white strains of the present day. Sired by
Nunsoe Little White Aigrette, his dam was Mrs. Megroz' Colerne
Down Black-Eyed Susan. Dandy Jim is still happily alive and, at
the age of fifteen years, is an honoured and loved member of the
Vulcan Champagne Kennel.

Monsieur Dagois, recently writing of the white Poodles
owned in the past by his father, the well-known breeder and
exhibitor, says that his father always clipped his Poodles himself
for showing—'the pinky skin showing up the snowy whiteness of
the white dogs'. He also states that the Corded white The Belioron
and all his puppies were pink-skinned with a few light brown or
fawn patches or spots not noticeable unless the dogs were shaved.

In 1916 Mrs. Arthur Hudson's name appeared in the *Kennel
Club Stud Book* for the first time with Mimi, a black Miniature
bred by herself, the sire being Champion Whippendell Negrillon,
the dam Little Judy. This bitch came from a brown strain, her
sire being Marco by Whippendell Tabac out of Cocoatina.
Cocoatina herself was sired by The Black Prince out of a dam

called Cocoa. Tabac's sire Snuffle was an unregistered dog; his dam Sourisette was by Miss Brunker's Whippendell Moufflon Bleu out of Petite Molly. Mrs. Arthur Hudson was fascinated by the blues and decided to specialize in them, and by the nineteen-thirties possessed a Kennel of blue Poodles which has never been excelled—one might say never equalled. She purchased Champion The Blue Boy from Mrs. Taylor, another great breeder of blues. The Blue Boy was sired by Chic of Watercroft out of Mrs. Taylor's Champion Arcangel, a most beautiful blue bitch. This bitch was sired by Mickey Free, her dam being Joan of Arc. Mickey Free was sired by Puck of Pré Fleuri out of Star Spangle.

Mrs. Hudson then added to her Kennel The Sprite, a grey bitch which had been sired by Whippendell Azor, a blue, out of Babette Grise, again going back to The Midshipmite and The Blue Girl. From The Sprite mated back to The Midshipmite Mrs. Hudson got Grey Mitten, a grey bitch. Mating her to Champion The Blue Boy produced that magnificent blue bitch Champion Blue Blossom, one of the finest Miniature blue Poodles ever seen in the ring. Mrs. Hudson then mated The Sprite to Champion The Blue Boy, the result being the unbeaten Champion The Silver Gnome. This dog was a pure silver and he excelled in head properties and graceful movement. He was always the devoted companion of Mr. Hudson. He lived to a great age, being found dead in his basket in Mr. Hudson's room.

With Champion The Blue Boy, Champion Blue Blossom and Champion The Silver Gnome, Mrs. Hudson possessed the pillars of her unsurpassed Kennel of blues. She now introduced some black blood with Puff of Smoke, a small bitch bred by Mrs. Tyndall, sired by Champion Naughty Boy, the dam being the same breeder's well-known Leila. Leila was bred by Miss Ormsby who also bred The Grey Billikin, another dog owned by Mrs. Hudson.

Mrs. Hudson was insistent that in breeding blues to get the true lovely soft blue colour no brown should ever be introduced. Pale silver bitches should always be bred to a dark blue sire, and every fourth generation black should be brought in. For preference silver bred. The best coloured blues, she maintained, are got from the pale silver dogs mated to dark grey bitches. Silvers mated together will, after four generations, inevitably have oyster-coloured eyes.

Warrior in Steel, also bred by Mrs. Hudson, sired by The Blue Boy, did a lot of winning.

This Kennel of lovely blues was almost wiped out in the late 'thirties by a mysterious disease; over thirty dogs, including Champions and young stock, died. Though greatly distressed and disheartened, Mrs. Hudson started to rebuild her Kennel with the few dogs she had left. She had a young bitch named Aura with which she hoped to re-establish her position in blues. She also began breeding blacks, with which she did a good deal of winning, amongst them notably Wigginton Daphne.

Both Mr. and Mrs. Hudson were in great demand as Judges, and although their views did not always coincide, their decisions were never questioned. Mr. Hudson died very suddenly during the Second World War and his wife did not long survive him. By her will all the Poodles in her Kennel were put to sleep, and thus ended a great achievement in the breeding of the perfectly coloured blues. Mrs. Hudson especially disliked the commercialization of Poodles and was never very willing to sell her dogs unless she was sure they were going to good homes.

Miss Fletcher, of the Campden Kennel, had helped to lay the foundations of the blue Miniatures. Her Campden Rena was sired by Chic of Watercroft, bred by Miss Nunn. This dog was concerned in the pedigrees of most of the best blues, being sired by Jacques of Hook out of an unregistered bitch called Betty. Campden Rhoda's sire was another unregistered dog, Prince out of Campden Josephine, which was sired by Shawl Joe out of Petite Lulu. These Campden and Watercroft dogs will be found in practically every blue pedigree.

Mrs. Taylor was another great breeder of blue Poodles. She was conspicuous in the Ring with Champions Arcangel and her daughter, Champion Angel of Mine, sired by Chic of Watercroft. A third generation of this strain came forward in Champion The Monarch, another grand little blue, the son of Champion Angel of Mine sired by The Diplomat.

Mrs. Audrey Tyndall's Vendas Kennel was producing many winners, some of them owned by other exhibitors. Bonny Forget Me Not owned by Mrs. Campbell Inglis was bred by Mrs. Tyndall. Mated to the International Champion Sparkling Jet, she produced in one litter Champion The Laird of Mannerhead and Champion Limelight. Bonny Forget Me Not was then mated to Blue Masterpiece and the result was the lovely Champion Flashlight of Mannerhead. Mrs. Tyndall's bitch Leila, bred by Mrs. Ormsby, was also responsible for the foundation of other blue Kennels. She was sired by Miss Brunker's Whippendell Crepon out of Babette Grise. Blue Masterpiece, bred by Mrs. Tyndall and first shown in 1934, was sired by Vendas Arrow of Silver, his dam being Leila.

The Sirius strain of silver Poodles was introduced into this country from Germany by Mrs. Crimmins. Irish by birth, Mrs. Crimmins was married to an American, and her frequent visits to the United States made her well conversant with the Poodles over the water. The Sirius Kennel was owned by Miss Kalendar. These dogs were of a pure silver colour much paler than the forget-me-not blues. Showing under the prefix of Barbet, Mrs. Crimmins had considerable success with her dogs in the Show Ring. She imported many dogs from the Continent, mostly from Germany. Her Barbet Chita, sired by Barbet Brer Possum out of Barbet Shadow, was her first Certificate winner. Another of Mrs. Crimmins's winning dogs was Barbet Silver Slipper, the sire being Barbet Vendas Silver Lancer, the dam again Barbet Shadow. Barbet Shadow came from Mrs. Hudson's stock, her sire being Champion The Blue Boy, her dam Bayford Bettine. Champion Mala Sirius was the best of Mrs. Crimmins's dogs. He came from Germany and had a great influence on the Barbets.

In 1932 Mrs. Twist came into the Show Ring with her Hunninghams, which were mostly silvers. Hunningham d'Argent was sired by Champion The Silver Gnome out of Hunningham Rikki Tikki. This bitch was by Whippendell Azor out of an unregistered bitch named Josephine.

In the same year Mrs. Vaughan and her son showed their Champion Somebody sired by Champion The Blue Boy out of their own bitch afterwards Champion Angelica. The Wymerings owned by the Vaughans were nearly all blue dogs and they achieved considerable success. They were largely founded on Mrs. Hudson's stock. Wymering Caddie was a very good small brown, bred by Miss Thorp by the black Champion Chieveley Chopstick out of Mimi of Newlyn, and Champion Wymering Brown Jack was another lovely brown. At this time it was still permissible to mate Miniatures to Standards, the resulting progeny being divided according to size. Thus Mimi of Newlyn's dam was a Poodle, her sire Champion Chieveley Chopstick a Miniature, and, as mentioned earlier, the well-known Leila was registered at the Kennel Club as a Poodle.

It was much later that it was decided by the Kennel Club

that this mating if carried out would have progeny which must be registered as inter-bred.

Mrs. Hudson made several breeding experiments which were most successful. In 1932 her Oberon was winning, being sired by The Silver Gnome out of Toy Princess, a black. Her Titania and Bandar were both winning small blues. Elfin Prince sired Wigginton Daphne, a beautiful black bitch and the first to carry Mrs. Hudson's prefix of Wigginton.

Wigginton Circe, which Mrs. Hudson called her coming star, was bred by her Mars, a grey unshown dog, out of Titania, a blue. Circe was a most lovely blue and won two Certificates before the outbreak of the Second World War. With the rest of the dogs at Wigginton she was put to sleep at Mrs. Hudson's death. Bandar was by Mars out of Mistletoe, a very dark grey bitch of fine quality but unshowable owing to her nervous temperament. Mrs. Hudson bred some of her best dogs out of an unshown bitch named Juno, sired by Champion The Blue Boy out of Puff of Smoke. Puff of Smoke was a very small black and a potential dam of good stock. It was unfortunate that Mrs. Hudson had no prefix until shortly before her death, so that her strain is not easily recognizable by present-day breeders. In the nineteen-thirties the blues were lovely, and were quite capable of winning in such company as the black Chieveleys and Piperscrofts.

Since the end of the Second World War very few blue Miniature Poodles have been exhibited and at the time of writing none that could compare either in colour or type with the splendid dogs owned by Mrs. Arthur Hudson. It is much to be hoped that breeders will work to establish a winning kennel of blues of the same calibre as the Wigginton dogs.

The Miniature Poodle Club had been formed in 1910, and it may be of interest to read the definition of the perfect Miniature Poodle as drawn up by Mrs. Hudson, Miss Brunker, Miss Bowring, Mrs. Glynn and Miss M. Y. Newall and Miss Moorhouse, when they were the Club's Committee:

Size.—Must be under 15 inches at shoulder but the smaller the better as long as the Poodle type is kept to.

General Appearance.—That of a very active, intelligent, smart, and elegant-looking little dog, well-built and carrying himself proudly.

Head.—To be as long, straight, and fine as possible; very slight stop; fine skull.

Muzzle.—Long and fine, not full in the cheek; teeth white and level; black lips not showing lippiness.

Eyes.—Oval shaped, very dark, full of fire and intelligence.

Nose.—Black and pointed.

Ears.—The leather long and wide, low set, and hanging close to the face.

Neck.—Well proportioned, the head being carried high and with dignity.

Shoulders.—To slope well to the back.

Chest.—Deep and moderately wide.

Back.—Very short, very slightly hollowed, loins not too broad, ribs well sprung and braced up.

Feet.—Very small and dainty, of oval shape, the toes not to open when set on the ground.

Legs.—The forelegs set very straight from shoulder with fine bone and muscle. Hind legs muscular and well bent; hocks well let down.

Tail.—Set on high, gaily carried, never curled or carried over back.

Coat.—For curly: very profuse, of hard texture, of even length; very frizzy, not at all open.

Colours.—Any even colour.

White Miniatures to have black eyes, black rims to eyes, black nose and lips.

The Red and Brown Miniatures to have brown eyes, brown nose and lips.

The Blue Miniature to have dark eyes, black nose and lips.

The Cream or Apricot Miniature to have black eyes, nose and lips.

FAULTS IN THE MINIATURE POODLE

Heavy build, clumsiness, long back, light and prominent eyes, bad stern carriage, coarse head, over- or under-shot mouth, flesh-coloured nose, coarse legs and feet. Open and rusty coats. White markings on black Poodles, lemon markings on white and coloured Poodles.

Chapter VII

THE MINIATURE POODLE

The Blacks

BEFORE the recognition of Miniatures at the Kennel Club there had been many small Poodles which won in hot competition with their larger brethren. Miss Brunker had some, but after this date several people took up the breeding of black Miniatures with much enthusiasm. Two of the earliest of these breeders were the Misses Newall; their very good small blacks with the prefix Ellingham were steady winners. Manikin, Jeanette and Ilona of Ellingham were among the first batch to be registered as Miniatures. The Ellingham dogs were always very well bodied, sound little dogs.

It was in 1912 that Miss Mary Moorhouse came on the Poodle scene to start breeding her famous Chieveleys, perhaps the finest Kennel of small blacks seen previous to the Second World War. Her first dog, Harcourt Jack, became a Champion very speedily. His sire was Megs Sambo, his dam an unregistered bitch named Jill. Megs Sambo was by Kiddye out of Diane, another unregistered bitch. In 1915 Champion Chieveley Choufleur was first shown, a lovely black bitch, her sire being Whippendell Chou, her dam Chieveley Bunty. Bunty had been sired by Champion Harcourt Jack, the dam being Harcourt Bijou. Another of the same breeding was Chieveley Beau.

Miss Moorhouse's first dogs carried the prefix Harcourt because at that time she was living in Harcourt Terrace, London. But when she increased her Kennel she moved into the country, to The White Cottage, Chieveley, near Newbury, and she altered her prefix to what was to become the famous one of Chieveley.

From this time onwards the Chieveleys came into the Show Ring in rapid succession, always covering themselves with honours. In 1922 we saw Champion Chieveley Cheeky Boy, Champion Chieveley Chuckles, Chieveley Charlotte and Chieveley Chuette and one blue, Chieveley Aura, competing against the

Whippendell's Boule de Neige, Marabout, Chevrette, Georgette and Tigrette.

With varying fortunes these dogs and bitches were always in the money. Champion Chieveley Grumps had also appeared, a rather larger dog than his Kennel mates.

The First World War had put a stop to most dog breeding; from 1917 to 1919 inclusive there were no Miniature Poodle registrations at the Kennel Club. But in 1923 Champion Chieveley Cheeky Boy took the Dog Certificate at the first three Dog Shows of the year, achieving great glory. This lovely black dog was considered by most Judges to be the best of the Chieveleys, though some of the others bearing this prefix ran him close. He was of a dense blackness with a beautiful dark eye full of fire, and his carriage in the Ring always earned him great applause—he was such a swanker! In 1925 Chieveley Challenger, Chieveley Chicot, Chieveley Chuckles, Chieveley Chintz and Chieveley Charlotte were all amongst the winners. In 1925 Chieveley Chaps, Chieveley Chela, Chieveley Chase, Chieveley Chiquette and Chieveley Chota Mem appeared and were all of the high quality now expected from this wonderful Kennel.

Another of the big winners of that day was Champion Naughty Boy, owned by Mr. G. H. Day, the well-known breeder and Judge. He was sired by Champion Chieveley Cheeky Boy out of Chieveley Peggy. His name appears in many pedigrees. In 1927 the Chieveleys were still staging fresh winning faces; Chieveley Cheg, Chieveley Chanteur, Chieveley Chaplet, Chieveley Cheverel, Chieveley Chunky, Chieveley Chicane and the famous Champion, Chieveley Chopstick, were all winning. In 1928 Chieveley Chinchilla, Chieveley Chivy, Chieveley Chaplet, Chieveley Chasseuse and Chieveley Chenille made their bows.

Miss Moorhouse loved her dogs and would never sell them to anyone unless they were assured of good homes. She had very decided views on the breeding of her dogs and the management of her Kennel. Her success as a careful, clever line-breeder speaks for itself in the long chain of winners bearing her prefix. The dogs were allowed all the freedom possible and had, in relays, the run of the lovely grounds at The White Cottage. It was the ordinary thing to sit down to lunch at The White Cottage with twenty Poodles in the room. Miss Moorhouse also insisted that such highly strung, lively dogs required a period of rest in the afternoons, when all the Chieveleys were shut up in their kennels.

Her methods were the correct way to breed lovely Poodles. To bring out many of their finest characteristics they need to play and to be happy.

One of Miss Moorhouse's best breeding bitches was Chieveley Chatty, sired by Champion Chieveley Chopstick out of the very small Champion Chieveley Chess. Chopsticks was bred by Champion Chieveley Chaps out of Chieveley Charmeuse. Champion Chieveley Chess was sired by Champion Chieveley Choufleur. Miss Moorhouse did not often go outside her own Kennel for breeding; it was extensive enough to make this easy. Her line-breeding was carried out on a large, calculated scale.

Her dogs were always densely coated and of a deep black throughout. Champion Chieveley Choufleur not only sired Champion Chieveley Chess but also Champion Chieveley Cheeky Boy. Cheeky Boy's dam was Desdemona of Monte Cristo, which went back to an unregistered dog called Tiny Tim out of Star Spangle.

With Chieveley Aura, Miss Moorhouse introduced some blue blood into her Kennel, for Aura was bred by Miss Fletcher by Chic of Watercroft out of Campden Rhoda. Chieveley Chatty carried a very strong Chieveley strain, and some of our best dogs at the present time are descended from this beautiful bitch.

After the death of Miss Moorhouse, Chatty passed into the possession of Mrs. G. L. Boyd. There is a direct descendant of Chieveley Chatty in Mrs. Ionides' Vulcan Champagne Panolfo, a dark grey dog. He is a son of Vulcan Champagne Platinum out of Fifi of Pilgrims. This bitch was out of Bal Rouge, a daughter of Chieveley Chatty sired by Platinum of Eathorpe. Chieveley Chou, a lovely little blue bitch, was given to Miss Bowring by Sir Harry Moorhouse; a winner whenever shown till her early death from heart disease. Chatty's most remarkable descendants are the Firebraves owned by Mrs. Harold Monro.

Anyone of experience who knew the Chieveleys cannot fail to recognize their reproduction in this present-day winning Kennel of blacks. Miss Moorhouse died in 1929 and left her Kennel to her brother, Sir Harry Moorhouse, hoping that he would carry on the high tradition of the Chieveleys until her little great-niece was old enough to take them over. But Sir Harry found this to be impossible. A dozen of the best of the Chieveleys were selected to form a small Kennel for him and with these he carried on for a short while. The remainder of the Chieveleys were either given to friends or, if elderly and unlikely to settle down, put to sleep. There were eighty Poodles in Miss Moorhouse's Kennel when she died.

Eventually Mr. Price of Boston purchased the dogs from Sir Harry and they were all shipped to the United States, including the celebrated dogs Champion Chieveley Chopstick and Champion Chieveley Chump which both became American Champions. These two were the only Miniature Poodles to achieve this double honour, though since then Mrs. Sherman Hoyt has accomplished this same feat with her Champion Bonny Bright Eyes of Mannerhead of Blakeen. Champion Chieveley Chess accompanied the dogs but I can find no record of her having been exhibited in the States.

This bitch and Champion Chieveley Chivy were amongst the big winners shown by Sir Harry after his sister's death, whilst Champion The Blue Boy, Champion The Monarch and Champion Kasha were all competing. These two blue dogs and little white bitch were in full competition with the winning blacks and were well able to hold their own in the hottest competition.

It was at this time that Mr. and Mrs. Willett made their appearance in the Poodle Ring to begin a long winning career. The Spriggan Bell owned by them won all the Dog Certificates in 1930 which were not carried off by Champion Chieveley Chaps. These two blacks dominated the scene, whilst in bitches Mrs. Arthur Hudson's Champion Blue Blossom presented herself and swiftly became a Champion.

Mrs. Hutchinson was showing a brown Miniature called Nymphaea Binnie. Her sire was Nymphaea Bruno, a Poodle, her dam a Miniature Whippendell Petite Brune, pure Whippendell bred. In 1931 Champion Spriggan Bell was still winning, as was Champion Chieveley Chump.

Mrs. Campbell Inglis now appears with her Dare Devil Dink, and Mrs. G. L. Boyd showed and won with Champion Louis of Piperscroft, the celebrated winner in Obedience Trials. This dog sired by Champion Pronto of Gotton out of La Pompadour of Piperscroft, which bitch was bred by Mr. Upton Robins and sired by The Aide de Camp out of Belinda Bleu. In 1932 Mrs. Arthur Hudson showed her first black dog, named Oberon. She also had considerable success with two other small poodles, Titania and Elfin Prince. Champion Spriggan Bell and Champion Louis of Piperscroft continued to share the honours, whilst Mrs. Campbell

Inglis brought out Eric Brighteyes, bred by Mrs. Taylor. His sire was Popinjay, his dam Bonny Forget Me Not, which was again by The Aide de Camp out of Belinda Bleu.

She also registered Sparkling Jet by Dare Devil Dink out of Crystal Bell. In 1933 Champion Spriggan Bell and Champion Eric Brighteyes were still carrying off the Dog Certificates, whilst the Willetts' The Ghost, another small black, had arrived also to become a Champion. In this same year Mr. and Mrs. Harper were introducing the Harpendales, originally bred from Whippendell stock. Champion Spriggan Bell continued to win throughout 1924. As at this time it was still permissible to breed Miniatures with a Poodle on one side, Vanity of Piperscroft was shown, sired by Mrs. Glynn's famous Champion Pronto of Gotton out of Black Beauty, a Poodle. Black Beauty was by the well-known dog Champion Naughty Boy out of Folette, a bitch sired by Whippendell Drapeau, another Poodle. In 1935 Mrs. Campbell Inglis's Champion Eric Brighteyes won all the eight Dog Certificates offered for Miniature Poodles that year, a record in Poodle history.

Mrs. Campbell Inglis had a great winning run at this time in the Miniature Poodle Ring. In 1936 she brought out the famous Champion The Laird of Mannerhead, sired by her Sparkling Jet out of Bonny Forget Me Not. This dog in the succeeding year took seven of the Certificates offered for Miniature Dogs, five of them off the reel, whilst his litter sister, The Mistress of Mannerhead, also entered the lists by winning a Bitch Certificate, accompanied by Sparkle of Mannerhead, another winning bitch. Sparkle was sired by Pierre, a Poodle, her dam being Psyche which goes back to Champion Whippendell Carillon on her sire's side.

Majoli de Madjigé, bred by Mademoiselle Galignani by Footit de Madjigé out of Joliette de Madjigé, was registered at the Kennel Club in 1939. Footit was sired by Champion Spriggan Bell out of Chieveley Chepress, whose sire was Champion Chieveley Chopstick. Joliette de Madjigé was sired by Ebbo Sirius out of Fausta. Here we have the combination of the best known English, French and German strains.

In 1938 the Challenge Certificates at seven Shows were all won by the Mannerheads, with Champion Flashlight, Champion Mistress and Champion Limelight, all of Mannerhead.

It was in this year that Mrs. Harold Monro founded the

Firebraves, those noteworthy descendants of the Chieveleys. The famous Champion Barty of Piperscroft was bred by Mrs. Monro, his sire being Monty of Piperscroft, his dam Manon of Piperscroft. He was originally named Firebrave Petit Ours, but on transfer to Mrs. G. L. Boyd his name was altered to Barty of Piperscroft. Manon of Piperscroft was by Petit Ami of Piperscroft out of La Pompadour of Piperscroft; Petit Ami was of Chieveley stock, having been sired by Chieveley Chanteur out of Champion Chieveley Chess. In 1939 Champion Barty of Piperscroft won four of the Certificates offered for dogs, whilst Firebrave Cupidon (his litter brother) began to win until the spread of the war ended the Championship Shows. Cupidon was thus deprived of the honours which might have been his. He lived to a great age and was the founder of the Firebraves. Even as an old dog his quality was great. Fine in head, he had also beautifully tiny feet. He dominated the entire Kennel, in which all acknowledged him to be their master. He died in 1950. Up to the day of his death no Firebrave dared to contest his leadership in their home.

There is no short cut to establishing a strain of dogs. Having an eye for the purchase of future winners is certainly a great asset not possessed by everyone. But skill, ability and patience must all go to producing a famous strain. We have an example of this in the Firebraves. Even through the discouraging years of the Second World War Mrs. Harold Monro persevered with her Firebraves, and it was nine years after she had first interested herself in Miniature Poodles that she brought out that great Champion Firebrave Gaulois, one of the most outstanding dogs of our time. His sire was Sienna of Piperscroft, his dam Firebrave Pepita (daughter of Firebrave Cupidon). Alida Monro died in July 1969.

Chapter VIII

THE POST-WAR POODLES

DURING the Second World War some of the greatest breeders of Poodles died, notably Mr. and Mrs. Arthur Hudson in 1941, and in 1943 Miss Millie Brunker and her sister, Mrs. Douglas Beith. It was, however, fortunate indeed for the Poodle that some of the well-known breeders of the pre-war days had kept steadily breeding on a small scale—the Piperscrofts Nunsoes, Vulcan Champagnes, Hockfords and Rathnallys amongst the breeders of Standards, and the Mannerheads, Firebraves, Piperscrofts and Adastras amongst the Miniatures. Also, Mrs. Audrey Tyndall had kept her Vendas Kennel going. In 1943 this breeder had registered in the *Kennel Club Stud Book* Vendas Somebody in Silver, and in the same year Mrs. Ionides had registered Vulcan Champagne Silvo. But in 1944 and 1945 no Miniature Poodles appear in the *Kennel Club Stud Book*. So when the war ended there was some very good Poodle stock in the country as well as some of doubtful origin.

From 1940 to 1945 the Poodle Club was in abeyance, but in the latter year a meeting was held at Hogge House, the Sussex residence of Mrs. Ionides, and the Club was resuscitated. In October, 1946, it was decided to send the following resolution to the Kennel Club:

"In view of the indiscriminate crossing of Poodles and Poodles Miniature, and the consequent degeneration of the breed, it is resolved to ask the Kennel Club to alter the present classification, and to make Poodles and Poodles-Miniature separate breeds."

It was further decided that it should be clearly stated on the pedigrees of the progeny of any crossings which parents are Poodles and which Poodles Miniature.

In 1947 a Resolution on the same lines was passed and again sent to the Kennel Club.

The Poodle Club, which had protected the interests of the breed for so many years, staged two Specialist Championship

Shows for Poodles in June and October, 1946. The President of the Club was Mrs. G. L. Boyd, the Honorary Secretary being Mrs. Harold Monro. The first of these Shows, held at the Scottish Drill Hall in Westminster, was held in conjunction with the English Shetland Sheepdog Club. Miss Bowring, being interested in both breeds, was Show Secretary for the Poodle Section, whilst Miss Day Currie carried out the same duties for the Shetland Sheepdogs. The Poodle Judge was Doctor Leach, better known before the war as Miss Rochford of the Berkham Kennels. The winner of the Dog Standard Certificate was Marcus of Hockford, owned by Mrs. Fife Failes and Miss English, whilst that for Bitches was won by Sunshine of Piperscroft, owned by Mrs. G. L. Boyd. In Miniatures there was a large entry, the Dog Certificate winner being Mrs. Harold Monro's Firebrave Gaulois, whilst the Bitch Certificate was carried off by Flip of Swanhill, owned by Mrs. Hilliard and bred by Mrs. Buckle, the dam being Firebrave Black Opal. At the October Show, where the two breeds again combined, the Kennel Club again offered Challenge Certificates. The Poodles were judged by Mr. Siggars and the venue was the Horticultural Hall, also in Westminster. The winner of the Dog Certificate for Standards was Mrs. G. L. Boyd's Shandy of Piperscroft, bred by Mrs. Bettridge, his sire being Mist of Piperscroft, a dog which has been a consistent sire of winners. The Bitch Certificate was awarded to Mrs. Saunders's Bewick Ballerina, whose sire and dam were both Nunsoes. The Miniatures at this Show again had a very large entry, the Dog Certificate being won by Firebrave Gaulois. Mr. Howard Price's Tresor de Madjigé was placed first in the Open Bitch Class, but the Challenge Certificate was given to Mrs. Vernon Tate's Firebrave Zizi.

The International Poodle Club, whose founder and President was Mrs. Campbell Inglis, now put on a Championship Show in November of the same year. The Judge was Mrs. Sherman Hoyt, who had come over from the United States and was a very welcome visitor. At this Show the Standard Certificate winners were Vulcan Champagne Darcy which won the Dog Certificate, bred by Mr. and Mrs. Ionides and owned by Mrs. Price Jones, whilst Mrs. Saunders's Bewick Ballerina took that offered for Standard Bitches. In Miniatures, Firebrave Gaulois repeated his two previous wins and became the first post-war Champion Miniature Poodle. An outstanding dog, he well deserved this honour. On this occasion he was accompanied by his Kennel

(*Casstine*)

Ch. Orchard Admiral (*Standard black*)

(*J. Wilkins*)

Ch. Orchard Diamond (*Standard black*)

Nunsoe Nellie von Lirrendenquai (*Standard black*)

Int. Ch. Nunsoe Chevalier Labory (*Standard black*)

Aunt Chloe (*Standard black*)

Nunsoe Dandy Jim aged fifteen years (*Miniature white*)

Int. Ch. Nunsoe Duc de la Terrasse of Blakeen (*Standard white*)

Int. Ch. Blakeen Eiger and his sister, Ch. Blakeen Jungfrau
(*Standard whites*)

companion, Firebrave Nicolette, which took the Bitch Certificate at this her first Show and was soon to become a full Champion herself. All the Certificate winners at this Show became Champions, testifying to Mrs. Hoyt's ability as a Judge of Poodles. Bewick Ballerina was the first post-war Standard Poodle.

The Vulcan Champagnes, owned at the present time by Mrs. Ionides and Miss Shirley Walne, emerged after the war to take a premier place amongst the Standard Poodles. Not only have they bred many Champions; their stock has been largely responsible for both the Frenches Kennel, owned by Mrs. Price Jones, and the Peaslake Kennel, owned by Mrs. Hilliard. Both these Kennels are now firmly established. Mrs. Price Jones has had remarkable success with her Frenches. She became the owner of Champion Vulcan Champagne Darcy, the beautiful dog bred by Mrs. Ionides. His sire was Copper Top of Astolat, his dam Vulcan Jean. Jean's sire was Champion Vulcan Champagne Pommery, her dam Nunsoe Damsel. Nunsoe Damsel brought in the famous Labory strain owned by Madame Reichenbach, for her sire was Nunsoe Chevalier Labory.

At the nine Championship Shows of 1947 four of the Certificates offered for Dogs were won by Champion Vulcan Champagne Darcy, whilst Vulcan Champagne Titan took the Dog Certificate at the Poodle Club's Show. This fine dog was sired by Vulcan Champagne Dragonfly out of a bitch named Judy. Dragonfly had been sired by an imported dog named Tommy out of Guestling Kiki, whilst Judy was by Nunsoe Tawny out of an imported bitch named Sheila. Guestling Kiki was sired by Brin of Rathnally out of Nunsoe Athene, whose dam was the well-known Champion Nunsoe Em'ly Brown.

In this same year Mrs. Price Jones's Frenches Blue Peter took the Certificate offered for Dogs at the International Poodle Club's Show and the Ladies' Kennel Association Show, whilst Vulcan Champagne Jocelyn took the Bitch Certificate at the two last-named Shows. Frenches Blue Peter, bred by Mrs. Price Jones, was sired by Mist of Piperscroft out of Frenches Vulcan Queen of Spades. This Queen's sire was Champion Vulcan Champagne Pommery, her dam Vulcan Dulcima. Vulcan Queen of Spades has had a most remarkable breeding career and she must stand high in any record of pillars of the breed. Champion Frenches Blue Peter, Champion Frenches Ferenita and Frenches Opulence, all of the same litter, are her children. Champion Black

E

Cherry and Black Tulip were in another litter bred from the Queen of Spades. Champion Blue Marvel, Champion Frenches Mighty Fine, Champion Frenches Rigoletto, Champion Frenches Lili Marlene, Champion Paulette and Champion Frenches Monique are all grandchildren of the Queen of Spades. Mrs. Price Jones has bred and owned eleven Champions since the end of the war. Champion Frenches Blue Marvel has now been exported to America.

One of the most beautiful blue Standard Poodles ever shown is Champion Vulcan Champagne Spinach. The sire of this bitch was Spitfire of the Chain, her dam being Vulcan Champagne Jocelyn. She has the soft blue colour we knew so well in the pre-war Miniatures.

Of Mrs. Price Jones's eleven Standard Champions five have a Vulcan Champagne sire or dam, whilst Mrs. Ionides and Miss Walne have six Champions in their Kennel, of which five are directly bred from Vulcan Champagnes. This is a remark-able achievement of the Vulcan Champagnes and one of which to be justly proud. Of the thirty-three Champions made since the end of the war fifteen have a Vulcan Champagne sire or dam.

Another good Standard blue is Champion Peaslake Storm, sired also by Spitfire of the Chain out of Helle of Piperscroft. The Peaslake Kennel owned by Mrs. Hilliard is also now well established in the front rank of Standard Poodles. It has been largely influenced by Miss Statter's strain of Rettats and the Vulcan Champagnes. Spitfire of the Chain was sired by Berkham Hansel out of Rettats Striptease. Helle of Piperscroft was by Mist of Piperscroft out of Vulcan Peony. Peony had been sired by Champion Vulcan Champagne Pommery out of Vulcan Verena. The pedigree of Berkham Hansel is of interest. He was sired by Rettats Spinner out of the American Champion Berkham Coquette. The Spinner was by Berkham Apollo out of Berkham Wilhelmina.

Champion Vulcan Lady Jane, bred by Mrs. Case, was sired by Champion Nunsoe His Grace out of Vulcan Repetition. Nunsoe His Grace is a magnificent dog bred by Miss Jane Lane. His sire was again Champion Berkham Hansel, his dam Nunsoe Maid of the Mists. His Grace had a most spectacular career in the Show Ring and up to the end of 1951 was an unbeaten dog. He excels in his lovely head and his superb carriage. He is the sire of Nunsoe The Duke, the dam being Toffee de la Terrasse, which lived to the age of twelve years. Champion Nunsoe The Pin Up Girl is the latest Champion to be made up by Miss Jane Lane.

Mrs. Proctor's fine Kennel of Standard brown Poodles, the Tziganes, now houses four Champions. Champion Tzigane Parhee was sired by Champion Vulcan Champagne Darcy out of Tzigane Lushka. Lushka brought in an entirely new line, her sire being Dry Sherry, her dam The Black Lily, an unregistered bitch. Champion Tzigane Parhee sired Champion Tzigane Dizar out of Roundoaks Bovary whose sire was Vulcan Militant. The Vulcan Champagne Kennel is at the back of these lovely dogs. The Tziganes are established as a most excellent Kennel of brown Standards now in their fourth winning generation.

In 1947 the Miniature Poodles had fifteen Championship Shows. In that year Mrs. G. L. Boyd's Top Hat of Piperscroft became a Champion. His sire was Ruffles of Piperscroft, his dam Harriet of Piperscroft. Ruffles had been sired by Champion Barty of Piperscroft out of Bijou of Rigi. This bitch was sired by Mr. and Mrs. Harper's Harpendale John Brown out of Harpendale Black Beauty, whilst Harriet of Piperscroft was by Vendas Black Gnome ex Peggotty of Piperscroft.

Mrs. Austin Smith has made her name in Miniatures with her Kennel of Braevals, which have been consistent winners at all the post-war Shows. Champion Braeval Bobo was sired by Champion Toyboy of Toytown out of La Poupée of Heatherton. La Poupée comes from Firebrave stock, a daughter of Firebrave André, a son of Firebrave Copperfield, and Firebavre Mamselle. Her dam Festive of Heatherton was by Russet of Piperscroft out of Heatherton Folly of Piperscroft. Champion Braeval Bobo sired Champion Braeval Brioche, the dam Braeval Brighteyes, a daughter of Harwee of Mannerhead whose sire was the great Champion Eric Brighteyes. The same breeding produced Champion Braeval Bolero. In 1950 Mrs. Austin Smith brought out Braeval Biscuit, a cream dog sired by Fircot Garçon de la Neige out of Wychwood Daisy. He created something of a sensation and was sold to America for a large figure, where he quickly earned his title.

Champion Glendoune Dapper and Champion Glendoune Dazzle, owned by Mr. R. McGill, were both sired by Champion Toyboy of Toytown, their dam being Braeval Brownbella.

The Firebrave Kennel owned by Mrs. Harold Monro had now come to the fore in Miniatures. They had been carefully line-bred over a period of years and were direct descendants of

Chieveley Chatty. Champion Firebrave Gaulois' dam Firebrave Pepita was sired by Firebrave Cupidon out of Firebrave Mamselle, whose sire was François of Piperscroft out of Chieveley Chatty. Champion Firebrave Nicolette, which had quickly followed Firebrave Gaulois to Championship status, was sired by Firebrave Copperfield, a lovely brown dog, prevented by the war from being shown. Champion Firebrave Pimpernel was a son of Firebrave Nicolette, his sire being Firebrave Alphonse who went to America to join the Blakeen Kennels of Mrs. Sherman Hoyt. The sire of Alphonse was Robin of Piperscroft, a son of Champion Barty of Piperscroft. Champion Firebrave Pimpernel has a famous son in Pixholme Firebrave Gustav who not only became a Champion but also made his name in Obedience Tests. A winner of six Challenge Certificates and the Best Poodle Dog at the Poodle Club Show in 1950, he has, in the ownership of Mrs. Atkinson, won a bronze medal A.S.P.A.D.S. with the title of C.D. and was one of the best-known Poodles in England. He has now gone to America and is already an International Champion as is his father Triple Int. Champion Firebrave Pimpernel. Firebrave Spiro of Braebeck is another remarkable dog of Mrs. Monro's breeding. In the ownership of Mrs. Fox he has sired three of the post-war Champions owned by Mr. Howard Price. Other well known Firebrave dogs are Champion Firebrave Guilbert and Champion Firebrave Fleurette, which became a Champion in the ownership of Lady Stanier of the Seahorses Kennel. Of the forty-three post-war Miniature Champions ten are either home-bred Firebraves or have a Firebrave sire or dam, whilst others have come from Firebrave grandparents.

Mrs. Atkinson, the owner of Pixholme Firebrave Gustav, has herself bred three Champions. Champion Pixholme Milada, a daughter of The Laird of Mannerhead out of May Queen of Mannerhead, is the dam of Champion Pixholme Muffin of Gatton, the sire being Pixholme Romulus of Mannerhead, and Champion Pixholme Pepé completes the trio.

Mrs. Coventon introduced an entirely new strain of Miniature Poodles from the Continent. Just before the war broke out in 1939 she imported Montet de Madjigé and her sister, Majoli de Madjigé. Montet went to the States to Mrs. Sherman Hoyt. These two bitches were sired by Int. Champion Footit de Madjigé out of the Int. Champion Joliette de Madjigé, a bitch sired by the celebrated Int. Champion Ebbo Sirius out of Champion Fausta.

Majoli de Madjigé was mated by Mrs. Coventon to Vulcan Iris Labory, which had been imported by her and sold to Mrs. Ionides early in the war years. This mating produced Adastra Black Magic, the sire of Adastra Aboyne and Adastra Banco. Adastra Aboyne is the sire of Champion Adastra Magic Action and Adastra Banco is the sire of Champion Adastra Magic Beau. Mia Footit de Ponthieu, a small black bitch imported by Mrs. Coventon also in 1939, was sired by Int. Champion Footit de Madjigé, which was by the great Champion Spriggan Bell out of Chieveley Chepress, the dam being Witor Sirius. This was a very good German bitch sired by Champion Sahde of Sirius out of Annima Sirius. Champion Adastra Magic Beau sired by Adastra Banco was out of Adastra Admiration. He won five Challenge Certificates in 1951 and was placed Reserve to the Best in Show at Cruft's Show, a position never before achieved by a Poodle, thus showing that Poodles had really arrived.

Mr. Howard Price's Montfleuri Kennel houses no fewer than nine Champions. Three of the Montfleuri Champions were bred by Mrs. Fox by Firebrave Spiro of Braebeck out of Kema of Piperscroft. These are Champion Braebeck Toni of Montfleuri and the two lovely bitches Champions Braebeck Jonella and Trilla of Montfleuri. Champions Figaro and Valentina of Montfleuri are Mannerhead bred, Figaro being sired by Champion Milord of Mannerhead out of Ninette of Mannerhead bred by Mr. Howard Price, whilst Valentina is by Meurice of Mannerhead out of Jill of Mannerhead and was bred by Mrs. Lyons. Champion Figaro is now in the possession of Mrs. Stevenson.

Mrs. Campbell Inglis has not done much breeding since the war, though the Mannerheads have had their say in breeding Champions for other people. The two Champions bred by her are Champion Milord of Mannerhead, by Champion The Laird of Mannerhead out of Miladi of Mannerhead, and Champion Lorna of Mannerhead by Harwee of Mannerhead out of Monica of Mannerhead.

Mrs. Audrey Tyndall's Vendas Kennel has produced two Champions since the war, Frenches Comet owned by Mrs. Price Jones and bred by her out of Vendas Starry Light, and Champion Vendas Silver Pickles whose dam was The Silver Bird. Both these Champions were sired by Silda of Eathorpe.

Mrs. Davies, who owns the Heatherton Kennel, has bred two Champions, Felicity and Highlight of Heatherton, the last named being now in the ownership of Mr. Howard Price. Champion Felicity comes of Piperscroft stock on both sides, whilst Highlight's sire was Firebrave Alphonse, the dam being Fidelity of Heather ton.

Among the most interesting events in the Poodle world of late years is the wonderful improvement that has taken place in the white Miniatures. Charming as they were in many ways, the small whites were, before the war, inclined to thickness in skull but this has now been almost overcome and the present-day white Miniatures are capable of holding their own in the best company. The first post-war white Champion Miniature was the lovely Champion Tarry-wood Starlight Glow owned and bred by Mrs. Birch. Recently Mrs. Hall has imported the American Champion Blakeen Oscar of the Waldorf which has already done a lot of winning in this country.

An attempt has been made to give a picture of the progress of the Poodle over a period of seventy-five years. In writing of post-war events comment has been confined to Kennels which have bred Champions. It would have been invidious to do otherwise.

Many changes have taken place during these years. The Poodle Club, which has consistently and sincerely championed the breed through all its vicissitudes, is now one of the oldest breed Clubs in England, having been founded in 1876.

The Curly Poodle Club, founded by Miss Millie Brunker to protect Curly interests as against Corded, has vanished under the stress of the war years. So has the Miniature Poodle Club, an offshoot of the Poodle Club and backed by its Committee. But this Club did not entirely disappear; the last Secretary, Mr. Vaughan, of the Wymering Kennel, has handed back the Club's records and trophies to the Poodle Club from which it stemmed, with the approval of the Kennel Club. In 1932 the International Poodle Club was founded by Mr. and Mrs. Campbell Inglis, and the latter still remains as the Club's President. Most of this Club's records were, I believe, lost in the bombing of Wimbledon. The Scottish Poodle Club still flourishes on its native heath and we have recently seen the emergence of the South-Western Poodle Club sponsored by Mrs. Sheldon and Miss Lockwood.

Looking back over the years one sees the Poodle as he has always been, the aristocrat of the dog world, the faithful, devoted companion. But it is the conditions which have changed, not the dogs. Enormously mounting registrations at the Kennel Club have resulted in more and more Championship Shows every year at which many dogs are exhibited which are not of the calibre of

Show dogs. And there is the growing impossibility of finding really good Judges for so many Shows.

Many people say the Poodle as a Show dog has improved in the post-war years. The whites certainly have done so. But if the earlier pictures in this book are studied it will be seen that some of the older Champions, if taken into the Ring now, would be hard to beat. And the nobility of character shown by many Poodles could well be an example to ourselves.

Since the war the increase in the registrations has meant an increase in Championship Shows. The figures for these are interesting, remembering that in 1939 there were only eight Championship Shows for both Standards and Miniatures.

	CHAMPIONSHIP SHOWS			REGISTRATIONS AT THE KENNEL CLUB		
	Standards	Miniatures	Toys	Standards	Miniatures	Toys
1964	16	31	30	368	13246	10572
1965	15	32	32	417	11377	9903
1966	15	32	34	376	8716	8514
1967	16	32	34	474	7499	8475
1968	17	32	34	495	6536	8510
1969	18	32	36	711	5986	7671
1970	19	33	36	740	5291	7926
1971	20	33	36	679	4497	6362
1972	22	33	36	959	4692	6941
1973	23	34	37	970	4104	6616
1974	23	34	37	894	4009	6041
1975	26	32	36	833	2941	5174
1965	26	36	38			
1977	26	36	39			
1978	30	36	35			
1979	33	36	34			

(In April 1976 the Kennel Club changed its system of registrations, thus preventing the continuation of the above method of listing annual totals)

It is clear that Poodles of all three sizes have reached their zenith in registrations and since 1963 there has been a steady decline. This is to be welcomed as many Miniature and Toy Poodles have been exhibited which were not worthy of the show ring. The Standards suffered a severe loss by the death in 1963 of the Hon. Nellie Ionides who had such a large Kennel of these beautiful Poodles. Her world famous Vulcan Champagne Kennel is now in the possession of her partner Miss Shirley Walne, but somewhat reduced in numbers.

Chapter IX

POODLES IN AMERICA

THE American Kennel Club Description and Standard of Points (in accordance with ruling of the American Kennel Club, July 13th, 1943, and amendments submitted by the Poodle Club of America to the original standard and adopted by the American Kennel Club, February 14th, 1940, and November 14th, 1950), for the Poodle are as under:

The breed of Poodle is divided into three varieties:
Standard.—15 inches or over at the shoulder.
Miniature.—Under 15 inches but over 10 inches at the shoulder.
Toy.—10 inches or under at the shoulder.

1. General appearance, carriage, and condition—that of a very active, intelligent, smart and elegant-looking dog, squarely built, well proportioned and carrying himself proudly. Properly clipped in the traditional fashion and carefully groomed, the Poodle has about him an air of distinction and dignity peculiar to himself.

2. *Head and Expression.*
   (*a*) Skull.—Should be slightly full and moderately peaked with a slight stop. Cheek-bones and muscles flat. Eyes set far enough apart to indicate ample brain capacity.
   Muzzle.—Long, straight and fine, but strong without lippiness. The chin definite enough to preclude snipiness. Teeth white, strong, and level. Nose sharp with well-defined nostrils.
   (*b*) Eyes.—Oval shape, very dark, full of fire and intelligence.
   (*c*) Ears.—Set low and hanging close to the head. The leather long, wide, and heavily feathered—when drawn forward almost reaches the nose.

3. *Neck.*
   Well proportioned, strong and long enough to admit of the head being carried high and with dignity. Skin snug at throat.

4. *Shoulders.*
   Strong, muscular, angulated at the point of the shoulder and the elbow joint, sloping well back.

5. *Body.*

The chest deep and moderately wide. The ribs well sprung and braced up. The back short, strong and very slightly hollowed, with the loins broad and muscular. (Bitches may be slightly longer in back than dogs.)

6. *Tail.*

Set on rather high, docked, and carried gaily. Never curled or carried over the back.

7. *Legs.*

The forelegs straight from shoulders with plenty of bone and muscle. Hindlegs very muscular, stifles well bent, and hocks well let down. Hindquarters well developed with the second thigh showing both width and muscle.

8. *Feet.*

Rather small and of good oval shape. Toes well arched and close, pads thick and hard.

9. *Coat.*

   (*a*) Quality: Curly Poodles—very profuse, or harsh texture, even length, frizzy, or curly, not at all open. Corded Poodles— very thick, hanging in tight even cords.

   (*b*) Clip: Clipping either in the traditional 'Continental' style or 'English Saddle' style is correct. In the Continental clip the hindquarters are shaved, with pompons on hips (optional), and in the English Saddle clip the hind- quarters are covered with a short blanket of hair. In both these clips the rest of the body must be left in full coat. The face, feet, legs and tail must be shaved, leaving bracelets on all four legs, and a pompon at the end of the tail. The top knot and feather on the ears must be long and profuse, so as not to lose the very essential Poodle expression. A dog under a year old may be shown with the coat long except the face, feet, and base of tail, which should be shaved. Any Poodle clipped in any style other than the above mentioned shall be disqualified from the Show Ring.

10. *Colour.*

Any solid colour. All but the browns have black noses, lips and eyelids. The browns and apricots may have liver noses and dark amber eyes. In all colours toe-nails either black or the same colour as the dog.

Grey Poodles whose coats have not cleared to an even solid colour may be shown up to the age of eighteen months. The degree of clearing shall count only in judging two or more grey Poodles

under the age of eighteen months when all other points are
equal, in which case the more completely cleared dog shall be
judged superior.

11. *Gait.*
A straightforward trot with light, springy action. Head and tail
carried high.

12. *Size.*
The Standard Poodle is 15 inches or over at the shoulder.

13. *Value of points.*

General Appearance, Carriage and Condition	20
Head, Ears, Eyes and Expression	20
Neck and Shoulders	10
Body and Tail	15
Legs and Feet	10
Coat, Colour and Texture	15
Gait	10

14. *Major Faults.*
Bad mouth either under- or over-shot.
Cowhocks.
Flat or spread feet, thin pads.
Very light eyes.
Excessive shyness.

15. *Disqualifications.*
Parti-colours.
Unorthodox clip.

16. *Description and Standard of Points of the Ideal Miniature Poodle.*
   (*a*) Same as Large Poodle.
   (*b*) Size—under 15 inches at shoulder but over 10 inches.
   (*c*) Value of Points—same as Large Poodle.
   (*d*) So long as the dog is definitely a Miniature, diminutiveness is
          the deciding factor only when all other points are equal.
          Soundness and activity are every whit as necessary in a
          Miniature as they are in a Large Poodle, and as these traits
          can be seen only when the dog is in action it is imperative
          that Miniatures be moved in the Ring as fully and decidedly
          as Large Poodles.

17. *Description and Standard of Points of the Ideal Toy Poodle.*
   (*a*) Same as Large Poodle.
   (*b*) Size—10 inches or under at the shoulder.
   (*c*) Value of Points—Same as Large Poodle.
   (*d*) So long as the dog is definitely a Toy, diminutiveness is the
          deciding factor only when all other points are equal;

soundness and activity are every whit as necessary in a Toy as they are in a Large Poodle, and as these traits can be seen only when the dog is in action it is imperative that Toys be moved in the Ring as fully and decidedly as the Large Poodles.

As long ago as the 'eighties, Poodles had been imported into the United States by American breeders. Fecken, which was whelped in 1873, belonged to a Mr. Rutan of New York. Michael Angelo, owned by Mr. Felder of Brooklyn, was whelped in the same year and this dog took a First Prize at the New York Dog Show. Both these dogs had been brought from England. Styx, the great Poodle bred by Monsieur Duchateau, was born in June, 1883. He was exhibited in England in 1885 and won many prizes, including a First in one of the largest classes for Poodles ever seen at that time in Great Britain, namely the Crystal Palace Show in 1886. He was then sent to America where he won the highest honours.

The earlier Poodles in the States were mostly imported from the British Isles. But they were not admired throughout America —it seems that they were most popular on the Eastern coasts. In the 'nineties there were several Kennels breeding what are now known as Standard Poodles. They were of very good type and size. A few of the Miniatures existed, but in the United States at that time the larger dog was preferred.

The Poodle Standard was drawn up on December 16th, 1885. A Club known as the Poodle Club of America was formed in 1896, but this was dissolved in 1898. The Poodle Club of America was reformed in 1931 and was then elected to membership in the American Kennel Club.

For some unknown reason interest in the Poodle declined in the 1900s and very few were to be seen, hardly any being registered at the American Kennel Club. They never really became popular, as they were in England at that time.

But there were some breeders who persevered; it would be hard for anyone who really loved Poodles to give up interest in such a breed. Amongst those breeders mention must be made of the Misses Alger, Mr. and Mrs. Trevor, Mr. Moulyon in Boston and Mr. Jacobson in Chicago.

As mentioned, the Poodle Club of America had been reformed and among those most anxious to place the Poodle on the map in

America were some of those who had been its original founders, notably Mr. and Mrs. Sherman Hoyt, Mrs. Byron Rogers, Mr. Loring Marshall, Mr. and Mrs. Putnam and Mr. Charles Price of Boston. The last-named breeder had purchased from Sir Harry Moorhouse all the best dogs which had been left in the famous Chieveley Kennel after the death of his sister, Miss Mary Moorhouse, in 1929. Among these were the three notable dogs, Champion Chieveley Chopstick, Champion Chieveley Chump and the bitch Champion Chieveley Chess. All these Poodles caused a definite influence on the Miniature Poodles in America. Indeed, Champion Chieveley Chess may be said to have laid the foundations of the beautiful little Toy Poodles now attaining such excellence in the American Show Ring.

Mrs. Byron Rogers had urged Mrs. Whitehouse Walker to allow her to let her import some Poodles for her from England. Those she brought over had been bred by Mrs. Hutchinson, who owned the Nymphaea Kennel. These Nymphaeas were mostly of German stock and had been imported into England by Mrs. Hutchinson and her daughter. Champion Nymphaea Jason was the best of these Standard Poodles and was the sire of many of the winning Poodles in the States. The most famous of his off-spring was Champion Blakeen Cyrano bred by Mrs. Sherman Hoyt. Cyrano's dam was Blakeen Vigee Le Brun, a daughter of Champion Nymphaea Jason, whose breeding went back to the English Champions Joyeux and Joyette.

Mrs. Byron Rogers also purchased the American Champion Whippendell Poli from Miss Brunker, as well as American Champion Stillington Klaus from Mrs. Murray Wilson, another successful English breeder. Many fine Champions were bred from these two dogs.

Mrs. Sherman Hoyt at this time imported from England Champion Harpendale Monty of Blakeen, from the Harpendale Kennels owned by Mr. and Mrs. Harper. Monty was an English son of Stillington Christmas. Mrs. Milton Erlanger's Champion Pillicoc Rumpelstiltskin was a son of Champion Cadeau de Noel, which was a son of Stillington Christmas then of Carillon.

Mention must also be made of the charming bitch Anita of Lutterspring which, mated to Nymphaea Pice, produced in one litter the two Champions Roulette and Paul of Misty Isles, which was Mrs. Byron Rogers's prefix. These two dogs passed, at the age of two months, into what was to become the world-famous

Kennel of Blakeen, owned by Mrs. Sherman Hoyt. This German bitch, Anita of Lutterspring, was imported and was later registered in America with the help of Mrs. Sherman Hoyt. She was a wonderful dam and in addition to the two dogs already mentioned she produced Champion Blakeen More of Misty Isles, also sired by Nymphaea Pice. Mated to Eric Labory of Misty Isles, imported by Mrs. Byron Rogers from Madame Reichenbach, Anita also produced Champions Ambroise and Ambroisine of Misty Isles.

In 1934 Mrs. Sherman Hoyt imported the magnificent white Standard Poodle International Champion Nunsoe Duc de la Terrasse. As previously stated, the Duke had been brought to England by Miss Jane Lane, his sire being the great Swiss dog International Champion de Beaute Prinz Alex von Rodelheim out of Leonore von der Seestadt. After his spectacular career in England he departed to the States with honours lying thickly upon his lovely snow-white coat. Mrs. Sherman Hoyt has given a charming account of the arrival in America of the Duke, in her recent book *Your Poodle* . . . his dignified bearing when she met him at the docks . . . the confidence he showed as he gently took her hand in his mouth. . . . In the States his reputation was finely upheld, for he excelled not only in beauty but also in intelligence. He created a furore in America and became a national figure. He was the first Poodle to go Best in Show at Westminster. His most famous children are Champion Blakeen Jungfrau, which went Best in Show at the Morris and Essex Show, the largest in America, and the Canadian and American Champion Blakeen Eiger. The Duke sired many other famous Champions and himself was never defeated in the breed in America.

The Swiss have had a great influence on Poodles both in England and America, Madame Reichenbach of Geneva having exported Poodles to both sides of the water.

Another great dog imported by Mrs. Byron Rogers was Eric Labory, the sire of Champion Giroflee of Misty Isles. Mrs. Milton Erlanger purchased this bitch from Mrs. Byron Rogers and gave her to Mr. George Frelinghuysen who, with his mother, owns the Smilestone Kennels. Mr. Frelinghuysen gave Mrs. Erlanger a puppy from the mating of Champion Giroflee to Champion Cadeau de Noel.

The Puttencove Kennels owned by Mr. and Mrs. George Putnam have produced many outstanding Champion Standard

Poodles whose breeding goes back to Champion Blakeen Cyrano and Champion Harpendale Monty of Blakeen. One of the best known of these is Champion Puttencove Impetuous sired by Champion Kaffir of Piperscroft, C.D. out of Puttencove Candida. Through Kaffir Champion Impetuous goes back to the Labory line. The best-known son of Champion Impetuous is Champion Carillon Colin of Puttencove, owned by Mrs. Putnam but bred by Mrs. Whitehouse Walker. His dam Champion Carillon Colline goes back to a blending of Whippendell and Labory stock.

Like the English breeders, the Americans permitted—indeed, encouraged—all colours in their Poodles and much interest was taken in colour breeding in the United States.

In Miniatures, Mrs. Sherman Hoyt imported American Champion Algie of Piperscroft, purchased from Mrs. G. L. Boyd, and Sparkling Jet. These two dogs, which have had a tremendous influence on the present-day Miniature Poodles in the States, were afterwards sold to Mrs. Byron Rogers. The great Pillicoc Champion Houdini was a son of Sparkling Jet of Misty Isles.

Champion Tango of Piperscroft was brought over to America by Mrs. Whitehouse Walker to join her famous Carillon Kennel. This Kennel included Champion Carillon The Jester, Champion Carillon Joyeux and Champion Carillon Epreuve. Champion Tango also made a great name for himself in Obedience Tests where he did remarkably well, being the proud possessor of the titles C.D. and C.D.X.

Champion Méchanceté of Misty Isles, a daughter of Champion Misty Isles Algie of Piperscroft, was purchased from Mrs. Byron Rogers by Mrs. Sherman Hoyt and, mated to Champion Vendas The Black Imp of Catawba, produced two well-known Champions from which have come a long line of winners. Méchanceté's sister Miette of Misty Isles, also mated to The Black Imp, produced a litter of equally famous dogs. The Vendas Kennel, owned by Mrs. Audrey Tyndall in England, has had considerable influence on the Miniature Poodles in America. The American Champion The Black Imp of Catawba was imported into the States by Mrs. Ruth Sayres for the late Mrs. James Austin and was then sold to Mrs. Sherman Hoyt. He was the sire and grand-sire of many of the best known Champion Miniatures, the most famous being Mrs. Sherman Hoyt's Champion Blakeen Eldorado, up to the present time the best brown Miniature in America. Eldorado's dam was Champion Vendas Winter Sunshine of Blakeen, a daughter of Champion Vendas Sunskista of Blakeen, both of which were imported from England by Mrs. Sherman Hoyt.

The best grey Miniatures in America go back to American Champion Platinum of Eathorpe, bred by Mrs. Harold Twist in England, and also imported by Mrs. Sherman Hoyt.

The Cartlane Kennels bred Champion Cartlane Once, one of the best Toy Poodles ever exhibited. Eight inches in height, she has a lovely snow-white coat with black points. It was these Kennels which imported Sparkle of Mannerhead, owned by Mrs. Campbell Inglis and bred by Mrs. Tyndall.

The Pillicoc Kennels owned by Mrs. Milton Erlanger include Champion Pillicoc Rumpelstiltskin and Champion Pillicoc Houdini and the Puttencove Kennels include, in addition to those already mentioned, Champion Puttencove Blaise and Champion Puttencove Grenadier.

The white Miniatures are still comparatively rare in the States and have been almost entirely developed by Mr. and Mrs. Sherman Hoyt. These whites come from Champion Arnim of Piperscroft and the apricot bitch Fifi of Swanhill, both imported by the Hoyts. This line, crossed with a more recent import, Champion Snow Boy of Fircot, is, I think, still the best white strain in America today.

It would appear that the Blakeen Kennel owned by Mrs. Sherman Hoyt holds a very high place in America. Not only did Mrs. Hoyt bring that great dog Champion the Duc de la Terrasse to the States; she has always been on the look-out for the best Poodles, and no one is a better judge than she as to what really is the best. Whilst breeding a splendid strain of her own, she had paid many visits to England and farther afield, and her importations, added to her own dogs, have produced an outstanding Kennel. Her dogs are known all over the world, and the Blakeen Poodles have won Best in Show over a hundred times at Shows in America. During the last ten years Mrs. Sherman Hoyt has bred thirty-nine Champions, this in addition to the honours carried off by her imported Poodles.

It will be seen from the American Standard of Points that Toy Poodles are recognized in the States whilst in England they have to take their chance amongst the Miniature Poodles. It is quite likely that in the future Toy Poodles will be registered as such at the English Kennel Club, though there has recently been a unanimous decision by members of the Poodle Club in England against such a step.

America has made great strides in breeding Toy Poodles and there are now a number of fine specimens on the Show circuits in the States. The little Toy Poodle Once, owned by the Cartlane Kennels, has achieved a wonderful Show record, but it is quite likely that younger dogs will eventually surpass her in type. One of the best known Toy Poodles is Champion Barnes Wee Winnie Winkle bred by Mrs. Evelyn Barnes. Her first big win was at the California Speciality Show in the Summer of 1951. Mrs. Sherman Hoyt, who was judging, afterwards bought this little bitch and later sold her to Mrs. Fleishman.

Mrs. Leicester Harrison's Leicester Kennels have produced some very outstanding Toy Poodles. The white male, Champion Leicester's 1811 Take Vanilla, has had a great career and was the sire of Blakeen Peek Boo now in the possession of Mrs. Fleishman. Some other Toy breeders of note in America are: Mr. C. K. Corbin with the Nibroc Kennel, Mrs. Audrey Watts of Pawling, New York, and Mrs. Gladys Hertel of California, whose Kennel name is Gladville.

Miss Lydia Hopkins of California has done outstanding work in breeding Toy Poodles from Miniature stock. The basis of most of this Kennel came from the English Chieveley lines and great credit is due to her. Her grand little Champion Sherwood Pocket Edition had a great, if short, career in the Show Ring where he was never beaten by either Standard or Miniature. Pocket Edition is now an old dog but he is the sire of the famous twins Champion Sherwood Vest Pocket Edition and Champion Sherwood Mademoiselle Bibi. Miss Hopkins had early appreciated the great qualities and potentialities of the Chieveley Champions which Mr. Charles Price of the Marcourt Kennels had imported. By clever line-breeding based on Champion Chieveley Chopstick she has evolved a strain of Toy Poodles which should immensely benefit these tinies.

It must be said that Poodles in the United States are on the whole far better displayed in the Ring than they are in England at the present time. They appear to be much smarter and their clipping is of a very high excellence. Many of the American breeders employ first-rate handlers to show their dogs, whereas in England most of the big breeders prefer to have the fun of showing their own dogs. In America the huge classes now seen in England

(Sport and General)

Ch. The Silver Gnome (*Miniature silver*)

(Peggy Cooper)

Ch. Eric Brighteyes (*Miniature black*)

Ch. Nunsoe Nickola's Christopher Robbin (*Standard white*)

Ch. Barty of Piperscroft (*Miniature black*)

(*Sport and General*)

King Leo of Piperscroft (*Standard brown*)

(*Fall*)

The Firebrave victory smile

Ch. Pixholme Firebrave Gustav (*Miniature black*)

Ch. Firebrave Nicolette (*Miniature black*)

are rare. The American breeders show only really good dogs, whilst in England many dogs appear in the Show Ring that are not, strictly speaking, of Show class. It should also be mentioned that the Dutch-clip is taboo in America and never seen in the Show Ring.

The American Judges are very popular in England and always draw a large entry. In the same way the English Judges are very welcome when they go to the States to adjudicate and are similarly esteemed.

The Interstate Club has now been closed down and disbanded by its founder Mrs. Sherman Hoyt. The Poodle Club of America reigns supreme and has twenty-four Affiliate Clubs. Doctor W. H. Ivens Jr has compiled a magnificent book on the American Poodles, sponsored by the Poodle Club of America of which he is a Governor.

It is interesting to note that the Toy Poodles were first introduced in the United States as a separate Breed, and classified among the Toys. In 1943 it was decided that henceforth the Toy Poodles could be considered to be Poodles, and judged as a Variety of the Breed. Champion Cartlane Once must take much credit for this. Handled by Mrs. Ruth Sayres of the Bric a Brac Poodles she was Best Toy Poodle and First in the Toy Groups at Westminster Show in 1950 and 1951. There is a 10 inch limit of height for Toy Poodles which is rigidly adhered to in America. This has led to some heart burnings over exports from England where the height limit is 11 inches.

The Americans having achieved a 10 inch Poodle are not likely to alter their size, but it seems a uniform size is most desirable.

There is a tendency now for an exaggerated long head amongst the American Poodles, and this could lead to disaster. A balanced head is essential, fine and moderately long but always well balanced.

Many Poodles are now flown long distances from show to show by their handlers their owners rarely seeing them and merely having the empty pleasure of notching up another win in their names.

In 1964 the three Varieties of Poodles in America registered the enormous total of 178,400. These vast numbers may not prove an advantage to the Breed. It is always quality and not quantity that is needed.

F

Chapter X

BUYING A PUPPY

WHEN you have made up your mind that you are going to own a Poodle, either Large or Miniature, the procedure is the same whether you are buying a puppy for Show or only as a pet. We will suppose that you are buying a puppy as a pet, to begin with. It is always best, if you can, to buy your puppy direct from a breeder. Although some dog shops are well run and kept as clean as possible, nevertheless there is always the risk that infection will have been brought either by a puppy or a visiting dog who has come to be trimmed and bathed. You can generally get addresses of breeders from the lists in the dog papers. However, you will be on the safe side if you ask your veterinary surgeon to put you in touch with someone whose dogs he knows. In this case there is very little chance that they will not be healthy.

Before buying, it is advisable to visit the breeder to see the kennel or the house in which the dogs are kept. If they appear to be clean and well cared for, you will probably have a very strong puppy. If you are not used to puppies, you should take someone with you who does know something. If this is not possible, then keep your eyes open and watch the puppies as they run about, giving a careful eye to their tails to see that they are clean and clear, and that there are no unpleasant messes about in their runs. The healthy puppy has healthy bowels, and you can see for yourself whether or not the litter you are inspecting suffers from any kind of bowel condition. When you have seen a puppy that takes your fancy, ask if you may handle him. Look carefully at his eyes and see that they are clean and free from mucus and that his nose is cold and moist. Part his coat, and look into his hair, and at various parts of his body, to make sure that there are no fleas or lice, and no signs of any skin trouble.

The puppy's stomach should not be hard and distended, nor should he have a pot-bellied look. It is advisable to enquire if or when he has been wormed, so that you will know what course to take when he becomes your property. Be very careful not to buy any puppy whose eyes are not bright and clear, as it is the eye that generally shows signs of illness first.

You will not want to own a nervous puppy even as a pet, so if the puppy shows signs of nerves it is advisable to handle him, and also in order that you can see that his bones are not rickety. If he appears to be nervous when you handle him this may be quite natural, as you will discover if you then ask the owner to handle him, and observe him. If he shrinks away and cowers down it is likely that he is nervous and therefore not really suitable for your purpose.

A dog that has to live in a big city has to be in tip-top condition in order not to pick up the diseases that are usually rampant. Personally, I think it extremely unwise to take a puppy out on the streets or into the public parks until it has been fully inoculated. You must not have this done too early or the teeth will be marked by distemper. Many veterinary surgeons will give the full inoculations to a puppy from eleven to thirteen weeks. Some, however, will not, considering that the puppy cannot develop sufficient resistance to make certain that the inoculation will hold. If you are in any doubt, consult your veterinary surgeon and he will advise you about temporary inoculations until the puppy is old enough to have the full dose.

A puppy under five months does not benefit particularly by being taken to walk about on the streets and roads. He will get all the exercise he needs playing about in the house.

The question of house manners has to be considered, but it is impossible to train a puppy to go out and make himself comfortable in the street at so tender an age. However, if you do not live in the country, or have no garden, you have to take other steps to make him house-broken. This problem is dealt with in another Chapter.

If you are buying a puppy not only as a pet but to show and to breed from, you will need to take greater care in selecting him. Generally speaking, if you want to breed and show, it is best to buy a bitch puppy or a young bitch and pay a stud fee to the dog of your choice.

Having made up your mind that you are going to buy a Poodle puppy, the next thing to do is to go to a number of Dog Shows and there to watch the dogs in the Ring, and try to pick up sufficient knowledge of the obvious points of the Poodle so as to have some idea of what *you* are looking for when you visit a Kennel to buy your stock.

When you visit Shows, study your catalogues with care, note

the parents of the winning dogs, and, having made a choice of the type you like, then make an appointment to see dogs at the desired Kennel. You will undoubtedly find most breeders very co-operative and anxious to help. Supposing that you greatly admire a certain dog and feel that you would like to own a puppy bred from him, then take steps to visit the Kennels where his parents are kept and do your best to see the grandparents and the great-grandparents. If you find that one or other of his parents or grandparents has some glaring fault, such as a round eye, a bad mouth, short leathers or poor feet, remember that every one of these faults is likely to crop up in the progeny. It might be that the dog of your choice was a sport, and had somehow missed these damaging features, but of course was capable of causing his descendants to produce them.

Before deciding that you will try another Kennel make a point of seeing some of the dog's puppies. There are sure to be some in the runs that you can observe and even handle. If you find that most of them excel in the points that were to be had in their predecessors, you may take it that the dog in question is very pre-potent and capable of producing stock as good in quality as himself. If you decide to buy a puppy from this particular Kennel you must then be prepared to pay a good price for a promising youngster or even more for a bitch ready to show and to breed from.

It is not always good economy to buy a promising puppy at three months old when you can buy an adult bitch, because, although the sum asked for the older bitch may sound a lot, it is not actually the case. A well-bred bitch that has reached the time at which she can be bred from is actually worth the price, and more, when you consider that she is the result of careful breeding over a large number of years. In buying such a dog or bitch you have to pay for the experience of the breeder selling it. It takes years of patient work, of trial and error, to produce a line that consistently throws a good type.

When you buy your Poodle for show and breeding you will be able to make use of the hints, given earlier in this Chapter, for signs of health or ill-health. When you have consulted the breeder in regard to whatever stock that there may be for sale and have enquired the price, do not make an appointment to visit the Kennels if you know quite well that you are unable to afford the price asked. Breeders do not like people who come to *bargain*. They would rather such buyers kept away. From the breeder's point of view there is no reason why he should reduce his price because you are hard up or have had bad losses from stock that you have bought from some other Kennel.

It is possible that the breeder from whom you wish to purchase your dog has had equally bad losses and has difficulty in keeping his Kennels going. If you approach a breeder in a perfectly open manner, stating what you want and what you are prepared to pay, you will generally find a very co-operative spirit. Most breeders are anxious to sell their dogs to good homes, to people who will appreciate them and who will give them every advantage in the manner in which they keep them, and also by showing them in the Ring. You may be quite certain that the serious breeder will have a definite price for all his stock and will not vary it according to what he believes to be the length of the buyer's purse.

The Puppy.

Now that you have bought your puppy and have taken him home, you will have taken steps to provide a suitable place for him to sleep, a bowl and so on for him to eat and drink from, etc. You must remember, if you buy an eight-weeks-old puppy, that he is likely to settle down very quickly. He has not had long enough to make serious ties with his family. If you have bought an older puppy, or even a young adult dog, you will need to be very patient, and to realize that it will take some time for him to adjust himself to his new environment and to become attached to you instead of the people he has known all his life.

Whether the dog is old or young he will require a comfortable bed, either a box or a basket, to sleep in in a quiet place. If he is young, it will be advisable to put him somewhere where he cannot do any damage when he begins to look about for something to do in the early hours of the morning or even after he has been put to bed. Also, you must take steps to make it all right for him to relieve himself during the night if he is too young to wait until you can put him out in the morning.

Many puppies will make use of the newspaper if it is put down, and will quickly go to the place once they have become accustomed to it. As they usually run to the door when they want to go out they easily learn if you put paper down in front of the door. Never forget that dogs must have water; leave a bowl with fresh water in it for the night.

When you decide to take delivery of your puppy do not do this without thinking carefully of the puppy's point of view. If he is to be your pet, and if you realize that you will perhaps be away from home for any length of time directly you have bought him, then put off his arrival until such time as you will have, say, a whole week in which to devote yourself to his care and training.

It is most important for his house manners that he should begin from the moment he goes into the house to learn that you want him to be clean and where you want him to go. If he is a puppy you will need to watch him with great care and to give him the chance to relieve himself directly after each meal. In the case of an older dog, you will have to decide whether to take him out or to let him out in the garden or whatever place you decide is suitable for his education.

Never lose your temper and punish a dog or puppy for being dirty unless you actually catch him in the act. He will not understand what you mean, and will only become frightened of you if you strike him for what he will consider no purpose. Always make sure to praise him enthusiastically every time he does the right thing and you will soon find that you have no difficulties.

Once you have decided where his special place is to be, and where you are going to put his basket, introduce him to it immediately on arrival and patiently put him back where you want him to be every time he leaves the place without permission.

If he is very young, and you want to confine him to a space, you can easily do this by making small frames of wire netting and batten wood. However, while the puppy plays about always keep your eye on him and attempt to anticipate the moment at which he is going to make a puddle; then take him to the paper you wish him to use. Poodles are particularly intelligent and, generally speaking, it does not take more than three days to train one to be clean on paper in a certain place. One good reason for getting a dog used to paper while he is very young is that he will always remember the training, and if at some time he becomes ill, and has a high temperature and may not go out, your training will stand him in good stead—it will be easier to induce him to break his adult habit and use the paper instead of going out of doors. Dogs vary very much in temperament and development; some very quickly grow up and can be weaned from the newspaper habit, others will have to be allowed to use it for a much longer time. However, provided the dog goes where you want him to, you will have very little worry one way or the other.

One of the easiest ways of training the young dog is to have a box or basket into which he can be shut at night. Most dogs will not soil their beds. Therefore if you get up early in the morning, take him out of the box and put him where he has to go and you will find in no time that he has got the idea. If you carry out this routine every time you feed him, and take him from where he has eaten and put him where you wish him to relieve himself, the lesson will be learned very quickly indeed. It may be that he will not always do the right thing for the first few days, but if he makes mistakes during this time do not punish him but let him know from the tone of your voice that you are very disappointed, and that he has not done the right thing.

As his aim in life will always be to please you and do what you want, to train him very quickly you have only to work on this will. One important point is that you must never relax this routine during the number of days required to get him to follow it. If you do, you will have to begin all over again.

After having trained your dog to be clean you will want to train him to a collar and lead. Some dogs make no difficulty whatever about this and will cheerfully suffer a collar to be put on, and will walk about at once with the lead attached. Others will fuss and jump and sit down and refuse to budge. Some may even get quite hysterical at the surprise and shock of finding themselves under control. The easiest way to get a puppy accustomed to such a control is to put on the collar and lead and let him run about the house with it on, even for a couple of days before you take up the end and request him to walk. It is sometimes a good plan when training a youngster to have him sit at your side wearing his collar and to keep the lead in your hand while you are reading or writing. By this means he will quickly understand what you want and will make very little trouble when you want to lead him about.

Another point about a young puppy is the fact that he will probably be very lonely and unhappy without his brothers and sisters, and therefore will cry and possibly bark and howl if he finds himself completely alone and without his human companion. You must be firm when dealing with this habit. It is no help to tell him to be quiet unless he knows he is making a noise. If you go out of the room and leave him and he begins to bark and howl, go straight back, speak to him firmly, order him to lie down and take a rolled-up newspaper in your hand. Every time he barks hit your hand smartly with the paper, making a loud noise. This will usually astonish him sufficiently to stop the bark for the time being. If, however, he persists, then you must go in and tap him smartly on the nose with the paper. Generally speaking, a few taps with the paper will show him that he has done the wrong thing and he will quickly settle down to sleep in your absence.

The basis of the training of all dogs and puppies is obedience to your wishes, and if you are firm and carry out the routine of your own making you will very quickly have a well-behaved dog. Spoiled dogs are as unpleasant as spoiled children.

It is very bad to encourage them to come to the table for pieces at meal times. It is much better for them to lie either in their baskets or at their owners' feet. If you train your dog to do this satisfactorily you will find that you can take him wherever you wish. The dog that disappears under his master's chair whenever he goes into a shop or restaurant is practically never objected to, and as you will want to take your dog about with you you will find that you are easily able to do this if you insist on obedience from the word 'go'. It is not very difficult to teach any dog to lie down and to stay where he is put, and such training will always repay you a hundredfold.

The kennel dog requires much the same treatment, except that he will have to get used to different surroundings outside the house. The procedure, however, of accustoming him to his new surroundings is always the same, either in the house or in the kennel.

There is quite a difference between training your dog for the Ring and bringing him up only as a pet who has to become accustomed to the ordinary life in a house. You will want to begin training him to a collar and lead very quickly. It is always a good plan to have a collar and lead in your pocket so that, as you go round your kennel, you can easily slip the lead on any dog or puppy. The method of training a dog for the Show Ring is dealt with in another Chapter.

Note for Novices with regard to purchasing foundation stock.

Many novices who hope to begin breeding are hypnotized by the idea of buying a good bitch and a good dog and thus producing a champion first go off. The great thing for novice breeders to remember is that if they buy a dog and a bitch that are closely related the resulting stock will be unsuitable to be bred together. It is a fallacy to suppose that stud fees make it almost prohibitive to breed a paying litter. The contrary is the case. If you pay ten or twelve guineas as a stud fee and your bitch produces three to five puppies, you will very nearly recoup yourself for your outlay on the bitch and the stud fee by the sale of the first litter. The stud fee is said to represent, generally speaking, the price of one puppy.

Buying a stud dog is a very different matter. Either you have to buy a young dog at three months old and risk it becoming a bad stud or you will have to buy an adult, or a dog at least nine to ten months old, and if you hope to buy a dog of any quality and merit you will have to pay a pretty stiff price at that age.

A good stud dog is a very valuable possession, especially if he comes from a famous line. Most novices faint away if asked to pay a large sum for a dog; yet if they would stop to think, they would realize that the dog has only to be used at stud a number of times for the outlay to be recovered. Of course, novices will say they have not got the price asked for, but then if they pay a lesser amount for a three-months-old puppy of a famous line they may find six months later that he is a monorchid or a cryptorchid. Therefore it is better to spend whatever capital is available on buying a good brood bitch perhaps two years old, who has already had a litter, than to buy a maiden bitch, younger and untried, for a good deal less, and to pay a fee for a suitable stud dog.

In the end it is obvious that the mature bitch is the better proposition. The best thing of all is, having selected the strain you prefer, to buy two bitches from the same strain with suitable lines, from different Kennels, or even from the same Kennel if it is adequately supplied with ancestors that will suit the selected stud. By this means the progeny of the two bitches will be able to be crossed, and if wisdom has been exercised in the selection they may quite likely produce the right stock to found a new strain based on their common ancestry.

One frequently hears novice breeders, and sometimes older breeders who ought to know better, state quite openly that it is no good crossing X's stock with Y's as 'they do not suit each other'. Such a statement is absolutely without foundation unless two stocks have been mated together without one common ancestor three or even four generations back. Even so, by mating two completely unrelated stocks it is possible to reconcile the X and Y strain but not, of course, in the first litter unless by some happy chance the fluke comes off, and a perfect example of one or other strain is produced.

What usually happens is that there will be an equal number of types, both of X and Y. If you have a preference for Y rather than X you will be able to achieve what you first set out to do when you decided to mate X and Y, by mating back the most typical Y to the most suitable dog in the Y strain. If you do this consistently, by the fourth generation you should have produced a good example of the best Y strain. Therefore, my advice to the intending breeder is: "Buy yourself one, two or three or more good bitches, but don't buy yourself a stud dog."

A warning to the novice. Before you set out to breed dogs that are show dogs, and not just puppies bred for sale, make sure that you possess an 'eye'. An eye for a dog is the one requisite necessary above all if you are going to have a successful kennel. You can easily find out whether you have this 'eye'; when you visit a Kennel, and see perhaps ten or twelve dogs all running together, unless you can quite clearly pick out the difference between each and every one you will know that you do not possess an 'eye'. How often people who go to buy a puppy from which they hope to breed a long line of champions give themselves away to the breeder by saying: "I can't think how you tell them apart—they all look alike to me!"

COMMON FAULTS IN THE POODLE

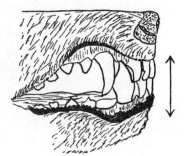

Correct mouth: level

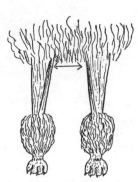

Incorrect front:
too wide

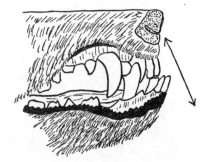

Incorrect mouth: undershot

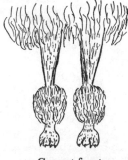

Correct front

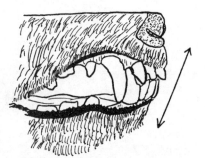

Incorrect mouth: overshot

COMMON FAULTS IN THE POODLE

Correct foot   Poor feet showing long
                            open toes

Correct stifle   Incorrect stifle: Incorrect stifle
                      straight   camouflaged by heavy
                                             clipping

COMMON FAULTS IN THE POODLE

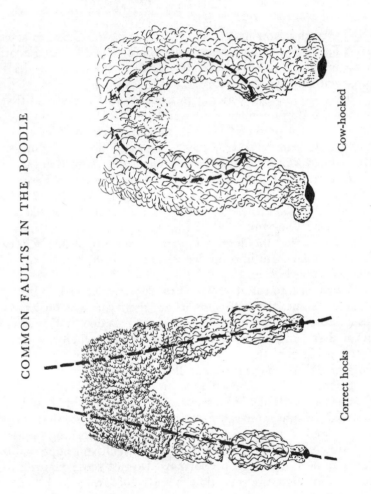

Cow-hocked

Correct hocks

Chapter XI

KENNEL MANAGEMENT

NOW that you have decided that you would like to start a Kennel and have bought the necessary bitches, a matter dealt with in a previous Chapter, you will have to consider the management of your Kennel, be it large or small.

There is only one way to run a successful Kennel, and that is to put the dog's comfort and well-being before everything else. If you are not prepared to work sometimes twenty-four hours a day and to remain tied by the leg perhaps for years while your Kennel is working itself up, do not undertake to breed dogs.

In actual fact there are two ways of conducting a Kennel. If you have the money, when you have bought your bitches engage a capable person or persons to run your Kennel—if you like to do it that way. They will do all the work. All you need do is pay the bills and register the dogs as in your ownership, and, if you care to do so, take them into the Ring. This is running a Kennel just like any other business.

If you wish to run it yourself as a Personal Kennel, and that is what I assume you will want to do, then you will be *personally* responsible for everything that goes on. This does not, of course, mean that you will not want to employ help when the Kennel becomes big enough, but it does mean that you will have all the work and all the pleasure of handling your own animals.

Before you buy yourself even one bitch make sure that your premises are suitable. It is useless to buy yourself a bitch and hope to breed the odd litter in your flat, and then find out that you are not allowed to keep animals there. The same warning applies if you are considering founding a Kennel which you hope will one day assume quite large proportions. Do not settle yourself in a house and then discover that because of Town and Country Planning, or some other local regulation, you cannot breed dogs there.

Again, do not buy or rent a house too close to other people if you are going to breed dogs, for dogs must be allowed to be noisy sometimes, and if you have neighbours too close you may find that they object to the noise. Then you will have to close down or

94

move to more suitable premises. Therefore make several enquiries before you buy your dogs. Remember that you may not put up even a rabbit hutch without the permission of the local authorities. So when you are looking for your premises find somewhere where there are some buildings that can form the nucleus of your Kennel.

If you are going to breed Poodles rather than Miniature Poodles you will be in a more difficult position as you must have outside buildings for the larger variety. Size alone will prevent you from keeping numbers of these in the house. However, if you have a reasonably large house you can keep quite a number of Miniature Poodles indoors provided you have adequate accommodation for them to run about in outside. It is most important when providing beds for your rooms indoors or kennels for outside that there should be adequate space for the dogs' comfort. A large Poodle requires a pen at least 8 feet by 4 feet in which to live in any degree of comfort. He will also require quite a large run.

Big dogs need a great deal of exercise; unless you are able to give your Poodles plenty of free exercise you will never keep them in condition for the Show Ring. Road exercise is not enough to harden muscles and to tighten feet if they are slack. If you are unable to find a house with a large enough paddock for exercise try to acquire one near a common or open land on which they can gallop freely at all times.

Miniature Poodles, too, must have free exercise. Provided there is plenty of open ground in which to run and play they will not damage their coats. In any case, freedom for their bodies should come first. Any dog that does not get sufficient exercise on his own to keep his muscles hard and tight will not satisfy a Judge who puts condition foremost. A dog that is all coat and soft muscle will not move correctly, nor will his feet be of the right type. He will be down on his pasterns, and though he may win under some Judges he will not get much stud work. Breeders, be they novices or experts, always have eagle eyes for feet and action; if they see a dog paddling about, wide at the back and close at the front, though he may get to the top he will not get the number of stud fees that his owner will probably think he deserves. Therefore, when you decide to found your Kennel, found it wisely.

If you are going to have only one bitch and breed from her, keep her where you can give her enough freedom to ensure that she is in perfect health when she is going to have her family. Once your bitch has been mated you will not find it necessary to make any change in the routine of her life until the time when she is nearly due to whelp. Let her lead her normal life and take as much exercise as she requires. If she lives in the country you will probably find that she will rat and rabbit up to the last minute and be none the worse for it, but when she does whelp you must give her all the attention she needs, as described in another Chapter.

You will have to run your Kennel, whether it contains one dog or a hundred, on a special routine. There must be regular hours for cleaning, feeding, grooming, exercising, etc. Dogs thrive on regular habits. They do not do well if they are fed at twelve o'clock one day and at two o'clock in the afternoon the next. You will find that if you feed the same quantity of food at the same time every day your dogs will remain in perfect condition.

There is much to be said for giving all food by weight, so that there is no chance that one day a 'handful' of biscuit may be four ounces and the next day six ounces, according to the whim of whoever is feeding the dogs. A dog's stomach will become accustomed to a certain amount of food and will be ready for it, and will thrive on this routine. For the same reason it is advisable to get them up at the same time every day.

After the dogs have been fed and have relieved themselves it is a very good plan to shut them up for one or two hours. Puppies, in particular, should be treated like this. A good routine is: let them out first thing in the morning to play either in covered runs or in the open, according to the weather, and after their morning meal shut them up again until mid-day, when they are again let out for an hour's play. Feed again at two-thirty p.m. and shut up again until four p.m., when they are released for exercise until about six p.m., the time for their evening meal, then bed for an hour (in the summer, of course), then more play and running about until nine p.m. or after, when they have their drink of milk and retire for the night.

Adults are treated in a similar manner except that they are fed at twelve p.m. and six p.m. and are always shut up after their meals for two or three hours, and after that are let out for exercise.

In the summer it is inadvisable to let any dog, young or old, lie out in the sun in the heat of the day. They should be firmly shut up or put in the shed from one o'clock until about five p.m.

Then puppies and dogs never suffer from touches of the sun and consequent summer diarrhoea. Poodles are very intelligent and sensitive animals; it does them no good at all to be kept in runs (sometimes too small) to jump and leap hour after hour. They are much better let out at intervals so that they do not have time to become bored with their surroundings and so take to jumping at the wire and yelping and barking at nothing in particular.

When you are building your kennels or buying ready-built kennels, whichever is the case, you will find it is a great boon to have several covered runs made for winter use. If you have them built with wire fronts and movable shutters you will be able to exercise your dogs all the year round. It does not do any good, either to adults or puppies, to let them get damp and wet, and then shut them up in kennels to dry as they sleep.

For young puppies it is usually advisable to put down straw on the cement to take the chill off during the winter, and also to put down sawdust to ensure cleanliness. Sawdust, too, is very warm, and it does no harm to the coats and does not get into the puppies' eyes, though of course you should not use it for the very tiny ones just out of the nest. Paper is much better for these.

Some people consider it necessary to have heating installed in their kennels. This appears to be quite unnecessary except in the case of illness. If your kennels are well built, and if the dogs have adequate boxes with sacks or straw or something similar in their beds, they will keep themselves warm. Poodles are very hardy dogs, have very good coats and very seldom suffer from cold. Even young puppies do not require any heat provided their beds are warm and their kennels draught-proof.

My own puppies are always born in the house, summer and winter, and kept there until they are about six weeks old, when they are put out with their mothers into draught-proof kennels. These kennels are built of wood and are lined with asbestos. The floors, too, are covered with asbestos. This is very strong, can be kept perfectly clean and can be thoroughly disinfected in case of illness. I usually put down paper for the puppies until they are about eight weeks old, when they are given sawdust.

When you are putting up your kennels be sure to provide them with adequate runs that can be wired off so that young puppies can get out into the air even in the winter on fine days. If you do this you will find that you have very hardy dogs. Because of a Poodle's rather foppish appearance those who do not

G

know him consider him to be rather a delicate creature. This is far from the case; provided he is sensibly treated (with no bits and pieces, if he is a house dog) he will go on year after year in perfect health.

If you do not place a good supply of clean water in a dog's kennel, as soon as he is let out he will rush to where he knows water is, and fill himself up with cold water and give himself indigestion. It must be particularly remembered that part of the male dog's sexual equipment is the raising of his leg to pass water. If he does not have drinking water in his kennel, or in the run, both day and night, he will cause damage to his kidneys because he will not eliminate the poisons in his blood as efficiently as if he would were he given a continual supply of water. Although this seems unnecessary to stress, it is a fact that the necessity of providing water at all times and in all places is one of the things that Kennel staff learn last. Personally, as an owner of a Kennel, I find it impossible to go into any room, kennel or run and not immediately notice whether or not the water dish is full. Yet this is the hardest lesson to teach student staff.

Disinfection of the kennels is an important part of the daily routine, and of course it is essential after illness. Even if a dog has only had diarrhoea as a result of worms the floor must always be scrubbed with very hot water in which a large quantity of soda has been dissolved. Ordinary washing soda is one of the most powerful deodorants and aid to kennel disinfection. If a strong soda solution is used to scrub out kennels every day there is little need to add any of the carbolic or other disinfectants on the market, unless serious illness has occurred, in which case it is advisable to use a blow-lamp on all woodwork and to scrub all floors and asbestos walls with a strong soda solution to which a good disinfectant has been added to make doubly sure.

There is no fear of damage to hands if a suitable scrubbing brush on a handle is used. Not only walls and floors must be scrubbed and cleaned; all dishes, cooking utensils, etc., that may have been used for sick dogs must be boiled for several minutes.

It is also a very good plan when you have dogs inoculated with the distemper virus not only to keep their dishes separate from all others but also to boil them every day in case of use by dogs that have not yet had the virus.

As contagious diseases in dogs are carried in the saliva, and urine and faeces, it is at once apparent that there must be complete disinfection of dishes and of the boots of anyone going into kennels used by dogs suffering from any illness, whether it is known to be infectious or not, and particularly where the dogs have been isolated for a distemper vaccine-virus inoculation. Therefore always have buckets of disinfectant standing outside runs in which inoculated or sick dogs are kept, into which boots should be dipped every time you go in and out. This is a good precaution in the case of any illness, whether known to be infectious or not.

Chapter XII

Part I

THE STUD DOG

(For the Novice)

IF YOU are going to use one of your dogs either for your own bitches or at public stud you will need to look after him very carefully. He must not be allowed to become thin or out of condition. He must always have a complete and adequate diet. A stud dog, according to his size, will need $\frac{1}{2}$lb. to 2lb. of raw meat a day. During the breeding season any dog required to be used once a week, or even twice over a period of time, will require a full diet of raw meat, raw eggs and milk.

The dog can give out only what is put into him; by this I mean that if a dog is expected to sire strong, healthy puppies he must be given an adequate supply of good, nourishing food. Generally speaking, a dog should not be used more than once a week. It is the practice of most owners of stud dogs to allow them to give each bitch two services. This, of course, is quite easy when the bitches come to stay or if the owners are willing to bring them twice. A full forty-eight hours should elapse between the first and second service. Contrary to the belief of many people, it is not dangerous or detrimental to the dog to allow him to mate a bitch twice within an hour, if for some reason the first service has not been satisfactory. It would be dangerous and detrimental to his health and to his capacity for producing strong, healthy stock if he were allowed to make a habit of this and to indulge himself in this way all day or at too frequent intervals. The reason is that the excitement brought on in the performance of the act is a great strain on the heart and will rapidly weaken the constitution of the animal if he is not disciplined.

Most dogs know exactly what to do when confronted, even for the first time, by a bitch ready to be mated. Some, however, are backward. Some are silly and have no idea what to do, but they all learn with patience and time. If it is at all possible it is advisable to allow a young dog to get his experience by mating an older bitch who has already been bred from. She will quickly show him what to do, and he will be equally quick in picking up her indications.

Sometimes the dog is very excitable and in his inexperience will fail to reach the right spot, so dissipating his energies to no purpose. It is quite probable that if you attempt to help him, and take hold of him and put him on the bitch's back, he will either resent this or will think that he is doing something wrong, and that you are trying to correct him. Always be sure that you never let the dog think he has done something wrong even if he attempts to mate a bitch though she is not in season. Most young dogs are anxious to find out what they can do, and if the bitch does not wish for their attentions she will quickly let them know without your interference.

When you are going to use a young dog for the first time, and a visiting bitch is brought for him, it is as well for you to satisfy yourself that she is fully ready and willing, by taking one of your older dogs to investigate the situation.

A young untried dog may be completely put off for some time if a snappy bitch turns on him when he is about to do his duty. An older and more experienced animal will know how to deal with such a bitch and will not be so easily put off. If you are not so fortunate as to have any other dog with which to test the bitch it is a good plan to tie up her muzzle so that she cannot snap, much less bite, and you will also be free to hold the scruff of her neck in your left hand while helping the dog with your right. It is quite easy to tie up a dog's jaws by using a length of strong material about 1½ inches wide. Double this in half; make a slip noose at the folded end; place the noose over the muzzle; pull tight, and secure ends by tying at the back of the neck. If the bitch definitely shows that she does not wish for the dog's attention, you will be advised to inform her owner that she is not ready and suggest coming back in twenty-four or forty-eight hours according to what you conceive to be the time arrived at in the season. Some bitches are ready for the dog at eleven days, others not until thirteen, and some even fifteen or seventeen days.

When attempting to use a maiden dog and a maiden bitch you will be on unknown tracks and will have to find out for yourself. Usually the owner of the bitch knows something about her and will tell you, when making the arrangements, when she is expected to be ready. Always supposing the bitch arrives at the psychological moment, you can then introduce your dog to her with every chance of success.

It is not good for a young dog to come in contact with a bitch in season unless he is going to mate her. If he suffers from frustration he will make his life and yours unbearable. He will probably refuse to eat, possibly for days, and will lose flesh and condition very quickly. It has always been my experience that, provided a dog does not actually contact a bitch when she is in season, he will not worry himself unduly and will be quite capable when he is at last taken to her. So do not let him meet her in the flesh until she is completely ready.

When accepting fees for the dog's services you must remember that the owners of the bitches will expect what is known as a 'satisfactory service' before they pay the fee. A service is not generally considered satisfactory unless the dog and bitch remain tied together for some time varying from five to fifty minutes. If it happens, as it sometimes does, that the dogs come apart as the male attempts to turn himself round, it is perfectly safe for him to give another service about an hour later.

It is better, however, in such a case for the owner to bring the bitch back in about twenty-four hours. If there is some doubt as to whether the bitch will be still in use at the later date, it is definitely advisable to allow the dog to have a rest and then use him again.

There are several schools of thought in regard to the manner of conducting a stud service. Some people just hold the bitch, produce the dog, and force her to be mated there and then.

Dogs that are kept very busy day after day presumably have no time to waste, but if you are using your stud dog in a considerate manner it is most advisable to allow the two to play about to get sufficiently acquainted with each other, to play happily and so to consummate with good-will on both sides. Many breeders believe that 'misses' are often due to the bitch having been forced to take the dog whether or not she liked him. It is a matter of fact that when the bitch is absolutely ready she will make no trouble at all about receiving a dog's attentions. It is usually a sign that the rhythm has not reached its apogee if she snaps and snarls and will not let the dog get very close to her.

When the bitch has been taken away the dog should be taken back to his quarters and given a rest and then a good meal of raw meat. A stud dog should never be fed for some hours before he is used, otherwise the effect of the pressure on his abdomen, induced by the sexual act, will make him sick. It is good policy to give him one or two raw eggs, according to his size, in the morning if he has to mate a bitch at mid-day, and to follow the service, as directed, with a good meal. An active, healthy dog will usually have a good sleep and then get up ready to begin all over again.

Anyone who has a dog at public stud runs a great risk of disease being brought by visiting bitches, and before he is put away it is advisable to disinfect him by cleansing his mouth with T.C.P. or some other suitable disinfectant, and also to disinfect his feet and every part of him that has come in contact with the bitch.

Part II

THE BITCH IN SEASON

(FOR THE NOVICE)

The bitch, like the stud dog, requires special care and attention, particularly when she is near the time at which she can be used. Most people would not dream of sending a bitch to stud unless she is in tip-top condition, but there are others who, through carelessness or ignorance, send their bitches away when they are ill or about to be ill. It is against these that one has to disinfect one's dog.

The normal bitch comes into use twice a year, and only at these times can she be mated. Young bitches vary considerably in the time at which they have their first season. Some will have it as early as seven or eight months; others perhaps not until they are fourteen months. If the season is delayed after a year a veterinary surgeon's advice should be sought. For the sake of the bitch's health, a veterinary surgeon usually wishes to give an injection to bring her into season, and if this is done she will generally come in season again at regular six-monthly intervals and can then be used.

It is not usually considered advisable to mate a bitch at an induced season, the reason being that she does not always conceive, and if you are paying a stud fee you will be anxious not to waste your money if there is not to be a litter. Once your bitch has had her first season you will be able to calculate when she will be ready to be mated. It is best to mate at the second season when a bitch is normally about eighteen months old. If, however, your bitch does not come into use until she is ten months to a year old, and if she is very mature and well-developed for her age, it is quite a good thing to allow her to have a litter at this time. The custom generally is to mate a bitch at her second season.

Once the date of the first season has been established, you will have to contact the owner of a stud dog. You will, of course, have considered the prospective father from every angle, and will have talked over his suitability with the breeder of your bitch. You will always find that serious breeders will gladly discuss with you the various stud dogs whose blood lines are likely to suit your bitch, if you approach them in the right way. Having visited as many Dog Shows as possible, you will have had the opportunity of seeing the dog in the Ring, and also some of his progeny as well, and will have some idea of the quality of the pups he is likely to throw. It is most advisable to visit the parents and the grandparents of the dog of your choice. The influence of the grandparents is even more important than that of the parents, especially the maternal grandsire.

As soon as you notice that the 'season' has begun, notify the owner of the dog. Most bitches come into use for the first time from ten to twelve months. The smaller Miniatures are usually later than Poodles or the larger Miniatures, except white Miniatures, and they generally come in much earlier than their brown or black sisters. Personally, I prefer to mate a bitch at her second season when she is between sixteen to eighteen months, unless she comes in at twelve or thirteen months and is very well grown and fully developed. When you tell the owner of the dog that your bitch has come into use he will usually tell you when, about, she will be ready for mating. The most usual day is from the eleventh to the thirteenth, but each bitch varies; some only stay in ten days, others twenty-one. I once had a bitch that was mated on the thirteenth day; she was then returned to 'purdah', and on the twenty-first day, as she appeared to be quite normal, she was brought back to the house. As soon as I put her down my stud dog ran to her and promptly mated her. She whelped to this mating and not to the first. From this mating was born the mother of Champion Firebrave Gaulois. Incidentally, my dog took no further notice of the bitch after having mated her that afternoon.

This experience goes to show how it is that sometimes a bitch fails to whelp although she has had a satisfactory mating. There is no doubt that there is a moment in the season at which the bitch can be fertilized. She can be served abortively once or twice, and although externally everything seems to have gone well, unless one happens to have selected the perfect moment there will be no pups. For this reason I prefer to give bitches, and particularly maiden bitches, two services at least. Nearly always a litter will result from the one mating, but I find it more satisfying to give my own and visiting bitches a second. I always urge owners to come a second time if they can, and I always keep unaccompanied bitches long enough to enable the dog to visit them twice.

If you yourself are unable to tell whether or not your bitch is ready, your veterinary surgeon will be able to tell you. To those who do not know how to tell for themselves, and have no other dog to show them, it is only necessary to say that when she is ready a cold object, such as a pencil, placed on the vulva will cause the bitch to turn her tail over partly parallel with, and partly at right angles to her back, in a most suggestive manner. As soon as she does this she is ready for the dog.

Unless it is absolutely impossible, take your bitch to be mated yourself. I know that sometimes one has to select a sire at a great distance from home, when the bitch must go by rail, but I maintain that where it is humanly possible it is much better for the bitch to be accompanied. I am of the opinion that with so highly intelligent a breed as the Poodle the change of quarters, the journey, the strange handlers, may have such a psychological effect upon her that she may, from sheer misery, fail to conceive. Most particularly is this true of nervous bitches.

We will assume that you have taken your bitch to a Kennel. If she is very nervous of strangers it may be well for you to ask the owner of the dog to let you handle her yourself. Some stud dogs are very touchy, and object to the presence of strangers, in which case you will have to hand over your bitch. Then you must ask the handler to call you as soon as the dogs are mated so that you can see the 'tie' for yourself.

In my own Kennel I have never yet had a dog that objected to anyone else being present at such a moment, as he himself is so keen on his job that he doesn't notice anything except the bitch herself. As soon as the service is satisfactorily concluded you must pay over the stud fee. Some breeders require you to send the fee when booking the service. This is because some inconsiderate owners book a service to a certain dog, arrange to bring a bitch, and then fail to turn up, or to tell the owner of the dog why they did not implement their undertaking. It must be pointed out that a stud dog, if he is to remain potent, can fertilize only a certain number of bitches, and if he is booked to a bitch for a particular day he will be unable to serve another for at least a week, especially if, as is common practice, he has to give two services to each bitch. During the breeding season the call on a fashionable sire will be heavy and if an appointment is not kept the owner will be that much out of pocket. It is therefore important not to make arrangements unless one is prepared to carry them out.

Once you have had your bitch mated you must take her home, shut her up, keep her quiet and let her lead a retired life for the next two or three days. After that she can resume her usual routine.

Chapter XIII

BREEDING

THERE is no royal road to breeding a good dog. The only way to be successful is to breed suitable lines together. This sounds very banal but it is the actual truth. Some people think that if they have a dog with short ears and a long nose, and they mate him to a bitch with long ears and not so good a nose, the ears of the progeny will be of the required length. This is not the case. The short ears and the long nose derive from some ancestor or ancestors who had either or both, and the converse is true. Some people think that if they mate a large bitch to a small dog the resulting progeny will be small. Such is not the case. They may all be very big or they may be half and half. The only way to be sure of getting what you want and correcting faults is knowledge of the pedigrees of the dogs you are mating. This, you will say, is very difficult to find out. How can one get to know details of the dogs in the pedigree perhaps for years back? There is only one way to do this—by studying the breed, and by studying I mean seeing and considering every dog in the pedigree as far back as you can, that is, alive at the time at which you are breeding. One excellent way is to ask some of the older breeders. They will have seen many of the dogs about whom you are enquiring. They will tell you that so and so had a coarse head, and such and such was short in the leg, or something else had lovely feet, another shocking feet, very heavy bone, and so on. If you keep your ears open, your notebook handy, you will find your study will repay you.

If you have bought a dog from A's Kennel and find that A uses B's dogs, then go to B's Kennel and ask if you may see your dog's relations. You will, without doubt, be very welcome. The same applies with A, from whom you bought your dog; go to him and ask to see as many of the ancestors as he may possess.

You can get to know your dog and your dog's ancestors only by this intimate study of their immediate predecessors. When you have discovered that the short ears and the long nose come from some great-grandpapa, and that most of the dogs coming down from him all have this particular fault, then you will know that there is no point in breeding back on that line however celebrated some of the descendants may be. What you will have to find will be the average good ears and good head descending from the progeny of great-grandpapa when he was mated to a bitch whose immediate ancestors carried good ears and good heads.

Those who are setting out to breed dogs—even people who intend only to breed a pet litter—frequently say: "I don't like all that in-breeding," and when you ask them what they mean by that they are usually unable to say. They generally think it is breeding fathers and daughters, and that it is wrong. In-breeding and line-breeding are two very different things. In-breeding, if it is incorrect breeding, is the mating of brothers and sisters. In fact, those whose parents and grandparents are closely related and have practically identical blood stemming from an identical source in both of them. Line-breeding is usually the breeding of a father to his daughter and a grand-daughter back again to a grandfather. In actual fact there is nothing wrong at all in breeding fathers to daughters and grand-daughters to grandfathers provided that you are breeding on a good, healthy line of typical stock un-marred by any serious faults.

It must always be borne in mind that each animal represents in itself the sum total of all its forebears, and each animal in itself is capable of reproducing both virtues and faults. When it is decided to breed from a certain dog it is important to remember that you are not making use of the seed of this stud dog alone; you are using the seed of his ancestors as well, and as it takes two parents to make a puppy the same is true of the dam. Both of them, dog and bitch, will stamp themselves and their ancestors upon their progeny. If you have a bitch bred from a long line of sound, well-constructed dogs that have consistently bred winning stock, and you decide to use a dog of the same quality, you can scarcely fail to produce really good stock, but it must be borne in mind that if you select a dog whose blood lines are entirely separate from yours it is unlikely that in the first generation you will get pups stamped with the appearance of either of the parents. Some of them will undoubtedly represent one parent, some the other. But the most common result of breeding two unrelated lines is over-sized puppies. One of them may, possibly, become a champion and a fashionable sire. Beware of using such an animal on your bitch if she is the descendant of a long, unbroken line. If you do you will probably be disappointed, because this dog, insofar as he resembles one or other of his parents, is not exactly what he seems. He is not only the sum total of your bitch's unbroken line but he is also the sum total of another line totally unrelated to yours. It will be some three or four generations before you will be able to look at your puppies and to see that they are typical representatives of your bitch's line.

When you decide to make use of a certain dog you must study the pedigree very thoroughly on both sides, and be certain that you have a definite affinity of type between dog and bitch. Blood lines in themselves are worthless unless there is that affinity. Some breeders go entirely by pedigree; if they are satisfied on paper that the lines are correct they do not bother to see the dogs in person or to find out anything from those who know the characteristics of the more important dogs. This method is likely to be successful if you, the breeder, have the capacity for visualizing in your mind the likely appearance of dogs that incorporate all the best points of the dogs in the selected pedigrees.

If a dog bred from a line that has consistently produced correct heads is himself the owner of an adequate but not a particularly good head, provided that he is mated with a bitch also coming from a line of good heads it is fairly safe to say that he can be used with confidence, and that the progeny will all carry the good heads of their ancestors. Certain lines, when crossed, tend to reproduce all bad points and no good ones; these pre-potent parents should never be used for breeding at all. It is a line stamped with the capacity for reproducing only the good points that is the valuable one for breeding.

You can never go wrong if you follow this rule. You will go wrong if you put together dogs that fail in identical points. It is not enough to use a dog with a good head with a bitch with a poor one in an attempt to correct the bitch's fault in the progeny. Unless the bitch has a line of good heads behind her you will quite likely find that she is the pre-potent partner in the mating and that all the puppies have inherited her poor head. Again, I must repeat that each parent is the sum total of its ancestors and in that sum it carries the virtues and the defects of the past.

You have to remember, when breeding, that every aspect

of the parents will be reproduced in their puppies. By this I mean temperament, action, constitution, general soundness and, most important of all, conformation. It is always a mistake to breed from a dog or bitch of a poor temperament however beautiful it may be in other respects.

It is equally bad to breed from any animal not perfect in conformation. The slab-sided, herring-gutted dog with the big coat and the long head will more than likely produce puppies with weak nervous systems. If the ribs are not well sprung there will not be sufficient room for the heart and lungs to do their work, so that the puppy, inheriting the poor conformation of his parent, will start life with a handicap, which may explain why it has nervous, cringing ways when anywhere outside its own accustomed surroundings. Indeed, it may behave like this in its home when confronted by strangers. I do not suggest that a bold dog, mated to a nervous bitch, will not produce bold pups. What I do mean is that a dog derived from parents and/or grandparents with poor temperaments will inevitably continue to pass on this temperament to some of the progeny. No amount of mating nervous bitches to bold dogs will produce a litter of 100 per cent bold puppies. If the nervousness is caused by some defect in the personal make-up of one or other parent, this defect may be pre-potent and will be reproduced in all the progeny.

It is no good at all mating a dog with a bad mouth to one with a good one, to correct the fault. A bad mouth is a terrible defect and no dog carrying this should ever be bred from by anyone who has the good of the breed at heart. Such animals are born to be pets; they should never be used to reproduce themselves.

I repeat—there is no doubt that temperament in itself is one of the most important points to breed for. It must be borne in mind that mental characteristics are in a certain degree more often transmitted than physical ones.

Once you have achieved the dog who fills your eye in his general appearance, then make sure that you mate him with another equally pleasing in appearance, equally bold in temperament. Only then will you be able to ensure that the good temperament of your line is carried on.

After this comes general appearance. By this I mean the dog that has a perfectly balanced appearance, so that when he goes

round the Ring in company with others the Judge's eye will fall
on him with interest because he is truly typical of the breed.
After that, when you take him out he must be sound. Soundness
comes second when you are breeding to a type. A dog with poor
quarters will never be a good, sound mover. Unless his quarters are
hard and he is well-ribbed up he will not be able to put his feet
down correctly and then his gait will be unsound. No dog should
ever be bred from, if you wish to breed sound stock, if he is out
at elbow and loose in shoulder; again, with these defects he will
be unable to move soundly in front and he will put his feet down
incorrectly.

It must be remembered when picking your puppy from the
litter that you cannot make strong muscle if the muscle is not there
to develop, and if you have bred from parents with soft, thin
muscle no amount of exercise will ever cause the dog to muscle-
up adequately.

Good feet are part of good conformation, and a good foot
cannot be made from a bad one. Parents, representing as they
do the sum total of their ancestors, will continue to produce bad
feet if bad feet are the characteristics of the ancestors. It is always
a fatal mistake to breed out one fault and breed in another. This
is very easily done.

The colour problem is another which creates great controversy.
Actually there is only one rule that can be stated, and must be
observed if you hope to breed true colour. That is—study your
pedigree. Chaos will ensue if, as so often happens, novice breeders
'experiment' in colours. It is a truism to say that whites will breed
whites and blacks will breed blacks. It is a fact that a true black,
and by this I mean a black-bred black (almost impossible to find),
bred to a pure white (almost impossible to find), may produce one
or two pure blacks; the rest will have white on their chins, white
on their chests, or white on their feet. If any of these whites are
mated to a pure black you will probably get pure blacks. But, as
has been said earlier in this Chapter, every parent represents in
itself the sum total of all its ancestors, and this black dog will be a
delusion and a snare. Bred to pure blacks he may produce silver
colour dogs, but he may also produce blacks with white hairs on
their chests or on their toes. He is not a true colour. The same
applies to the white, bred to a black.

This does not mean that it is impossible to breed a pure white
strain from mixing blacks and whites. What it does mean is that

until the strain is established not one of these puppies should go outside the breeder's Kennels. These litters are raw material, and after the third and fourth generation you can be fairly safe in establishing your white strain, which will be all the better for the admixture of the black. But if, while you are manufacturing your pure white dog you are led away into using a stud with silver or brown ancestors, you will be laying up trouble for yourself. You must be careful that your third generation whites are mated only to whites or you will find every kind of parti-colour, from the 'brindle' to the mis-marked, cropping up.

I cannot overstress the fact that the first generation is of no breeding value whatever outside his Kennel. The progeny of such breeding is always a sport and must not be used or put into the Ring until the third or fourth generation. This is not prejudice; it is a scientific fact. Although you may get a beautiful apricot from mating a brown, accidentally bred from black parents, with a cream bitch do not think that you have established an apricot line. You will probably get a shock when you mate the dog with a silver bitch, as frequently happens, and find that all your apricot puppies have brown noses, correct in their brown ancestors but ludicrous in the apricots when they clear to cream as they invariably do. A cream is a white and should have black pigmentation.

Never mate a brown to a blue. The resulting progeny invariably have light eyes, and if they are black at birth, within a year or so they usually clear to a dirty smoky colour, generally described by their proud owners as 'blue', instead of the bad black that it actually is. Black dogs that carry a brown strain can safely be mated to browns, but it is always a lottery and it is safer to mate self-colours to self-colours. It is, however, a fact that a black line which carried a good brown can be relied upon to reproduce this colour when mated to another line that also carried a good brown strain. It is to be deplored only when the brown itself comes from a blue or silver line and is therefore not in itself a true colour.

It should be remembered that the Kennel Club Standard lays down that all coloured Poodles must be solid; this means that any dog with ears carrying darker or lighter hair than the body, or toes and hock rings which carry darker or lighter hair, cannot be described as solid in colour, and should not be exhibited until they have cleared. Any silver dog that has patches

Ch. Vulcan Lady Jane (*Standard white*)

Ch. Vulcan Champagne Darcy (*Standard brown*)

Ch. Lorna of Mannerhead (*Miniature black*)

Ch. Pixholme Pepè (*Miniature black*)

Ch. Braebeck Toni of Montfleuri (*Miniature black*)

Firebrave Lulu, Zeeta, and Nadia (*Miniature blacks*)

THREE CHAMPIONS OF THE 1970s

(Diane Pearce)

Ch. Roushka's Pacific
(*Standard black*)

(F. E. Garwood/Dog World)

Ch. Jolanta By Jove
(*Miniature black*)

(Thomas Fall)

Ch. Sudbrook Sunday Glad Rags
(*Toy white*)

of white on the chest, under the tail or on the feet is definitely mis-marked and should not be used for breeding.

If one gets down to bedrock while breeding colours and using what I have described as raw material, the best thing of all is to put painlessly to sleep every whelp that is born mis-marked or is not true in colour. By this I do not mean that the first generation white, from a black and white mating, should be destroyed in its entirety, but that all 'brindles', all blacks with odd patches of apricot, grey or blue should be either painlessly put to sleep or given away to homes where there is no possibility of their being bred from.

This raw material is dynamite in the wrong hands. If a chemist experiments with gases of whose reaction he is not sure he will undoubtedly blow himself up. If a novice experiments with colours he will undoubtedly do harm to the breed he has taken up. Therefore if you intend to attempt colour breeding do not do so until you have consulted some established breeder who, after many years' acquaintance with a line, is able to state as fact what will be the results of mating Such-and-Such with So-and-So. Again I say—study your pedigrees and make notes of all the information you can get from experienced people who have known the dogs personally.

Before leaving the subject I feel I must once more stress that you cannot get what you want by breeding a bad coat with a good coat. It does not follow that the progeny will all have good coats. Nor is it right if your dog has good feet but poor ears, and not too good a coat, to put it to another that has wonderful ears, gorgeous coat and poor feet. There is no point in correcting your own faults and then introducing, for instance, a bad foot where your line has a good one. Also, remember that mental characteristics are hereditary just as are the physical ones, and that temperament comes before all things if you are breeding for Show.

There is no sense whatever in breeding from typical dogs with poor temperaments. There can be nothing more galling than to have a dog wonderful in appearance but poor in temperament. You often see stud advertisements extolling the wonderful temperament of a dog and stating that he is the sire to correct nervousness in bitches. As I have said before, I do not mean to say that a bold stud dog with a gay temperament will not produce progeny like himself, but as the dam is also the sum total of her ancestors her nervousness will be there, latent, as will be the

H

chance of mis-marks in the case of a poor black dog derived from black and white parents. She, too, is dynamite as far as a transmission of the sire's temperament may go. No one would dream of breeding from a horse with a poor temperament and therefore, hard as it may seem, I am quite sure that one must steel oneself and refrain from breeding from nervous strains as one would from breeding from bad mouths, if one wants to perpetuate one's line and to see it carrying the qualities that give the necessary personality and quality of the successful Show animal.

One of the important sides of breeding has been very prominent lately—the breeding of very small Miniatures that will not exceed ten inches at maturity. For many years Miniatures of twelve inches have been no rarity. It has been the practice of many breeders constantly to breed the 'tinies' of litters to each other. It often happens that when breeding two lines not suitably related some of the puppies will be very big, some correspondingly small. These 'smalls' are often wrongly described as 'toys'.

It is impossible to establish any characteristic in a line as permanent under five or six generations at the very least, and it must always be borne in mind that in order to fix desired characteristics only dogs that are known must be used to throw the desired characteristic points. There are, for instance, certain stud dogs, Miniature-bred for generations, who although fourteen inches in height themselves will, when mated to the correct strain, always throw puppies very much smaller than themselves. These puppies will all carry the typical points of the true Poodle. These are the lines to breed from.

As mentioned before, it often happens that there is a great discrepancy in size between members of the same litter. In such a case the smaller puppies can generally be described as 'runts'. It is the mating of the 'runts' together that has produced the round-headed, pop-eyed, short-legged 'tiny'. Many of these 'tinies' would not measure the ten or twelve inches at the shoulder they do were it not for the fact that length of leg is too short for length of body.

There is no short cut to breeding a desired type; it needs patience and it needs time.

In recent years there has been a movement to induce the Kennel Club to change the classification and to add a new variety, the 'Toy' Poodle under eleven inches. As the classification reads at present, every Poodle is a Miniature up to fifteen inches, irrespective of size. In America there is a separate classification for the 'Toy' Poodle and it has to be under ten and a half inches. On the Continent they have three sizes. These are: under thirteen inches, and under eighteen inches, and over eighteen inches. These being described as 'miniature', 'medium' and 'large' Poodles.

Enthusiasts who wish to have the separate classification probably are not aware that in order for their ambition to be achieved it would be necessary for the progeny of the mating of a Miniature Poodle of fourteen inches with another of perhaps eleven inches to be registered as cross-bred or Miniature-bred for four generations before they could be finally registered as 'toys'. The difficulties in acquiring this status are immense. For instance, it would be impossible to register any small Miniature until it had been officially measured and found to be of the desired height; not before then could it be given its appropriate standing with the Kennel Club. Then again, the progeny would have to wait twelve months for official measurement before they, in their turn, could be described as 'toys'. After all this procedure it would be necessary for a suitable number of registrations to be made for a certain length of time, number and length of time being determined by the Kennel Club before it would give its sanction to the new variety of Poodle. I think the following, written by Mr. Will Hally many years ago, gives the final word on the matter:

"As it is almost impossible to judge the larger Miniatures along with the very tiny ones, to my mind the suggestion (to give them a separate classification) is not feasible; to be of any real value it would call for the recognition of a third variety, and besides that being hopelessly bad for the Miniatures as a whole, it would lead to such complications as would in themselves counteract the whole aim of the idea. The reason for the suggestion is that the tiny Miniatures are different in type, or, in other words, so much inferior in type to the larger Miniatures. That is a complete explanation of the difficulty in judging the tiny ones and the larger ones in one and the same section, but it is no reason at all for such separation as is suggested. Indeed, it is a sufficient reason for not separating them. A Poodle, whatever its stature may be, must be a Poodle in type, and to provide separate classes for tiny exhibits because they are not the required Poodle type would not only be thoroughly retrogressive and make hay of the standard but would also mean that there would be no real standard by which to judge the tiny ones. If you say that they could be judged according to their nearness to the Poodle ideal, or, as it would be in this case, the prizes going to the exhibits which were the least far away from the idea, then you are only providing Show Ring opportunities for exhibits which do not deserve and should not get such opportunities. If the very tiny Miniatures of today are really as bad as some people say, that is no reason for them being provided with opportunities to win on their badness. Isn't at least some of this difficulty, if I may put it in that way, of judging the very small with the up-to-size Miniatures caused by a slight lack of focus? I am only suggesting a possibility, but I have sometimes known the very tiny ones in the past to be criticized for certain features, whereas in actuality these features were every whit as perfect as on their larger fellows—it was the very diminutiveness of the very tiny ones which was misleading. Besides, if you are going to provide classes for Miniatures under, say, twelve inches, you cannot logically leave out the Poodles which are from fifteen and a half to, say, eighteen inches. The latter bunch are barred out, for the most part from both sections of their breed, though no criticism of their type can be levelled against them. One dividing line is quite enough, and we have got it already."

With Mr. Hally's point of view in regard to the preservation of type in the Toy Poodle I am in complete agreement and so are other breeders both of Toys and Miniatures. With this object in view a number of enthusiasts met together in March 1956 and made tentative plans to establish a Toy Poodle Club to further the recognition of Toy as a third variety of Poodle. So successful was the effort that the British Toy Poodle Club was definitely founded in May 1956 with Lady Stanier as Chairman. With the backing of a large membership the Kennel Club agreed to recognize Toy Poodles as a separate and third variety of Poodle on March 1, 1957. In order to compile a separate Register for the new variety breeders were asked to transfer all their under eleven-inch stock which had been registered, perforce, as Miniatures prior to that date. The Kennel Club further stipulated that after that date (March 1, 1957, subsequently extended to July 1, 1957) no dog could be registered as a Toy unless both its parents had been transferred from Miniature to Toy Register. If either of the parents were registered in one or other Register then their progeny must be registered as inter-bred, and would only be eligible for Registration as pure-bred Miniature or Toy after four generations. This regulation caused a great deal of discontent among serious breeders because it was clearly recognized by them that as the variety was only just born, so to speak, some admixture of small Miniature stock must be permitted if type were not to suffer.

The general practice, prior to recognition of the Toy, had been to breed the tiny runts of litters together to produce tiny stock, and of course type and stamina were in danger of serious weakening if such practices should go on.

In writing thus I do not include the serious breeders of Toys, for they were always anxious to improve the quality of the variety. In November 1957 the Kennel Club recognized the difficulties of breeders thus handicapped and amended the regulation so that dogs bred from Toy sire or dam and a Miniature dog or bitch could be registered according to the variety they most resembled.

Poodle history was made at the West of England Ladies Kennel Society's Show in April 1958, when Challenge Certificates were first offered under Mrs. E. C. Thomas, *judge*. The Dog Challenge Certificate went to Summercourt Papenan Romeo, owned by Mrs. Burton and bred by Mrs. A. C. Carrie; the Bitch Certificate went to Sudbrook Sunday Morning, owned and bred by Mrs. H. Cox. The next step in Toy Poodle history was made in November 1958, when Mr. Joe Braddon gave the qualifying Certificate to Poupon of Braxted, and he became the first Toy Poodle in Great Britain to become a Champion. He is owned by Mrs. Spence and was bred by Mrs. Wrenn.

The Monorchid

For many years since the War a great deal of discussion has gone on in the Dog Press and among breeders as to whether or not the condition known as monorchidism is hereditary or not. (A monorchid is a dog that has only one testicle descended and in the scrotum.) Opinion among breeders is divided and, as far as one can tell from their published utterings, so are veterinary surgeons. It is a fact that certain lines in all breeds are known to produce this condition, but one is continually reminded that the great Judges of the past, or at any rate pre-war, paid no attention to this fault, or failing, whichever it may be deemed to be. It might be argued that just this failure to take heed has produced a large number of monorchids in many of the breeds that are in the Ring today. As regards the Show Ring a Dog Show is first and last a beauty competition, and any dog that lacks a certain attribute must lose points to another that is equally beautiful in every other respect. Nature intended the dog to have two *visible* testicles, and if only one is visible he is wanting in that one respect. There we stand on firm ground. For many years I held the view that monorchids should be banned from the Ring, which meant that they would therefore be banned from breeding. Later experience has made me not so sure. As I became more interested I made enquiries regarding the situation in countries where monorchids had been banned from exhibition for many years, and monorchidism, instead of disappearing, had become more apparent as more incomplete dogs were being born. An incomplete dog is one that has not both testicles in the scrotum. I have judged in Europe, Canada and America and found Monorchids rife in Poodles of all varieties. I enquired of judges both here and from overseas and they all confirmed that the number of Monorchids was on the increase. This led me to the belief that Monorchidism is a *condition of Nature* and cannot be corrected by man-made regulations. But—and this is the crux of the matter —no breeder in Europe, America or Canada or Australia has been able, for some years, to take a dog into the Show Ring until he has passed the veterinary surgeon, who will have examined him and found him to be *entire*, i.e. having both testicles in the scrotum. Such being the case, the Kennel Club decided that as from January 1, 1959, no monorchid dog may be taken into the Show Ring, and this edict was issued to all Show secretaries for the information and action of the veterinary surgeons officiating at Shows. This regulation has brought the British Kennel Club into line with those in other parts of the world. Before a dog can now be sent out of this country a form must be obtained from the Kennel Club which must be filled in by a veterinary surgeon stating that the dog has both testicles in the scrotum. If only one, or none, is in the scrotum the veterinary surgeon is required to give this information and before the Export Pedigree can be issued the Kennel Club must have written evidence that the purchaser is aware of the condition of the dog.

THE CRYPTORCHID

A cryptorchid is a dog that has no visible testicles and is therefore incapable of reproducing himself. He is, however, perfectly capable of performing the sexual act. For this reason breeders (novice ones, of course) are led into thinking that puppies may result if their bitch is served by such a dog. It is a scientific fact that for the semen to be fertile it must be secreted at external body temperature. Therefore if a bitch, served by a cryptorchid, does produce a litter she has invariably been served by another dog without the owner's knowledge! *There can be no progeny of the mating by a cryptorchid.* I need say no more.

Chapter XIV

THE WHELPING BITCH

(For the Novice)

THE normal period of gestation is sixty-three days. You count the day the bitch is mated as one of the sixty-three. There is no need to make any alteration in the bitch's customary routine during the time she is in whelp. She can take her usual exercise and be treated in the normal manner, but about ten days before she is due it is advisable to introduce her to the box in which she will whelp and the place in which you intend to keep it.

Whether you have a Poodle or a Poodle Miniature the procedure is just the same. My pups are always born in the house, and I bring the bitch in (if she has been living in the kennels) and get her used to the other dogs, and to the noises of the house, at least ten days before her date so that she will not be unduly alarmed when she hears them from the seclusion of the 'maternity ward'.

Her diet does not vary and she shares the life of the house dogs in every detail. It is essential to watch her bowel movement for the week preceding whelping, and if she is in any way costive, or the reverse, give her whatever remedy you usually use. A little liquid paraffin or Milk of Magnesia is the most suitable. Bitches of the Poodle Miniature variety do not always go the full sixty-three days. In fact, I have found that the first litter is usually born on the sixty-first day. As this Chapter is intended for the owner whelping a first litter it will be best to assume that the bitch is expected to produce her family any time after the fifty-ninth day. For this reason, from this day onwards the bitch must be under constant supervision so that as soon as she shows signs of whelping she can be immediately taken to the room where she is intended to whelp, and to which she has already been introduced.

For a Miniature Poodle I find that a tea-chest makes an admirably warm place in which to bring up the pups. For the actual whelping itself get a soap box, or any open wooden box about twenty-four inches square. It is essential that you should be able to see what the bitch is doing, and able to go to her aid if she requires help. A coarse sack, such as a coffee sack, tacked tightly to the bottom provides a good resistant surface for the bitch to scratch and bite on before she whelps, and for the first three days for the pups, as its roughness makes it easy for them to get sufficient purchase whilst they try to keep themselves on the teats. Once the bitch has finished whelping I give her a hot bottle wrapped in a blanket to provide a warm bulwark on which the pups can lean, to counteract the excessive iciness of the world in which they find themselves after the warm embrace of the uterus— particularly in the winter.

Have the box all ready from the fifty-sixth day onward, and introduce the bitch to it as early as possible and encourage her to lie in it.

May I assure her agitated owner that normal whelping is the rule rather than the exception, and Poodles with their fine heads are particularly easy whelpers?

The first sign that labour has begun is when the bitch begins to dig and scratch her bed. She sometimes begins to do this some hours, sometimes even twenty-four, before she really means to whelp in earnest. The next real sign that a puppy is actually on the way is when the rigors begin. These rigors are waves or trembling that move down all the aisles of the body; they cannot be mistaken. They are caused by the movement of the pups, and the digging is part of Nature's effort to assist the muscular pains.

As the time approaches when the bitch feels the pup about to arrive she will begin to give more frequent digs in her bed and will keep gazing at her tail and violently licking. After a time you will notice that she seats herself in the box in a very suggestive manner. She pushes violently downwards with all her abdominal muscles. They can be seen bunching themselves up for the push down. Do not attempt to interfere with the bitch. Merely sit and watch. She will feel comforted by your presence. Do not become unduly alarmed if no puppy appears even within an hour.

First whelpings are very often more prolonged than later ones. In due course you will see some green discharge staining the bedding, and shortly after this you will notice the water bag protruding from the vulva. Keep your eye on this but do not attempt to help. The bitch will go on straining and pushing, the bag will gradually shoot out into the box, and quite suddenly the whole pup will come forth and the mother will immediately begin to tear the bag to release the puppy. As soon as the puppy struggles out of the bag the bitch will begin to bite the cord; she generally succeeds in doing this for herself.

It sometimes happens that, with a first litter, the pup arrives and the mother does not know what to do. Then the owner must slit the bag and release the pup. This is done by taking it with the thumb and first finger of either hand and slitting the membrane sharply. The pup will then fall out. If the mother still does nothing, take it in one hand and hold it to her mouth, and she will infallibly begin to lick. As she does this the pup will cry and nature will come to her aid and she will know what to do. She will then undoubtedly bite through the cord. If she does not the owner must then take a pair of sterilized scissors and cut it about two inches from the pup's body. In case there should be any haemorrhage from the cord, induced either by the bitch's bite or the scissor's cut, have ready some crystals of permanganate of potash and apply some. This will stop bleeding at once.

Sometimes the after-birth does not come down with the bag. It gets separated and slips off, and therefore the puppy may be born and be lying in the box while its cord is still attached to the after-birth inside its mother's body. Wait to see that the after-birth appears, as its retention after the birth of the last puppy may cause trouble later.

There are several schools of thought in regard to the disposal of this after-birth. Nature intended the bitch to eat it, as is easily understood when one considers that in the long ago past the bitch had to lie up in a hole by herself and was unable to go out foraging for food. Nature therefore decreed that she should have sufficient food for at least twenty-four hours by eating and digesting the after-birth. Veterinarians of the past always taught that eating the after-birth was beneficial to the bitch. It is natural for her to do this; the placenta contains valuable products that are good for her in her condition. In the home and in the kennel the bitch will not lack nourishment but the natural value of the placenta remains and is necessary to her health.

After the first pup has arrived your part is still that of observer. If the bitch moves about a great deal before the arrival of the next one, and is not too careful with her feet, you must then steer the new-born pup away so that it is not stamped upon. But do not handle the pup more than is absolutely necessary. It gives the mother real pain to have her whelps handled at all. As soon as she is occupied with the imminent arrival of another pup see that the others are well out of the way, then await results.

The bitch will probably lie down and rest in between each pup's birth. She will lick them over and over again. This massage with the tongue is life-giving and stimulates the vitality of the whelps. As soon as she has had three or four pups, and seems to be resting peacefully, fill a hot water bottle with very hot (not boiling) water, if the weather is cold, wrap it carefully in a blanket and place it in the box so that the warmth radiates from the front of it on to the pups.

There is usually some interval between the arrival of the first and second puppies—twenty minutes, sometimes an hour, and sometimes six puppies will be born in an hour and a half—there is no telling.

When you think she has finished whelping give her a drink of warm milk to which you can add Lactogal or Glucose as a stimulant. Lactogal is very good for helping the milk supply, and most bitches love it.

When you think the last puppy has been born try to find out for yourself whether or not there is one left—as far as an inexperienced person can do so—by gently pressing the abdomen and finding it soft and resistant, in complete contrast to what it felt like a few hours previously. You may feel what appears to be a hard bulge at one side, but that is probably only bunched-up muscles. After the bitch has had a drink of milk leave her by herself to sleep for some hours.

Some mothers are so devoted that they have to be forced to go out to relieve themselves. It is always as well to take the precaution of arranging the room in which they whelp so that they can relieve themselves there, if the need is urgent before you go in to let them out.

Some bitches have plenty of milk before the puppies are born, some develop it as soon as they have come, some do not produce any for twenty-four hours after the birth. In any case, a pup can live twenty-four hours without suckling, but it is not normal for it to have to do this. If the milk is not there within twenty-four hours consult your veterinary surgeon. One usually sees the pups happily nursing in a neat row very soon after birth.

The first three days are the most important and it is inadvisable to leave the bitch for any length of time until they are over. Many a valuable pup has been lost because the bitch has been left unattended too long and has not noticed that one of the pups was not sucking, or that he has been pushed out by one of his hardier brothers.

The best method of all, if it can be arranged, is to have the bitch and whelps in one's room, or to arrange a bed in the whelping-room so that one can see on the first night that all the pups are getting their share of food. I defy anyone to be able to sleep through the crying of a hungry pup or pups.

There is a very distinct difference between the cry of the normal puppy as it sucks and the miserable wail of the hungry one who is starving in the midst of plenty. If you are there on the spot for the whole of the first twelve hours you will be able to see that the smallest and weakest of the litter gets its chance at the nipple. It is a good plan to hold such a pup to the teat for a definite length of time every two hours. If you succeed in getting three or four good meals into it within the first twenty-four hours it is more than likely that the puppy will survive. Anyhow, a weak puppy will require constant supervision for the first three days.

As soon as the puppies are three days old they can have their tails docked and the dew claws removed. They need not be done before five days if it is difficult for some reason, but it is as well not to leave them longer than five days as up to that period the puppies' nervous system is not sufficiently developed for them to feel anything but very slight pain when the tail is docked. You must call your veterinary surgeon in to do this job as it calls for skill in cutting and experience in the length of tail to be removed. It is possible to mar a puppy's appearance for life and render it almost useless in the Show Ring if the tail be cut too short. A tail that is too short destroys the balance of the dog and prevents a proper pompon being grown. If a tail has been left too long it is possible to have the tip removed when the dog is about six months old. My veterinary surgeon tells me that, contrary to usual belief, it is not a painful or dangerous operation. If a tail has to be redocked an anaesthetic is of course used.

By the time the puppies have passed their first three days they should be transferred from the bed in which they were born to the tea-chest, taking care to transfer the blanket from the first box or the bitch may resent the 'clean' smell of the new bed. The bottom of the tea-chest must be covered with thick newspaper, which is easily removed and replaced. After a time the blanket can be taken away and there will be nothing more to be washed—the bed will always be clean and sweet.

A box is better than a basket because it is solid and prevents any moisture dripping through. The box, however, should be stood either on blocks or bricks to provide air space between it and the floor, otherwise there is a danger of damp destroying the lino or similar floor covering. Into the bottom of the box put some thick newspaper, then a piece of blanket. Take care that the blanket is not too big or the bitch may push it up into folds and a puppy may become entangled and die of suffocation because it is too young to wriggle out again or cry out. Some bitches will have nothing whatever on the bottom of their box; they will tear up the paper and throw it out, and will throw the blanket out too. If they do this one can only bow to their wishes and allow them to keep their puppies in their own fashion.

It is as well to tack a strip of wood about six inches wide across the box at the bottom and about half an inch up, so that dirt or cleansing water can be easily got out.

After the pups have been born the mother should have all the extra food she needs to give them a good start in life. A pint of milk a day is essential. If you have it, a raw egg beaten up in milk each morning and either Glucose or Lactogal should be added to subsequent milk drinks. For nursing mothers, both Poodle and Miniature, five meals a day are usually required.

The rule of thumb method is to give a meal per pup. Two of the meals a day should be milk. At least two pounds of meat for a Poodle and at least half a pound for a Miniature, according to the size of the litter. This should be given daily, raw, the bulk being made up by feeding biscuit meal, shredded wheat or whatever kind of cereal is in general use. For the first two weeks I usually scald the meal with hot water and give it soaked, with a teaspoonful of Glucose added, and just enough milk to make it crumbly but not soggy. As the puppies get older I feed it dry and in a larger quantity. I generally give some of the meat about ten-thirty a.m., the remainder at six-thirty p.m. At two-thirty p.m. I give the biscuit meal, rice pudding, suet pudding or whatever is preferred. This is a subject about which I feel very strongly; I consider it vital that all meals for nursing mothers, puppies and adults should always be given in the same quantity and at the same time each and every day. The less it varies, the healthier will the animals be.

Between three and four weeks, according to the bitch's make-up—and they all vary—she will probably begin to regurgitate her food. As soon as she does this you will know that the puppies are ready for weaning. In any case, as soon as the puppies are four weeks old they should begin to eat scraped raw meat. Some puppies show that they are ready to be weaned earlier by trying to eat their mother's food. I begin my Miniatures with an ounce of raw meat daily. As they begin to eat the meat the amount is increased week by week. Some of them will at first try to suck the meat; the less advanced will tend to give up trying to swallow the tiresome stuff, much preferring their mother's milk, but in a few days their taste for their natural food begins to assert itself and they eat greedily.

It must be emphasized that as soon as it is noticed that the bitch is vomiting her meals only food of a size that can readily be swallowed by the whelps should be given or, and I know from experience, the tragedy of a puppy choking to death will be enacted. From three weeks onwards it is best to be on the safe side and never give any food, meat or biscuit, that is not small, soaked, and finely chopped.

Once the puppies have begun to eat meat there is no need to scrape it, but it must be chopped into very small pieces about the size of minced meat.

When the daily meat meal has been established the puppies can slowly be put on to some milk—cow's milk reinforced with a little suet, or goat's milk, which is best of all and does not need reinforcing. The size of these milk meals can be gauged only by observation of the puppies. A rough guide is to give a tablespoon-ful to each Miniature pup and double this for a Poodle puppy, and as soon as this seems too little double it until, at five to six weeks old, each pup has three or four tablespoonfuls at each meal. When they are used to the milk and meat introduce the starch meal. One of these daily, to two of meat, is best to begin with. They will usually eat one of the fine puppy meals if it is well scalded and then fed with a little cold milk.

As a help it is advisable, especially in winter, to give one or two drops of cod-liver-oil—veterinary standard—to each pup in its food once a day. This tiny dose will be found much more successful than giving half a teaspoonful, most of which will not be assimilated. The biscuit meal can be varied with stale crumby bread or groats or Farex.

If the pups have diarrhoea, when they begin eating, Allbran will be found invaluable. It is not possible to give quantities, but a tablespoonful to a small handful for a puppy, according to his size, is usually enough. It can be given twice daily for a time instead of biscuit. It is important to put on cold milk but not to put it on until one is ready to put the meal down, otherwise it gets sticky and the puppies find it difficult to swallow. This cereal is most valuable for dogs of any age if the bowels are loose, and for the puppies while they are teething or when they have worms.

All puppies must be wormed at eight weeks whether they show signs of infestation or not. They all have worms, however healthy they appear to be—and of course they are healthy; a strong pup can resist the toxic effect of worms but he cannot do so if he has to wait too long for treatment.

Sometimes puppies have them very badly at three or four weeks. One of the signs is from the bowels, which are very pale in colour, and the belly is very hard and distended. There are one or two vermifuges on the market that can be given with complete safety at three or four weeks. These are those with an oily base. Your veterinary surgeon will help you here. Naturally it is inadvisable to worm at such a tender age unless it is absolutely necessary. If the puppies are really bad, so young, they will die unless you can clear them. It is a case of kill or cure. If nothing untoward has occurred dose the litter at eight weeks and again within ten days. The puppies should then be clear for some time.

It is perhaps not generally known that the indication that all is not well with a puppy, or indeed with an adult dog, is to be found in the temperature. The normal temperature of an adult dog is 101.4°F. (38.5°C.); the normal puppy temperature is about 102°F. (39°C.). If a puppy is not as keen on his food as usual, or if he is sick or has diarrhoea, it is advisable immediately to take his temperature. If it is over 102.5°F. (39°C.) something may be wrong. It may be only a digestive upset; it may be worms, or it may be the beginning of an illness. There is no need to worry unless it goes up to over 103°F. (39.5°C.). A young dog's temperature will run up and down very easily.

If you have recently wormed a puppy and he has been out in the cold and damp he may have a chill. He may have eaten something that has upset him. Therefore as a preliminary it is advisable to give a small dose of some mild corrective, such as milk of magnesia; for Miniatures, the dose recommended on the bottle for infants, for Standards, that for a small child is probably the right amount. If the temperature remains at 102.4°F. (39°C.) or 102.6°F. (39°C.) for more than twenty-four hours it is as well to call in a veterinary surgeon.

If you have a bitch due to whelp, and you think she is going to do this before the right day, you can generally determine whether this is likely by taking her temperature; if she is about to whelp it will probably have dropped below normal. This is not true of every bitch but it is generally accepted as an indication if there are no other signs. Again, if after a bitch has whelped she does not settle down and appears restless and excited, take her temperature. If it is up, 103°F. (39.5°C.) or over, it is possible that she may have some inflammation, or some of the after-birth may not have come away and is setting up a toxic condition. Once more, do not delay—send for your veterinary surgeon.

Always have your thermometer handy, and do not hesitate to use it. It is a simple matter to do this. See that the mercury is shaken down to the right place before using; dip the end in some vaseline or similar grease, then gently insert into the rectum, holding the dog's tail firmly in your left hand while you do this. Be careful not to push it too far into a puppy or you may hurt him. If inserted gently, usually no dog protests. Keep it there, right inside the rectum, for at least one minute and then gently withdraw it. It is most important that the mercury be right inside the dog's body for the whole of the time in which you are taking the temperature.

Poodles are very excitable dogs, particularly the Miniatures, and when they are under a year old their temperatures run up and down very easily. I remember once taking the temperatures of five young puppies under seven months old after they had experienced their first clipping with electric clippers. They were all very excited; while not frightened, they were nevertheless keyed up the whole time the clipping went on. Before returning the pups to their kennels I decided to take their temperatures as I was of the opinion that any such experience might cause a big rise. One was 105°F. (40.5°C.), and the other four ran from 103.5°F. (39.5°C.) to 104.5°F. (40.5°C.). They were put back in their kennels and left quietly for two hours, and when temperatures were taken again they were all normal. It is quite an experience to take a temperature before some excitement and then to take it after. If, for instance, the veterinary surgeon comes to do some inoculations you will find, if your dogs are some distance apart in different kennels, that as he proceeds to test before giving the inoculations, the dogs done first without any worry will be normal while those done last, after ten minutes of excitedly running and jumping and barking, will be found to be up to as much as 102°F. (39°C.) to 102.5°F. (39°C.).

It is important to remember this before getting too het up about a rise in temperature. It is not suggested that a rise is not serious; but merely to point out that there is no reason to worry unduly until some cause for the rise has been found. If you can remember something that has happened that might have caused the temperature to go up, you will know what to do. If you know of nothing, and it does not go down within twelve hours, that will be the time to send for the veterinary surgeon.

If a puppy or adult dog seems to be out of sorts and you find his temperature is over 102.5°F. (39°C.) call in your veterinary surgeon at once. If there is only one degree of fever it may be that the dog has some digestive upset or a mild chill. If you remember that he has not been quite himself for a day or two do not delay—call in your veterinary surgeon.

Always make sure there is plenty of fresh water available; in some cases puppies will toss their bowls of water over or even blow themselves out by drinking too much, in which case it is advisable to give them a bowl and stay with them while they have a drink—but do be sure they have sufficient, especially in hot weather.

At ten weeks, if they have been well reared and are healthy, they are ready to go to their new homes. I do not think it is a good thing to sell them at six weeks unless they are going to an owner used to rearing tinies, otherwise tragedy will ensue, or the puppy will grow up weedy and possibly rickety, and may become the prey of distemper or some other fell disease.

A puppy should be allowed to stay with his mother so long as she is willing. I have known bitches that refused to feed their puppies a day after four weeks, and others that had milk for them at eleven weeks. There is no better way of fitting a puppy to withstand disease in later life, and of making him strong and healthy, than to leave him on his mother as long as she allows. Let him have his mother's milk in addition to the meals you are giving him. If you keep the puppies until ten weeks and after, you will have satisfied customers. If you sell at five to six weeks you will probably hear of sickness, diarrhoea, worms and whatnot. I know that it is very expensive to keep them long these days, but as you are responsible for having brought them into the world it is your duty to keep them until you can send them out as strong and healthy as possible.

As soon as you see that the pups are quite normal in every way, moving about well and strongly at, say, six to seven weeks, invite the owner of the sire (if addresses are not too far apart) to come and see them and advise. You will be sure to get some real help. Actually, I do not think it is possible really to give an opinion until a litter is at least eight weeks old, as most pups have not full control of their limbs until then. If the owner of the stud is unable to come to you it may be possible for you to go to him. If he offers you a reasonable price for some or one of them, take it. A reasonable price between breeders is usually assumed to be the cost of the stud fee, but this is of course a variable fee. Some fashionable dogs ask a very high fee, but if their progeny does not find favour with the public you may not be able to get as much as the stud fee for a single pup. Anyhow, if the owner of the stud offers to buy two puppies, or perhaps the whole litter, remember it is more profitable to sell them at a lower price than you hoped to get at eight weeks than to keep them until they are perhaps three or four months old, and then get only a pound or so more. Besides, it takes time to establish yourself, and if you want to make a success of breeding you will need to gain experience, something you can get only in the passage of time.

One important fact that is frequently forgotten by the novice breeder is that puppies become adults, and if a lower price than is hoped for is offered, and not accepted, the puppy may hang on until it becomes an adult, and an adult dog is far more difficult to sell, unless it is an outstanding one, than is a puppy eight weeks old. £20 in hand at eight weeks is very much better than a possible £40, if it can be obtained, at ten or twelve months. Before the war, breeders used to say that the average cost of raising each puppy to twelve months old was £10, taking everything into consideration. If this estimate was a correct one, and it undoubtedly was, today the cost of raising a puppy from infancy to adulthood must be well in the neighbourhood of £50 to £100 according to whether it is a standard, miniature or toy Poodle. Such a price is absolutely by some happy fluke, a buyer happens to fall in love with a particular dog, and is prepared to pay a large sum to obtain it.

SELLING

The 'Dog Press' is an ideal medium for advertising young stock but, generally speaking, unless your dogs are very well known, and are by winning dogs on both sides, you are not likely to sell them at much of a price through advertisements. These are largely trade papers, read by fellow breeders who will buy only for the breeding lines of any stock, whereas the owner of the stud is likely to find it easier to sell his own dog's progeny than you are. Also, as he probably has a larger Kennel he can more easily afford to wait. If you are breeding in your home you will not want to have five or six young puppies to clean up after and to feed for any length of time. Therefore dispose of them as quickly as you can after they are eight to ten weeks old. An advertisement in a local paper is more likely to put you in touch with people in your district who may be looking for pets, but it is important to realize that you cannot expect that you, without any experience and without the background of a reputation built up through years, will receive the same price for your puppies as do the long-established breeders. It very often happens that the novice buyer goes to the novice breeder and pays far more for the novice's pup, probably of mediocre quality, than he would if he went to an established Kennel and stated clearly what he wanted.

Again, it often happens that the novice buyer is very disappointed when he discovers that the novice seller has asked a big price for a puppy not worth more than half, as it is only of pet standard, and is consequently very disillusioned when he finds out the truth. The moral of this is: if you are a novice breeder take advice from the established breeder and ask a price suited to the type of pup you are selling. If you have good puppies, and are content to sell them, at reasonable prices, to other breeders who are already established, you will find that you yourself will slowly be able to work your way up on the strength of the good puppies you have sold, which had the advantage of getting into understanding hands and perhaps of attaining honours in the Show Ring, which would have been impossible had you tried to do this yourself.

Establishing a Kennel and selling good puppies takes years; it cannot be done by just breeding one or two litters.

Your time will come if you are patient and if you breed carefully and with thought. There is no quick road to success with any livestock; if you get the purchase price of your bitch back in a year you will be fortunate. I have yet to hear of any other venture in which one can get one's capital investment back in so short a time.

When you have bred a winner you will be on the road to success, but it is a long road and one beset with pitfalls, and only serious people ever get to the top. So go ahead confident that you have bought a good bitch, mate her to a good dog and take the advice of those who know. Don't use a fashionable dog because he has sired a number of winners. Analyse the pedigrees of the bitches that threw those winners and find out whether there is a common factor on both sides that made for the success. Then look for the same factor in your bitch's pedigree and if it isn't there don't use him. By a fluke he may throw a winner but the chances are that the progeny will be a combination of the *differences* in the parents, and then you may not have winners. Remember that like breeds like, and only by observation and study, and making use of the experience of others, will you be able to mate parents that will enable you to produce a type, so that people will say, looking at your dog: "Why, that must be from X's strain."

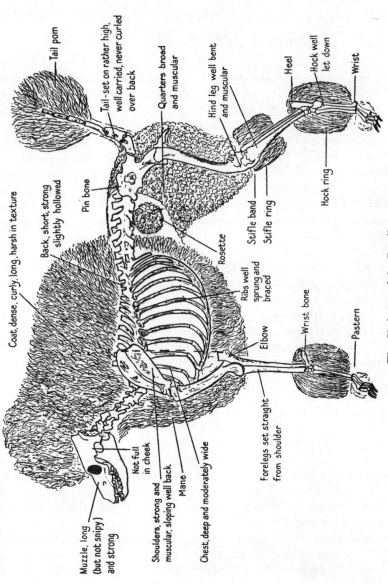

Tail pom

Tail-set on rather high, well carried, never curled over back

Quarters broad and muscular

Hind leg well bent and muscular

Heel

Hock well let down

Wrist

Pin bone

Back, short, strong slightly hollowed

Coat, dense, curly, long, harsh in texture

Rosette

Stifle band

Stifle ring

Hock ring

Ribs well sprung and braced

Wrist bone

Elbow

Pastern

Muzzle, long (but not snipy) and strong

Not full in cheek

Shoulders, strong and muscular, sloping well back

Mane

Chest, deep and moderately wide

Forelegs set straight from shoulder

The Skeleton of the Poodle

Chapter XV

PREPARATION FOR SHOW

WHEN you have clipped your poodle the time has come to continue the toilet required for the Show Ring. Miss Bowring has written a comprehensive Chapter on training your dog for Show, so I will confine myself to some technical points.

It is necessary to give your dog a bath three or four days before the Show takes place. If you do this only one or two days beforehand, you will find, particularly with young dogs, that the hair remains quite silky and will therefore count against him in the Ring with regard to texture. When you are showing a white dog you are in somewhat of a predicament. If you bath your dog too soon the weather may be wet and he will become dirty. Generally speaking, you have to bath a white dog only twenty-four hours before a Show. You are allowed to use a cleaning block or a white powder to clean the coat, should it have become soiled before the Show, but it is not permissible to use large quantities of powder and leave it in the coat to make a cloud when the Judge's hand descends in examination.

Also, it is essential to bear in mind that you are benched irrespective of colour, and if you have a white dog benched next to blacks or browns you will not find yourself very popular when clouds of white descend upon the black dogs. Therefore be sure that you have brushed out all powder before you get to the Show, that is to say, all the powder contained in the big coat. The bracelets and hock rings can be protected by winding bandages over the hair. Some exhibitors put bandages on their dogs, fore and aft, to ensure that the coat is not soiled on the journey. If by chance the feet and hock rings, and so forth, are soiled it is a simple matter to powder them and to brush it out without causing annoyance to fellow exhibitors.

There are many different schools of thought concerning the use of shampoos to enhance the beauty of the coat. It is generally a matter of personal taste. There are several soapless shampoos for dogs on the market which are excellent in every way. Most of them are very suitable for whites, but with blacks it is sometimes difficult to brush out what remains in the coat after it has been shampooed and dried. Personally, I have found that the soapy shampoos stick in the coat and are extremely difficult to remove. This applies mainly to post-war types of soaps and shampoos.

The manner in which you dry your dog is again a personal one. Most people, particularly those who own the larger variety of poodle, make use of one of the many electric hair-dryers. Others favour the old-fashioned fire, which, of course, is not available in the summer. At that time of year the sun, if it is kind, will very quickly dry any coats. However, if you do decide to dry yourdog in the open air in the sun be careful to have him either on your lap or on a table so that he is not able to roll and immediately get grass and mud into his coat.

Whether you use an electric dryer, a fire, or the sun, you must keep brushing him gently all the time, to ensure that he dries as quickly as possible right down to the roots. Once he is dry, give him a very careful grooming. Brush and comb the hair just as it will appear when he goes into the Ring. Then cast your eye over the coat and clip off with the point of your scissors any hairs that destroy its even length. Do the same to the quarters, the rosettes, stifle and hock rings and bracelets, and last but not least, comb out the tail pompom. First of all, comb this with a perpendicular motion, then comb so that it lies like a chrysanthemum, then cut off any hairs that stand out and destroy the round effect. If you comb all of the pompon in this manner you will find that there are invariably little clusters of hair which hang down towards the body and which must be gently cut off to get the tuft with hairs standing all in the same direction. When you have satisfied yourself that all is as it should be, then take a silk handkerchief and rub the coat all over. This will give a wonderful polish.

When you get to the Show, as soon as you have benched your dog give him a thorough grooming. You will have taken your collapsible table with you, and also sufficient brushes and combs, a pair of clippers for the last-minute finish round the toes, and a pair of scissors to cut off any odd hairs that may still offend your eye.

No dark rinses that may improve the colour of a bad black or brown are allowed by the Kennel Club rules. Nor may you use grease or white of egg (as is sometimes done by novice exhibitors) to keep back the hairs from the eyes. No Judge, who knows his job, will allow his favourable opinion of an animal to be interfered with because a few hairs have come out of the top-knot. Remember that it is only the traditional clipping and scissoring of the Poodle that is allowed by the Kennel Club.

For the benefit of exhibitors who are novices, it may be necessary to mention some of the following points:

No dog can be exhibited at any dog show held under Kennel Club rules, unless registered with the Kennel Club, except in the case of Exemption Shows which are held in aid of charities.

If you have bought a dog that has already been registered on the Active list, then all that is required is to transfer him at the Kennel Club into your name. In most cases a form will have been given to you with his registration certificate, etc.

Should the puppy have been registered as one of a litter, on the basic registration only, then it will need to be registered on the Active list before being shown, used at stud or bred from. Then an application form must be sent for from the Kennel Club, duly filled in and returned with the appropriate fee.

You cannot show a dog under six months old except in Litter Classes.

Dog Shows are run by clubs specially formed to advance the benefit of a particular breed, and also by large Canine Societies.

If you wish to become an exhibitor you should study the Dog papers, in which you will find particulars of all Shows at which your particular breed is being exhibited.

If you write to the Show Secretary, a schedule of classes will be sent to you. The number of Classes varies at all the Shows but generally speaking there are always some Classes for beginners, the beginners being the dogs. There will probably be a puppy Class, and one for the novices, and so on up to the higher Classes such as the 'Open Dog'. This Class is open to all dogs of the breed, of all ages and colours. These are what are known as the Senior Classes and you usually begin by entering your dogs in the 'Juniors', that is, the 'Puppy', the 'Novice' and the 'Maiden'.

After you have exhibited at a few Shows you will soon understand what is meant by all these expressions.

During the spring and summer Shows are held out of doors, and it is generally advisable to start a puppy on his career at such Shows as the noise and bustle is so much less than it is in a large, echoing hall, and is unlikely to cause him to feel shy or nervous. Also, if you are exhibiting a young dog he will stand much less chance of picking up infection in the open air than he will in the germ-laden halls in which Shows take place in late autumn and winter.

It is not often advisable to show a young dog unless he has been inoculated against distemper; after a year the risk of infection is much lighter. Some people are prejudiced against the use of anti-distemper inoculations, in which case they must use their discretion. Experience over a large number of years has convinced most exhibitors and veterinary surgeons that the chances of a dog who has not been inoculated of picking up a disease is very great. It has also been found that dogs which have been inoculated with the Burroughs Wellcome method of inoculation against distemper do not take hard pad so badly, if they pick it up, as do dogs that have never been inoculated. In fact, dogs that have been inoculated with the anti-distemper virus invariably recover perfectly from an attack of hard pad.

A thing to remember when you go to a Dog Show as an exhibitor is that you must arrive in sufficient time to avoid hurrying yourself or your dog. It takes quite a time to get a Poodle ready for the Ring, and if you are flustered and in a hurry your dog will feel your mood, will become flustered himself and will not do you justice.

As soon as you have arrived at the Show, and have benched your dogs, be certain to find out where your Ring is, and at what time judging will begin. Always remember that if you miss your Class it is your own fault. There are Stewards, of course, whose duty it is to see that exhibitors go into the Ring, but if you are away exercising your dog, or having a chat with someone, and miss your Class it is not the Steward's fault.

Remember, too, that it is bad manners to keep the Judge waiting. When you go into the Ring keep your eye on the Judge, ready to do whatever is required of you without delay.

Most Classes nowadays are very big and Judges have an arduous task. Although you can relax between your Classes, the Judge cannot. He has to concentrate the whole time, and if you do not keep your attention on him, and happen to have your dog with his back turned and with his feet splayed out at the wrong moment, you are likely to lose a place that might otherwise have been yours.

Do not keep on brushing your dog when you have entered the Ring. Nothing is more irritating to a Judge who is looking round at the contours of the exhibits before him than to have his attention distracted by the constant movement of a brush.

Keep your place in the Ring. Do not crowd your fellow exhibitors: they also have paid an entrance fee.

Do not keep moving your dog backwards and forwards, and up and down, in an attempt to ensure that the Judge sees your exhibit. He can see him much better if he is standing still. Before you enter you dog at his first Show you should give him Ring training so that he will stand still with tail erect and his eye upon you until you give him leave to relax. There are training classes held in most areas, usually run by the nearest canine society. It is worthwhile taking your prospective puppy along where you and your puppy will be given helpful instructions. The Kennel Club or perhaps your veterinary surgeon would be able to give you the address. If your dog is inclined to be nervous and shy of being handled by strangers, you must help him to overcome these drawbacks. As he will have to stand steady on a table if he is a Miniature, or on the floor if he is a Poodle, he will have to allow a stranger to handle him from head to foot—to peer into his eyes, to measure his ears, to look at his tail, to handle his feet, to feel his quarters, to put weight upon his back to test his firmness.

Some dogs are entirely willing to have all this done; others are not. Therefore, if your dog does not like standing on a table (if he is a Miniature) give him his meals on a table every day, encouraging visitors to the house to handle him there and to give him his food. He will then soon become accustomed to this and will even jump upon the table, thinking of the meal he is about to partake. The same method is suitable for a Poodle if he is shy. Do exactly the same as you do with a Miniature, but do it standing on the floor and not on the table.

You will find when you attend your first Shows that experienced exhibitors will be only too pleased to help you in every way if you ask assistance. Do not assume that because it is not offered they are stand-offish or unfriendly. As you know, English people are very chary of interfering with others, and the exhibitors cannot know that you are in a state of nerves because of ignorance. When you have asked for advice and received it, take it. Do not go to five or six different people, seek guidance from all but be guided by none. No one likes to feel that advice has been asked for but ignored.

If you do not win, do not think it is necessarily the Judge who is wrong or unfair. Your dog may be at fault; it may be that you have not mastered the art of presentation and in consequence have not done him justice.

It is not encouraging for a Judge to see, as sometimes happens, an exhibitor tear up the card just handed to him, because disappointed that it is green instead of red.

Just as you train your dog to have manners in the Ring so you must train yourself to maintain calm whatever happens.

There are many regulations, drawn up by the Kennel Club, governing the running of Shows. These relate to placing, conduct in the Ring, time of judging and time of leaving. If it is stipulated that no exhibit may be removed from the Show before a certain time do not use your ingenuity to get out before the time permitted, or you may find yourself disqualified from your wins. The fact that your dog has, or has not, been placed is immaterial. A Show opens at a certain time and closes at a certain time, and by making an entry you have undertaken to remain there all the time. Novice exhibitors frequently appear very disgruntled when they have to stay until perhaps five or six o'clock in the afternoon, their dog having been judged in the morning. Dog Shows are Beauty Competitions and all the exhibits are there to exhibit their looks; the public, having paid to go in, is entitled to see the full bevy of beauty entered for its delectation.

Do's *and* DON'TS *for the Intending Exhibitor*

Do groom your dog daily, being careful to brush and comb gently to avoid pulling out hair unnecessarily.

Do keep his teeth cleaned. Brush them at least once a week and give some hard tack daily.

Do have his nails cut if they grow too long; then he can put his feet down correctly. A sound mover with well-shaped feet seldom needs his nails attended to.

Do clip him, or have him clipped, three or four days before a Show and then bath him.

Do find out where your Ring is as soon as you have benched your dog.

Do pack all your dog's equipment in one container and don't forget some paper bags. They are invaluable for train or car sickness.

Do have your dog ready in time for his Class—don't keep the Judge waiting.

Don't brush your dog while you are in the Ring. Nothing

is more distracting to the Judge than a wildly moving brush. Your dog's toilet should have been completed before he goes in. The Judge confirms his visual impressions with his hands, and no amount of 'arranging' a coat will deceive knowledgeable hands.

Don't brush or handle your dog while the Judge is going over him. The Judge will ask you to help him if he thinks help necessary.

Don't crowd the other exhibitor. He, too, has paid for his entry.

Don't throw a ball or squeak a toy. You may cause other exhibits to stand at attention too!

Don't talk to the nearest Ringsiders. Keep your attention on your dog and on the Judge.

Don't try to leave before the authorized time.

PREPARATION FOR SHOW

One of the most important pieces of property necessary when you are getting your dog ready for the Show Ring, particularly if you are clipping him yourself, is a big looking-glass. Place your dog on a table in front of a looking-glass and have handy a really good photograph of a perfectly clipped Poodle. All the time you are doing the clipping look into the glass. You will quickly see whether you are working in the right direction. The looking-glass is an essential when you are tipping off the coat and doing the 'squaring-up'. By keeping your eye on the glass as you cut the coat you will very quickly see when you have done enough.

Toenails. The well-made foot properly put to the ground will always have a well-worn toenail, and cutting will be unnecessary. Many dogs, however, that have feet that look quite well do not consistently use them correctly; consequently the nails are inclined to grow.

When judging one is frequently amazed at the length of toenail some dogs are allowed to carry. If the nail is long enough to touch the ground, and if the foot is not put down correctly, it will grow and cause great disfigurement to the feet. It is a simple matter to keep the nails down if one takes them in hand in time. As soon as it appears that the nails are a little long they can easily be shortened with a suitable nail-file. The proper way to file the nail is not from the top of the nail downwards but from the bottom of the nail to the top. When cutting, the reverse is true; one has to begin from the top. Great care must be taken to avoid cutting to the quick when using nail clippers. It is not easy to see the quick in a black dog's foot, but much easier with whites. Although white dogs are supposed by the Standard to have black toenails in actual fact only a few have nails so coloured. The majority have white or slightly brown nails. If you have a white dog, look at his toenails and you will see exactly what is meant. The horny part of the nail is opaque and the part where the quick is, looks pink. It is easy, therefore, to practise clipping toenails on a white dog.

Take your nail clippers in your right hand. Hold the dog's foot in your left and place your first finger under a nail. Then put your clippers parallel with the side of the nail, the centre of the clipper being at the top of the nail, and cut off a very small piece at an acute angle. Do the same with the other side, making two acute-angled cuts instead of one across the nail, and parallel with the body.

If you cut across the nail you are in great danger of cutting the quick. If you do a sideway cut correctly you will see the quick projecting very, very slightly up to the point of the nail. In a few days all roughness will be worn off and the nail perfectly prepared for the Show Ring.

If you have let your dog's nails grow very long you will have to ask your veterinary surgeon to do the cutting. The quick grows right down to the end of the nail, and if there should be half an inch required to come off you will not be able to do this in one operation—that would cause your dog intense pain and make the nail bleed badly.

Incidentally, while on the subject of nails, puppies' nails should be cut when they are quite tiny, at two or three weeks old. The nails are like little needles and quickly scratch their mother unless they are cut back.

If you take the puppy's foot in your left hand and run the first finger of your right hand under the pad in a downward direction you will feel the sharp curve of the nail. Cut off the little white tip and the bitch will be much more comfortable. I have often heard novices complain that their bitch is not a good mother, that she growls and swears at her puppies when they feed. An experienced handler who picks up the bitch will see at once all the scratches and sores the tiny claws have made. It is no wonder that mothers do not like nursing if they are so scratched and sore. Therefore always keep an eye on the bitch to see that she is not becoming red round her teats. If she is, it will most likely be the result of scratching toenails.

Care of the Teeth. No dog should ever be allowed to go into the

Ring with dirty teeth. Apart from the fact that dirty, discoloured teeth detract from the beauty of the dog in a Beauty Competition it is not good for the dog, or the teeth, if tartar is allowed to accumulate. A wise owner will attend to teeth once a week. If this is done weekly, no tartar will accumulate.

When a dog's teeth have tartar on them it may be possible to get it off quite easily with a toothbrush and some precipitate of chalk. A little peroxide is also useful; having used the precipitate of chalk it is wise to dip a piece of cotton wool in the peroxide and carefully wipe all round the teeth and gums.

If a small amount of tartar has collected it can easily be removed with a suitable instrument. Most suppliers of dog equipment will have such an instrument in stock. It is quite easy to use and needs only a certain amount of experience for the operation to hold no terrors for patient or performer. If you take hold of the muzzle with your left hand and put your first finger into the mouth, right across it under the fangs, you will be able to control any but the most temperamental animal. If you are afraid of being bitten—most unlikely, but you may be—put on your finger a leather one from an old glove.

Tartar comes off quickly and easily unless it is very heavy and of long standing, in which case it is better to call in a veterinary surgeon. If most of the teeth are badly coated it is essential that he should be called in; he will most likely give a slight anaesthetic and clean up the whole mouth. Once this is done, you will be able to keep it perfectly clean by the weekly use of the toothbrush.

Care of the Ears. The ears of the Show Dog must always be perfectly clean. These can be kept free from parasites and canker if they are wiped out once a week as required. If an eye is kept on them they will probably never require any but the most perfunctory attention. A good soothing cleanser is a mixture of one part liquid paraffin to two parts methylated or surgical spirit. If this mixture is kept in a small bottle and well shaken before application it will be found to be most efficacious. A very small quantity dripped into the ear and gently massaged down will generally clear out the most obstinate wax. A tiny piece of cotton wool twisted on a match or an orange stick is one of the best implements for cleaning out the tiny orifice. After you have wiped out the passage clean the flaps until perfectly clean. If any dead hair is in the passage it is as well to take it out. If you cannot reach it easily with your fingers a small artery clip, which can be bought at most chemists, is invaluable for safely pulling the hair out. A little penicillin powder dusted into the ear and well shaken down will keep the ear free from germs. When you have put a little powder into the ear-hole you will find that it will shake down very comfortably if you gently hold the flap in your left hand and lightly tap the passage on the outside until all the powder has disappeared.

If you are in any doubt as to the state of your dog's ear, and if he persists in shaking and scratching although you can see nothing, consult your veterinary surgeon. He may have a grass seed or some other foreign body at the bottom of the passage, which will set up an abscess or, at the best, cause such intense irritation that the dog will not be able to eat, sleep or sit. If, by some unlucky chance, you neglect such an ear the dog will rapidly scratch off large patches of hair from the flap, so barring himself from the Show Ring for some months. If the hair on any part of the ear comes off in its entirety, it may be six to eight months before it has grown again adequately for the Ring.

Never show a dog unless he is in perfect condition and full bloom. If he is a bit short of coat, or if his ear feathers have disappeared for one reason or another, or if his eyes are not as clear as usual, do not take him to the Ring. Someone is sure to see what you do not want seen. The Judge, in his report, will probably say 'poor in coat' or 'short of coat' or 'fails in ear feathers' or 'not in condition' and you will find there is 100 per cent truth in the saying: "Give a dog a bad name and hang him." It is amazing how easily hypnotized some people are. Having seen So-and-So's Tommy poor in coat he will continue to be poor in coat under some Judges for the rest of his career, notwithstanding the fact that he now has an adequate one. It is easy when in doubt between two dogs to say of one you already know, and about whom two other Judges have pronounced that his coat should be longer, to repeat the same thing to yourself and so give yourself a good reason for rejection. It is difficult for an animal to live down a report of some fault that may, or may not, be accurate. So bear this in mind, and realize that it is better for your dog in the long run to miss one or two Shows than to run the risk of having him labelled for ever as 'poor in coat', and so forth.

Chapter XVI

HOW TO SHOW YOUR POODLE

THE object of this Chapter is to show novices how to train dogs to ensure that the animals, when shown, will exhibit to the best advantage all their potential winning-dog qualities. It is not enough to have the finest dog. It must be properly shown. A dog that will not show starts under a grave disadvantage. It is up to the owner to get the best out of his dog. A dog that refuses to allow himself to be handled in the Ring by the Judge, pulling away and behaving stupidly whilst being shown, may easily be beaten by a dog not quite so good but which shows himself off and, aided by his owner, gives the Judge every chance to appreciate all his good qualities.

Most dog Judges will give a novice every opportunity to show his dog, but at big Championship Shows a Judge has the right to expect that exhibitors should know how to handle and show their dogs. With large classes it is impossible for any Judge to allow for the stupidities and idiosyncrasies of untrained exhibits. Therefore you should endeavour to give your dog a really good training, enabling him to come into the Ring unafraid and eager to show himself off. If your dog happens to be of a nervous type this training may mean much patient work, but with perseverance you should win in the end.

If destined for the Show Ring it is as well to commence training a puppy before it is three months of age. From an early age the dog should be accustomed to noises of every kind. You will find that an electric vacuum cleaner, and the wireless set, can be used to advantage. The young dog should also be taken out to the nearest town and made familiar with the sound of traffic. Many dogs are afraid of traffic; the owner should remember that the dog is down amongst the wheels, which is not a pleasant position for anyone. It is quite a good idea to take the dog sometimes to a railway station where he can hear the sound of trains, especially if he is likely to have to do much travelling. From an early age it is a good plan to place the dog in a travelling box every other day for a short while. This accustoms him to being shut in a box and he will learn that there is no cause for alarm. With one dog it may be easy for you to take him with you in a railway carriage, and he should frequently be taken in local buses. It is the old story of familiarity breeding contempt. A nervous dog, terrified by every sound, stands a bad chance at a big, noisy Championship Show. Perhaps you will be travelling to the Show by motor; if so, the dog should have previously been taken out in a car, so that this mode of travelling is familiar to him.

In training a dog commands should always be given by the same words, said slowly in the same tone of voice. Great patience is needed; however provoked you must never lose your temper. A dog should never be punished unless you are certain that he has deliberately disobeyed you. A dog quickly senses if you are annoyed. You should never call a dog back to you and then punish him when he does come. And, above all, never whip a dog. If a dog refuses to come when called, stoop down, speak very gently, and hold out your hand.

Instruction should not be given for long periods. A quarter of an hour, or even ten minutes, given regularly every day is far better than a longer period given at long intervals.

The dog should have a good romp before you start a lesson. This will take some of the bounce out of him and make him more amenable and attentive. If a tit-bit is carried in your pocket, and the dog knows he will get it as a reward if he does well, it will teach him to watch your hands. If you watch the shepherds at the Sheep Dog Trials you will see how their dogs are directed by their owners' hands. Shouting and a loud voice only terrify a dog and a naturally nervous dog will be made far worse by such methods.

A firm, sharp tone of voice is much more effective in training a dog than any hint of unkindness, which would destroy the dog's trust in you. How often one sees in the Show Ring a dog which has obviously been bullied, and is so terrified of doing wrong that he shows himself at his worst. A dog really fond of his owner will soon get to know what the boss is thinking and will be only too anxious to please him. Poodles of all dogs are such sensitive, intelligent beings that is is easy to gain their love and confidence.

To start the training of a puppy, give him a game first, then put a lead on him and walk slowly across the space where you are teaching him, making him keep to your left heel. As you do this say the word 'Heel' very clearly over and over again. At first patience will be needed to make the dog understand what he is required to do. To keep at heel is the foundation of all training and the dog must clearly realize what is expected of him. See that

K

he always keeps to the left hand. Never allow him to get on your right side. As he gets more accustomed to this exercise you can let the lead become looser, until he is keeping to your left heel without any control.

It is best to carry out these earlier lessons whilst the dog is on a lead. He will be on the lead whilst in the Show Ring, and it is necessary that he should be thoroughly accustomed to its use. If you find that the dog persists in trying to pull ahead gently pull him back, saying the word 'Heel' in a very decided, clear voice. If you find that it is difficult to cure him of pulling you can take out with you a folded newspaper, and when he tries to forge ahead give him a slight tap on the nose to restrain him. If the dog is inclined to drag backwards you should encourage him with your hand to keep up with you. Carry out this heeling exercise every day until your dog follows closely at your left heel. You will probably have been teaching this exercise in some quiet place, such as your garden. Now take your dog out to the road and carry on with the same exercise. If you see another dog coming, repeat the word 'Heel' in the same quiet tone, so that he knows that he must pay attention only to you.

If you have a yard or a lawn take the dog there and mark out, in your mind's eye, a circle of a size equivalent to that of a Show Ring. The Kennel Club has laid down in its Show Regulations that a Ring must contain at least five hundred square feet of clear floor space and be not less than sixteen feet in width.

Allowing for this, you should be able to work your dog inside the correct space. Walk him in a circle, accustoming him to move at an easy pace, being careful to keep him on the side nearest to the Judge, who will be in the centre of the Ring. Now mark out in your eye a run across the Ring about two feet wide and sixteen feet long. Some breeders go to the trouble of marking this out with a piece of tape to train the dog to keep always within the limits. Most people can do this exercise by eye. Now take the dog to the end of this pathway and make him walk, slowly at first, in a straight line down the pathway. Practise this repeatedly, so accustoming the dog to move easily in a direct line across a Ring.

How often one sees an untrained dog pulling and yawing all over a Ring, making it quite impossible for a Judge to see how he really moves. Watch the tail carriage to see that this is correct. A Poodle should carry his tail jauntily at a right angle—as some say, at ten to or ten past the hour if you were standing the dog before a clock. Tail carriage is most important in a Poodle. If your dog is inclined to carry his tail over his back try the rolled-up newspaper, gently touching the tip of the tail. To many Judges nothing is more annoying than to see an exhibitor continually fiddling about with his dog's tail, which should have been correctly held, without assistance from his owner, at the time the Ring was entered.

Encourage your dog by talking to him, and when he does his exercise well be sure to praise him. Most dogs love to be praised— above all, a Poodle.

When you have taught your dog how to walk in a circle and in a straight line, bring your previous lesson on heeling into practice. Say the word 'Heel', stop, make the dog stop instantly and remain standing where he is. See that his legs are correctly placed and his head well held up. If you have a friend to help you ask him to act as if he were the Judge. Accustom your dog to being handled by someone else yet not be afraid. If a Miniature Poodle, accustom him to being placed on a table and handled whilst there. Never scold your dog. Carry in your hand some small tit-bit and when he does well reward him. But do not overdo this.

Do most of the training with your hands so that by watching them the dog knows what you want him to do. You must always be very patient and never, never lose your temper. If you begin to feel irritated because you think your dog is being stupid, stop the training for a few minutes and then start again. As said before, a short period of training regularly every day is the best way to teach your dog.

To get your dog's coat to perfection is a matter of brushing, brushing and again brushing. Too much combing can do a great deal of harm to a Poodle coat; if the coat is regularly brushed every day there should be little need for the comb. It will be found that a good rub over every day with an old silk handkerchief will put a wonderful sheen on the coat. The following is a prescription for growing a coat; it was long ago given to me by one who was a master at exhibiting a dog to perfection:

> 2 drachms Oil of Rosemary
> 2 drachms Tinct. Cantharides
> 2 drachms Liquid Ammonia
> ½ oz. Glycerine
> add water to 8 ozs.

The day of the Show has come. Leave plenty of time for the start so that you have everything you want and do not have to get off in a hurry. It is as well to have ready the evening before all the things you will need: Food for yourself and your dog, your brush and comb, a couple of bath towels, the dog's rugs, his collar and lead and a smart piece of ribbon to put on his head. And take a paper bag with you in case your dog is sick en route. These are all essentials. You will know what tit-bit will be most appreciated in the Ring. But do not take squeakers, balls or toys.

Have your entrance tickets ready before you arrive so that you and your dog can pass easily into the Show. It is always sensible to arrive in adequate time so that you can go in quietly and do not have to push and shove as this may easily upset your dog.

It is inadvisable to take a puppy under ten months to an indoor Show during the winter.

A wise exhibitor will take the precaution of having a small spray with a good disinfectant with which to spray his bench before use. Benching firms are supposed to do this, but any extra precaution is worth while. Wipe the flaps of lips with spirit and paint the throat with some throat paint.

You will have left plenty of time for brushing and grooming your dog; when his turn arrives to go into the Ring you will be ready and not in a fluster. In the Ring the Steward will give you your number, which you should put on your coat or in your hat in a position where it can be plainly seen. And if you are showing more than one dog do please see that you have on the correct number for each dog.

The Judge will probably ask all the dogs in the Class to walk round the Ring. Here your previous training should stand you in good stead. Walk your dog quietly round, keeping a fair space between you and the dogs before and behind you. And be sure your dog is on the side nearest to the Judge. Watch the Judge and when he holds up his hand for the dogs to stop, stand at ease.

Each dog will now be examined. Have your data ready— such as the correct age of the dog. When the Judge asks to see your dog's mouth pull up the lips and show the mouth with the teeth shut. Most Judges avoid handling the mouths of dogs in order to avoid, if possible, any carrying of disease.

Your dog will now be asked to move alone across the Ring and here your previous training will prove its value. When the Judge has finished examining your dog take your place amongst those dogs which have also been looked at. Do not get in the way of other dogs showing off their paces. Do not try to jockey other dogs out of the way. Concentrate on showing your own dog to the very best advantage. Do not try to spoil the chances of other dogs. If the Judge is a good one he will know all about your dog and the others too, and an exhibitor trying to push his own forward to the detriment of others does not make himself popular with either Judge or other exhibitors.

If your Poodle has been well trained he will have no eyes for anyone but you, and if he shows well reward him with a tit-bit and words of praise. Whether you win or whether you lose, accept the decision of the Judge. After all, you have elected to show under him. You should be ready to accept his decisions. If you feel you and your dog have not had a fair deal . . . well, you need never show under that particular Judge again.

When the Judge has made his awards do not rush out of the Ring as soon as your card is handed to you. Remain as you have been placed until the Judge tells you to go. He may wish to make some notes on the winning dogs. It is disconcerting to a Judge to find that whilst he is attending to the first and second winners the third and fourth placings have vanished, sometimes without having had their numbers taken.

If you are a loser do not show your feelings. You can always ask the Judge afterwards why he rejected your dog; most Judges are willing to give reasons for their placings. If you just pipped for the Challenge Certificate it is customary to congratulate the owner of the winning dog or bitch in a sportsmanlike, generous way.

If, however, you are fortunate enough to win the Certificate come, at the end of the judging, to the table to receive your card. This also applies to the Reserve Certificate winner. Your aim whilst in the Ring should be to show your dog off to the very best advantage, whilst being fair and courteous to other exhibitors, to help the Judge as much as possible, and to carry out the instructions of the Ring Steward. By such observances you will enjoy showing your Poodle.

Do not pester the Show Secretary for an early removal pass unless you are entitled to one. A Show is open to the public who pay for admission and have a right to see the exhibits, especially the winning ones.

Another important point is: be very careful to guard your dog as much as possible against disease. A big Dog Show is always a risk for a valuable dog as there is always the possibility of infection. Never take your dog to a Show if he is at all off colour. If every exhibitor did this there would be far fewer outbreaks of illness after Shows.

It is quite a wise plan to give your dog a treatment for one week before and after a Show, by the administration internally of a reliable disinfectant. Inoculation is a matter of personal preference; many breeders never exhibit a dog that has not been inoculated. A good veterinary surgeon should be consulted about these matters. And when you get home after the Show, perhaps tired but happy, do not forget your dog.

A final tip: if you have some give him a sip of brandy or whisky. Many an illness has been warded off by this small attention.

The Poodle Council

In 1963 the Poodle Council was set up with the approval of the Kennel Club. At the time of writing (January 1973) all the twelve Poodle Clubs have joined the Council. It is hoped that this will enable them to speak with one voice on matters affecting the breed. It is a consultant body with no executive powers and the Kennel Club has the final word on all matters. Two delegates attend the meetings from each club comprising the Council and these meet twice yearly, alternately in the north and south of England.

The Kennel Club Liaison Council Representative is elected by the Poodle Council, nominations being received from all the Member Clubs. Chairman, Vice Chairman and Secretary are elected on alternate years by the Council. The Council will also maintain the Standard up to date and monitor Judges Lists.

Poodles have become very successful in Obedience Tests and the British Toy Poodle Club has been much to the fore in this matter with great help from Mrs. Nora Andrews. Poodles need special training as they are swift to learn and easily get bored with too much repetition. It is not surprising that Poodles with their wonderful intelligence should shine in the Obedience Ring.

Chapter XVII

CLIPPING STYLES

(For the Novice)

THE clipping of Poodles is usually represented as the 'bug-bear' and difficulty in keeping them. In actual practice this is not the case. The Poodle is the only dog permitted by the Kennel Club to have his coat clipped and fashioned for the Show Ring. The clipping of a Poodle is not a whim or a fashion; he has been clipped for centuries, and the style known today as the Lion-clip, is as old as the dog. There is a famous example of this particular style on a column erected to the Emperor Hadrian in Rome, and we ourselves have a very interesting example in a tapestry in the Victoria and Albert Museum.

Before one can perform the operation of clipping one must be equipped with the right tools. First and foremost are the clippers. If you are fortunate you will have a pair of electric clippers. Most of us, since the war, are not in such a position. We have to depend on the hand variety. There are a number of these on the market in varying sizes. The most suitable for the average dog is the size known as ooo. The oooo size is very useful in the hands of an expert, but in the hands of a novice it is liable to cut too close, and may cause sores and scratching. Next to clippers, you require a pair of hairdressing scissors. It is important to have this particular type because they are constructed to cut with the tips, and it is the tips that are needed to tidy up the odd parts of the tail, quarters and feet after the clippers have done their work.

The next requisite is a steel comb with widely spaced teeth— $\frac{1}{4}$-inch gaps make the ideal size—but one difficult to come by nowadays, because of the steel shortage. It is best to buy the nearest you can to this.

You will require a table about 2 feet 6 inches in height. A folding card-table is very useful, but it must be sufficiently heavily made to be steady when the dog lies upon it. If you have Standard Poodles as well as Miniatures you will require a similar table, but one of much greater width and strength. If you have several dogs and intend to show, it is best to buy one of the many tables on the market specially constructed to take Poodles of both sizes.

Having equipped yourself, the next step is to master the use of the clippers. Novices often say to me that their clippers do not cut. They seem to pinch. This is because they have not mastered the knack. It is important that the blades should be opened and closed completely at each stroke. If you practise this you will find that with a quick, staccato action of the fingers the blades do not

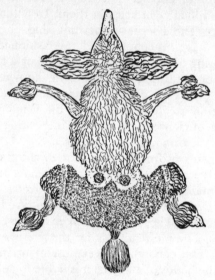

'Clipper's eye' view of the Poodle

close completely at each movement. A very firm, slow movement, opening and closing deliberately, will illustrate my meaning.

Once having acquired the knack, you will have no difficulty. Next, you must be careful not to put any weight upon the clippers as they work, or you will cut too close to the skin and cause great irritation and scratching that may take days, weeks—perhaps months—to heal. You will have accustomed your dog to grooming, from his earliest days, so he will be quite used to lying on his side on the table while you perform his toilet. This is important as you will rely on his steadiness for the success of your clipping.

We will begin with the Lion-clip.

The dog should stand on the table with his back towards you, the light falling over your left shoulder. You begin by lifting one of his back feet. Here I must point out that it is essential that the feet should be absolutely dry before you begin to clip. Do not allow him to run on wet grass or wet ground for some time before you wish to begin, or you will quickly find that your clippers are 'bunged up'. Wet and grit are particularly bad for them.

Now take a foot in your left hand and begin to clip the back of it behind the big pad. Clipping of the hind foot continues for about an inch beyond the toes, up to what is known as the 'waist'

The Lion-clip: 1, English saddle

of the foot. You will see this in the illustration. Having done the back of the foot, gently edge your clippers round the side towards the front. Here you may turn your dog towards you; if you feel he will be more comfortable let him lie on the table. You will then be free to clip in towards the toes without any difficulty. I always find it best to do both the hind feet first. I then clip the tail.

The clipping of the tail depends on the type of tail, its length, and the shortness of the dog's back. Take the tail in your left hand, and about a quarter of the length from the tip of the tail, not of the hair, clip down towards the back *against* the hair, right on to the back. Then do the sides, and as the under-

neath of the tail is particularly sensitive always clip this part *with*
the hair. If you are clipping a puppy for the first time it is advisable
not to use clippers on the tail but to cut gently and closely with
scissors. Many dogs and puppies are particularly sensitive about
their tails and you will find by experience whether or not your
dog is one of these.

If you find that several days pass before he carries his tail
firmly after clipping, then, when you are going to clip for Show,

The Lion-clip: 2, English saddle

be sure to do the tail well in advance of the period he takes to
recover from clipping. Indeed, some dogs are so sensitive that for
the first few times it may be a week or more before they cease
to walk like crabs or to keep wildly dashing about nosing their
posterior. In fact, people who buy a Poodle, and who have never
before owned one, often rush anxiously to the veterinary surgeon,
declaring that there must be something wrong as their pup keeps
sitting down and whimpering. Only experience will show that
there is nothing wrong and that it is the normal reaction of some.
These are the few. Most Poodles take no notice whatever when
their tails are clipped.

Having finished with the tail, you are ready to begin with the

Stifle Band and the Hock Ring. You will see by the illustration that the Stifle Band is about a quarter to half an inch in width. The Hock Ring should be double the width of the Stifle Band. You begin clipping the Hock Ring from the 'heel' of the leg, marked on the illustration. You clip up about one inch, just to where you feel the swell of the muscle begin. This Band must be clipped inside and outside the leg. The same applies to the Stifle. If you run your hand down the edge of the Stifle you will find a flat bone. This is where you put your Band.

For the Stifle Band, before using the clippers comb out the hair on the joint and cut to an even length, roughly half an inch,

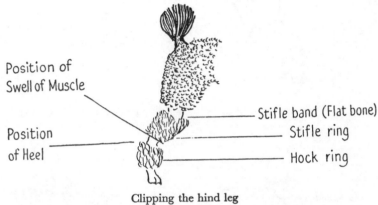

Position of
Swell of Muscle

Position
of Heel

Stifle band (Flat bone)

Stifle ring

Hock ring

Clipping the hind leg

then comb the hair down towards the foot. Take your clippers, place them flat against the leg and gently notch a line from one side of the leg to the other, as shown in the illustration. Having done this, take your clippers and clip up towards the notch. This will be seen very clearly if you have done the job correctly. When you have clipped the Band on the outside of the leg, comb the hair down again towards the foot and cut off in a straight line. Conversely, comb the lower part of the hair up towards the Band and cut that off straight. You will then see that you have a clear, straight line above and below the Band. This, as in the case of the Hock Ring, should be clipped off inside as well as outside the leg. When you have done both hind legs you are in a position to scissor off the hair on the back of the quarters.

While it is quite a simple matter to clip the Band and to cut down the quarters, it is a matter of experience whether or not to

leave the hair long—or short—on the quarters or the back. A
great deal can be done to improve the appearance of the dog by
balancing the hair according to whether he is well muscled-up or

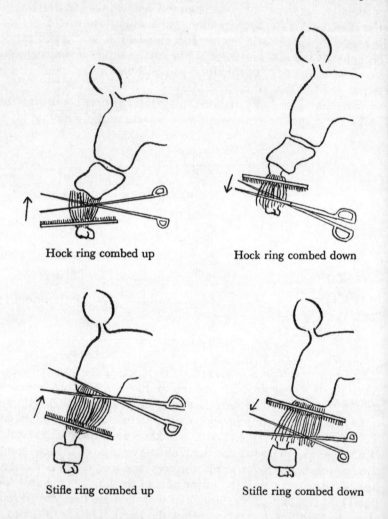

Hock ring combed up   Hock ring combed down

Stifle ring combed up   Stifle ring combed down

fails in this particular respect. Of course such trimming can only
deceive the eye; it can never deceive the knowledgeable fingers of
the expert. But it will greatly add to the appearance of the animal
when it goes round the Ring, and that is half the battle.

What is known as 'good presentation' will always help a dog

who may not be as beautiful as his opponent; because of the stylish manner in which he is presented he may manage to get himself a good place.

Before you scissor off the quarters comb up the hair and see that there are no knots anywhere. If you find knots they must all be teased out or you will never get the correct length, or even cut. To get the Astrakhan effect the ideal length is roughly half an

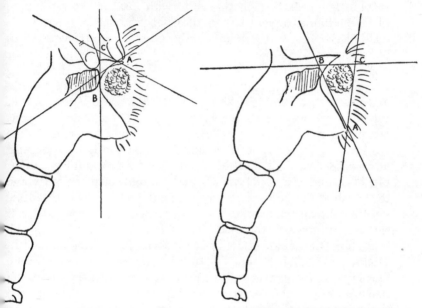

Clipping the saddle: first triangle. Base of triangle = *BC*, point of triangle = *A*

Clipping the saddle: second triangle. Base of triangle = *BC*, point of triangle = *A*

inch all over. Before you begin to cut brush the mane up towards the head and feel with your fingers for the last rib. This is where the mane must end and the Astrakhan begin.

It is always advisable not to cut too closely to begin with. It is as well to leave about half an inch below the last rib and gradually cut off to avoid going above. If you have the mane too far forward you will make your dog appear to be long in back although he may not actually be so.

Having scissored off the quarters, you may decide that you will put what is known as a 'saddle' on the back. This is not necessary, but it has a slimming and pleasing effect. For the very young, and for the small sizes of either variety, it is inadvisable. The young dog, immature and not sufficiently muscled, looks better with his hair plain all over.

The 'saddle' seems to be almost impossible to achieve without practice. Actually, after a few times it is done quite simply. The important thing to remember is that you have to make a triangle with the 'pin bones' as the base. This is shown in the illustration. Having got your dog on the table with his back towards you, place the thumb of your left hand on one pin bone and first finger on the vertebrae at the mane as the point of the triangle. With your comb make a parting in the hair from your thumb to your finger-tip and neatly clip down this with your scissors, so producing a straight line. Do the same between your first and second fingers, and if you then comb the hair on both sides towards the front of the body you will clearly see your triangle. Then again take your comb and from the pin bone on the right make a parting to the rib towards the elbow of the right leg, and gently clip the hair along this. You will then have another triangle with the right pin bone and the vertebrae as the base and from the vertebrae to the rib as the point. There you have the nucleus of the 'saddle' rosette. Clip off the point of the triangle against the rib and comb the hair up towards the back. Then from the vertebrae clip the hair off down the side of the body for about half an inch in width, as shown in the illustration. Clip off the corners until you have the four clipped away. You will then see the circle appear. Comb the hair up towards the centre of the ring and gradually clip off the tiny portions until you have all the triangle bare except for the ring in the middle. Having done one side, match it with the other.

The next step is to do the front legs and the feet. Cut off the hair of the legs from the elbow joint almost to the wrist bone, leaving it about half an inch in length. You will then be able to clip it off quite easily. If you do not do this you may find it difficult to stop your clippers from being 'bunged up' if the hair is knotty or thick with mud or grit.

You will see by the illustration that the front bracelet extends an equal distance above and below the joint. The rest of the hair above the bracelet is clipped to the skin. This is a simple operation, and useful as practice in acquiring the knack of using clippers.

You now come to the clipping of the front feet. Many dogs greatly object to having their front feet clipped. This is probably because they are more sensitive than the hind, being used for digging, etc. I have known some who firmly refused to have the electric clippers anywhere near their front feet although they would tolerate them, even on their faces.

'Clipper's eye' view of the Poodle

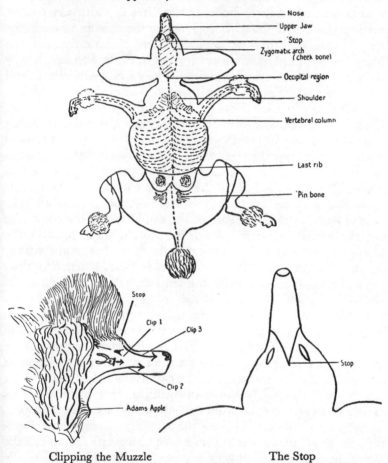

Clipping the Muzzle   The Stop

Take the foot in your left hand and begin clipping the back towards the pastern. You can easily tell when you have clipped far enough up the back of the foot as you will encounter a little bumpy pad. Then clip the front up in a line with the back, clipping carefully in between the toes, back and front of the foot.

In order to get the toes completely clear of all hair it is advisable to take the odd bits between your fingers and pull them up so that the clippers can even them off. You will probably find it just as well to go round the toes, back and front, with your sharp scissors to tidy everything.

One word with regard to the use of scissors. They must always be kept parallel with the body or feet—indeed, with any part of the dog you are clipping. If you incline the scissors towards the body you will find that you are liable to nip the skin and to make 'holes' on the quarters when cutting. This, again, is a knack very easily acquired. All you have to do is to watch your scissors and see that they never point towards the body but remain parallel.

Now that you have done the back, the legs and feet, you are at liberty to attack the face. Strangely enough, you will find that while some dogs will resent you doing their feet they will remain quiescent when you clip their faces. You will see by the illustration that you again employ a triangle when clipping the muzzle and throat. This time the base of the triangle comes from the middle of the ears, and the point is at the Adam's Apple. First of all, take your clippers from the corner of the eyelid to the middle of the ear, clip against the hair towards the muzzle, then clip from the Adam's Apple up towards the end of the lower jaw, and continue clipping like this until the whole area is clear. Then take your clippers and place them with the left side at the front corner of the left eye, and the right corner of the clippers against the stop. Then clip off down and towards the end of the muzzle. Do this on both sides so that you have a triangle from the corners of the eye to the point of the stop. You can increase the appearance of length of muzzle by clipping off the hair towards the stop, as is shown in the illustration. The appearance of a dog with a short fore-face will be greatly improved by adjustment of the length of the division you can make from the bottom of the stop to the top.

When you have completed the technical parts of the Lion-clip you must do what is known as 'squaring-up'. Comb out the tuft of the tail. Hold it in your left hand firmly and cut off all the uneven lengths of hair. Then comb the tuft again in a fan shape and lightly clip all the hair off in a circular direction. If you then comb the hair out to the four points of the compass you will see that it is all level. If it is not, round it off again. Next comb out the Hock Rings, and comb and cut them evenly, beginning at the top and cutting down towards the foot. If you comb out the

hair in an upward direction towards the Stifle Band, and place
your hand round the dog's leg, all hairs not level will extend
beyond your hand and can be cut off. Do this again, combing
down towards the foot, and again place your hand round the
dog's leg and cut off all projecting hairs. The length of the Hock
Rings depends on the size of your dog in either variety. If you
have a small dog of either type you will need to leave the hair of
your Hock Rings shorter than with a larger dog. If your dog has

The Puppy-clip

not a very luxuriant mane, then do not leave him with very
luxuriant Hock Rings or you will draw attention to the lack of
length of hair on his body.

The length of hair on the quarters should be the same as that
on the Stifle Rings. It is very bad for the appearance of your dog
if you leave, as some novices are inclined to do, the hair on the
Stifle Rings longer than that on the body. This gives your dog the
appearance of being bandy-legged and of curving outwards
where he should be straight.

The appearance of the Poodle in the Show Ring should be
that of a very elegant animal, and this appearance can be achieved

L

only if the 'tailoring' is done in as mathematical a manner as possible.

The front bracelets should be combed out and cut in the same way as the Hock Rings. You will probably find it necessary to have your dog clipped by a professional in the first instance; you can then follow out these instructions about three weeks after the clipping, and gradually teach yourself to keep your dog in perfect trim.

The Royal Dutch clip

The only clip other than the Lion-clip allowed in the Show Ring in England, Europe, America and South America for all dogs over twelve months is what is known as the Puppy-clip for those under twelve months. For this clip you require to have only the face, feet and tail clipped, the rest of the hair being untouched.

What is known as the Dutch-clip is very fashionable for Poodles. It certainly gives no idea of the traditional style and in my opinion is far more trouble to deal with in the home than the Lion or the Lamb-clip. The hair on the legs, back and front, is left long. The animal is clipped down from the tail to the neck, and all round the body, part only of the face being clipped, and the feet and tail done in the usual manner.

Again it is a question of clipping to bones, as for the Lion-clip. For the hind legs the pin bones are again the base of a triangle, the hair being clipped down from the pelvic bones over the pin bones, down the front of the thigh bone, and right off all round the body and up to the withers, where the hair is taken down short to the breast bone, leaving a high 'leg-of-mutton' sleeve from the withers over the ribs to the elbow, and then long on the leg to the foot. The hair up the back of the neck, as far as the occipital bone,

The Continental-clip (1)

is cut off. Usually the top-knot is left, but some people like to have what is known as the Dutch Cap—the hair cut off from the top of the ears in a circle in front of the occipital bone and left about half an inch long. The face is clipped from the ear to the middle of the muzzle, the moustache and beard being left on the front of the jaws. The hair on the back and front legs can be left at normal length (about nine inches) or cut down to within an inch or two from the body, as preferred.

It is a curious fact that many people who are anxious not to own a dog that looks as fantastic as a Poodle are quite willing to go out accompanied by these grotesques. But if one does not wish to have a Poodle with the traditional clip it is better to have one cut in the 'Lamb' fashion. This consists in having the hair cut off all over the body to about an inch in length, and having the face, feet and tail clipped in the usual manner. This is a tidy, neat and most fascinating way of keeping a Poodle. Barbering is easy to do oneself, and the coat requires attention only about once a month to keep it the right length. Dogs cut in this fashion are

The Continental-clip (2)
(English style)

particularly useful for towns; with their clipped feet and short coats they do not take up a great deal of wet and mud. They also have the advantage, as do those with the Lion-clip, that, having no hair on their muzzles, they do not smell of milk, bones, meat, etc., as is the case with those who sport the long moustache and beard.

There is a variation of the Lion-clip for the Show Ring that is most becoming to the big Poodle and to his smaller brother when he has big, well-muscled quarters; this is known as the Continental-clip. This clip is absolutely essential for the Show Ring all over Europe. It consists in having every hair clipped from the body, from the last rib down to the stifle. In this country, exhibitors who favour the style usually leave about an inch in radius round the tail. This is very becoming to a short-backed dog. Sometimes a rosette of long hair is left on the body; that is what is known as the English Style Clip.

GROOMING.

You cannot begin grooming a dog too young. From about eight weeks old a puppy should be groomed every day.

For the young animal you require a soft bristle brush and a fine wire comb. The type of comb with a handle and close teeth is useful for keeping down livestock in the young puppy.

The correct manner of grooming a Poodle is to lay him on his side on a table. It is important that the table should not move at all or the dog will become nervous. Lay your Poodle on the table with his legs towards you. Brush the hair from the lower part of the body away from you, then brush it down again towards the table.

When brushing and combing your dog the brush or comb should always be used down *towards* the body. If you brush the hair and give a flick of the wrist at each stroke you will quickly break hairs off. The hair must always be brushed and combed down on to the body. By this I do not mean that you should put weight on the brush. You must use the brush lightly and gently. Always have in mind a plan to keep a definite 'squaring' of the hair. Part each section, brush it carefully from the base of the body to the elbow. It is difficult to acquire the art of grooming correctly. It may take several months. When you are confronted with a dog with a very big coat, and a very dense one, you will have all your work cut out not to lose your place each time you mark out another section.

Having groomed one side of the body from the lower part to the pin bone, take the hind leg and deal with that in the same manner, making a particular point of combing round the tail and again round the elbow and the armpits.

The directions about combing round the tail concern puppies in full coat intended for the Ring and not yet cut down, when the hair is inclined to knot and mat here and is easily overlooked. The same is true of the elbow and the armpit. Before turning the dog over and grooming the other side, be careful to deal with the chest and the hair round the throat. This area knots and mats very easily; if neglected for more than a few days mats may be made that cannot be dealt with other than by cutting out, and thus ruining the dog's appearance for some months.

It must always be borne in mind that it takes nine to twelve months to grow a full-length coat; if for any reason you are compelled to cut out lumps you will not be able to put your dog in the Ring for a long time. If you do not comb right down to the roots every time you groom your dog you will find, after a week or two, that the lower part of the hair, close to the body, has become felty and cannot be combed.

Some novice exhibitors are foolish enough to let this happen—to brush out the top only, so that at first sight their dog appears to have a dense coat. It must be remembered that points are given for coat, and as soon as a Judge feels mats in a coat he will make that dog lose marks against another exhibit whose coat is satisfactorily groomed and presented. Therefore take as your watchword in grooming: "Down to the roots every time!"

Having completed one side of the body, treat the other side identically. When the mane has been carefully groomed, stand the dog up and brush the hair gently and strongly towards the head. Next comb out the ears, paying particular attention to the feathering.

With Poodles, as with all long-eared dogs, it is necessary to keep the ears clean after feeding, or to provide bowls into which their ears cannot dip. Some dogs, if their ears are not washed after meals, are in the habit of chewing off the feathers; one can find with dismay that a dog with great length of ear feathering has suddenly had two or three inches removed in this manner. The hair on the ears takes the longest time to grow, and if for any reason it has to be cut off near the leather you will be forced to keep your dog out of the Ring for twelve months.

An important point, though one it may seem unnecessary to mention, is the fact that when combing and brushing one must always have one's eye on the skin in order to detect any livestock that may be there. Nothing is more detrimental to the dog's coat than fleas or lice. It is amazing how much coat a dog can get out by half an hour's good scratching. When teaching kennel maids to groom I have nearly always found that they fail to keep their eyes on the coat all the time. It is very boring and very tiring to have the eye directed on to the body for an hour or more at a time, but it is most essential.

One more hint on the grooming of puppies : begin by grooming the puppy on your knee but, from the outset, do not allow him to play with the brush or comb while you are using them. As soon as possible lay him on the table and he will very quickly get used to this and will enjoy it ; he will probably go to sleep.

Chapter XVIII

POODLES IN THE SEVENTIES

by Shirley Walne

Standards

IN STANDARDS, as nature no doubt intended, many changes have taken place in the seventies; affixes as well as dogs have changed hands. Vulcan Champagne is now in the capable hands of Miss Ann Coppage, having been transferred from me. Vulcan Champagnes are still to be seen in the show ring and continue to be bred with the Vulcan Champagne tradition.

It is nice to think that Leighbridge, so well known and belonging to Mrs. Skeaping, is being carried on by Mrs. Sanders who was Mrs. Skeaping's partner during the latter years of her life. It was Champion Leighbridge Catmint, among many others in the seventies, who kept Leighbridge to the fore by winning the Reserve Best in the Utility Group in 1978 at Cruft's.

Mrs. Ashwell's Torpaz Poodles have been producing many winners; so have Mrs. Beswick's Balnobles and Mr. and Mrs. Nathan's Supernovas. Another well to the fore is Mrs. Cleaver with her Groomars; also Mr. John Cottrell's Warwells, and Mrs. Flatt with her Tragapanz. Mrs. and Miss Gibbs' Montravia Poodles can be seen in all three sizes, so too can Mrs. and Miss Sillito with Malibu as their affix. The Vicmars of Mrs. Marshall have made themselves felt. Miss Barbara Peake continues with her Chestalls, well known in the earlier days. Beguinette, belonging to Mrs. Iggulden, must be mentioned; Mrs. Kellard's Alpendens, who has a soft spot for Apricots; Mrs. Streatfield with her Leanders, although not a big breeder of Poodles, imported Champion Acadia Detonator of Leander and Champion Acadia Stagedoor Johnny from America to give the British stock an out cross.

One must also remember Mrs. Holbourn's Shanpave—she is a breeder who concentrates on Apricots. So too does Mrs. Coxall, another who has all three sizes in Apricots, as well as Blacks. Messrs. Stone and Thompson's Vanitonia affix has been very noticeable in the seventies, another kennel with all three sizes.

Vistella, Miss Hincks' affix, is a small but select kennel of Standard Poodles since the fifties, interested mostly in Blacks; and Mrs. Geeson, a recent but successful breeder, has her Janavons. Another is Mrs. Timpson with her Kelrarmos; her Champion Kelrarmo Lily the Pink probably being one of her best. One of the proudest of our Standard Poodle breeders must surely be Mr. D. Thomas who bred Champion Roushka's Pacific, so ably handled by his partner with this dog: Roger Bayliss, who not only piloted him to a Champion but to the record holder of thirty-one Challenge Certificates for the breed, beating Mrs. Price Jones' Champion Frenches Rockavon who had previously held the record. The Frenches' Poodles, so well known for their Standards, now concentrate on the little ones only.

MINIATURES

Changes have taken place in Miniatures too—and one has the pleasure of seeing some truly beautifully presented dogs. Names connected previously with Miniatures are now to be found within the Toy Poodle world. One can still see the well known Montfleuri affix, piloted now by Mrs. Howard Price. In Silvers and Blues the Walditch Miniatures, owned by Mrs. Gundry, have kept their name in the front line. Mrs. Laughlin's Junius affix can be seen mostly with Blacks; at one time Mrs. Laughlin had a number of Mrs. Monro's Firebrave breeding. Well known, among others, one must mention Mrs. Howarth's Idadoun affix and Miss K. Rees' Conersks, and Mrs. Rose with her Miradel, one of the few white breeders who has made up Champions in that colour.

One of the newer breeders in Miniatures, Mrs. Porter, had the thrill of winning the Utility Group at Crufts, 1979, with her Champion Jolanta By Jove. To win any Group, which Poodles frequently manage to achieve, does great things but to win a Group at Crufts is an added thrill.

TOYS

Now to the *Toys*: how they have improved! Gone are the apple-headed Toys one used to see with their round pop eyes, and on the whole they are as a breed a joy to look at—which says much for their dedicated breeders. From the start Sudbrook, the affix of Mrs. Cox, has concentrated on Whites and has been among the winners during the seventies; also in Whites are the Panavons, belonging to Miss Pantlin. Mrs. Barratt with her

Great Westwoods, in all colours although in fewer numbers, towards the end of the seventies has made a name to be remembered in Champion Benidorm Daisy's Image of Great Westwood, bred by Mrs. Austin but campaigned in the Great Westwood colours. I must also mention Mrs. Conn's Montmartres and the Wemroses of Miss Machon, another one of the first breeders of Toys. Mr. Butcher and his Tuttlebees could be seen in all three sizes of Poodles. With Merrymorns Mrs. Ellis has recently concentrated on Apricots, a difficult colour whichever size one has. In Silvers Mr. D. Wickens has his Silcresta Toys; he is another who has been in Toys for some time. Mr. and Mrs. Gregory, with the Snowstars, and Miss Dunn, with Valetta, are often seen in the winners' enclosure. Mrs. Francks, with her Stonesby, usually concentrates on Blacks.

It is nice to see the Drumaids, so well known in Mrs. Ringroses' days, now being taken into the ring by her daughter, Miss P. Ringrose.

The registration figures have declined in Toys in the seventies, but when I say that there were almost eighty exhibitors who showed at Crufts in 1979 (and no doubt quite a few more who had qualified but who, for one reason or another, were not able to be there) one can still see that Toy Poodles have many dedicated breeders, with a number who are still well up in the charts.

As I have already indicated, I could not possibly include all the breeders' affixes, but one has only to look at the lists of Champions in the first three appendices to see the top-bred Poodles of all three sizes to know that there were many good dogs in the seventies and Poodles will, I am sure, continue in the same vein in the eighties.

ADDENDUM

In 1978 the Kennel Club amended the regulation regarding the registration of Miniature and Toy Poodles. As from 1 January, 1979 the Toy Poodle can only be registered as a Toy Poodle if both parents are Toy Poodles, the progeny of which will be placed in the register of the breed of the parents. Should the Toy Poodle grow oversize, that is to say, over 11 inches, then he/she may be re-registered as a Miniature. This also applies to the Miniature Poodle who may be re-registered as a Toy Poodle should he/she not grow to within the limits set out for the Miniature, that is 11 inches to 15 inches at the shoulder.

At one time it was a disqualification should either a Miniature or Toy Poodle be found to measure oversize in the show ring, but this has now been amended so that it is a fault and not a disqualification.

Previously the standard said Show Judges had been able to please themselves as to whether they would measure exhibits before making their final placings. Henceforward the Kennel Club decreed that Show Secretaries would in future have to provide a measure for each size and Judges were instructed to measure the dogs selected as winners before making their final placings. If a Judge did not wish to measure personally he could depute the steward to do this for him.

Miniature Poodle height *should* be under 15 inches at the shoulder.

Toy Poodle height *should* be under 11 inches at the shoulder.

S.W.

APPENDIX A

STANDARD CHAMPIONS, 1966 to 1978

(From 1975 I have included the champions' sex (*D* or *B*), colour and date of birth—S.W.)

Sire	Dam

Bibelot's Tall Dark and Handsome
Owned by Mrs. S. R. Fraser
Bred by Mrs. S. R. Fraser

Can. Ch. Wycliffe Virgil   Can. and OSA Ch. Lady
     Joan of Lowmont

Chestall Moonrocker
Owned by Miss B. Peake
Bred by Miss B. Peake

Ch. Frenches Rockhaven   Chestall Susannah

Frenches Eynsham Master Gunner
Owned by Mrs. R. E. Price-Jones
Bred by Mrs. P. Nightingale

Ch. Frenches Rockavon   Hellfire Witch

Beguinette Vulcan Champagne Silk
Owned by Mrs. M. R. Iggulden
Bred by Mrs. M. R. Iggulden

Vulcan Champagne Admirer   Ch. Vulcan Champagne
     Dimity

Leighbridge May Sunbeam
Owned by Mrs. M. Skeaping
Bred by Mrs. M. Skeaping

Ch. Leighbridge Mystic Star   Ch. Leighbridge Partita

U.S. Ch. *Martindell Alekai Kalania*
Owned by Miss Katania H. Martin
Bred by Alekai Kennels (U.S.A.)

U.S. Ch. Alekai Kila   Can. Ch. Tambarine
     La Fontaine

	Sire	Dam
Parkhouse Playhouse Christmas Carol Owned by Mrs. B. Hiddlestone Bred by Mr. & Mrs. S. W. Jobson	Valeroyal Tarquin	Ch. Nunsoe Black Mantilla
Vulcan Champagne Misbehave Owned by Miss V. S. Hincks Bred by Miss S. Walne	Ch. Vulcan Champagne Taffy	Vulcan Champagne Rosetta
Jonbir Courteous of Olingborne Owned by Miss J. Johnson Bred by Mrs. O. Bailey	Ch. Frenches Rockavon	Ch. Annabell of Olingborne
Vulcan Pacemaker He's a Tramp Owned by Miss S. Walne and Miss A. Coppage Bred by Mrs. H. Mitchell	Ch. Bibelots Tall Dark and Handsome	Vulcan Champagne Rosabel
Vicmars Follow That Owned by Mrs. P. Ashwell Bred by Mrs. V. Marshall	Ch. Bibelots Tall Dark and Handsome	Pethmelys Bracken Brown
Vulcan Psyche of Gayshaws Owned by Miss S. Walne and Miss A. Coppage Bred by Mrs. V. Inglis	Ch. Vulcan Champagne Taffy	Aphrodite of Gayshaws
Alpenden Golden Sand Owned by Mrs. V. Kellard Bred by Mrs. V. Kellard	Ch. Vulcan Golden Light	Ch. Alpenden Owstonferry Golden Oriel

173

	Sire	Dam
Bibelots Polar de la Fontaine of Springett Owned by Miss M. Willis and Mrs. Fraser Bred by Mrs. Ellis and Mrs. Corbin	Ch. Can. Ch. Loyal Pledge de la Fontaine	Zouki de la Fontaine
Josato Evorglens Star and Garter Owned by Mrs. J. McDermott Bred by Miss D. Snelgrove	Ch. Bibelots Tall Dark and Handsome	Ch. Evorglens Bonnie of Olingborne
Springett Darken Democrat Owned by Miss M. M. Willis Bred by Miss M. Willis	Am. and Can. Ch. Wycliffe Kenneth	Bibelots Magnificent Maxine
Frenches Saraven Owned by Mrs. R. Price Jones Bred by Mrs. S. Marshall Foster	Ch. Frenches Rockavon	Ch. Tullerone Sarita of Monclova
Bibelots Rich and Rare Owned by Mrs. S. Fraser and Mr. B. Pritchard Bred by Miss Radley Fraser	Am. and Can. Ch. Black Rogue of Belle Glen	Can. Ch. Bibelots in Style of Hi-Crown
Tryphaena Tramella Owned by Mrs. P. Harrington-Gill Bred by Mrs. P. Harrington-Gill	Pethmelys Flambeau	Ch. Tryphaena Humewood La Tricoteuse
Beechover Brilliance Owned by Miss R. Gregory Bred by Miss R. Gregory	Burntoak Vulcan Champagne Bacchus Boy	Beechover Frolic

	Sire	Dam
Sylphic Fiddler Owned by Mr. R. Dicker Bred by Mrs. and Miss Lowdell	Sylphic Welcome	Sylphic Vulcan Champagne Flautist
Beguinette Moonstone Owned by Mrs. M. R. Iggulden Bred by Mrs. M. R. Iggulden	Ch. Leighbridge Mystic Star	Ch. Beguinette Vulcan Champagne Silk
Springett Darken Endearing of Montravia Owned by Miss Walne and Miss Coppage Bred by Miss Willis	Am. and Can. Ch. Wycliffe Kenneth	Am. and Can. Ch. Bibelots Magnificent Maxine
Gosmore High & Mighty Owned by Mrs. Dallison and Miss D. Lloyd Bred by Mrs. P. Ashwell	Pacemaker Snowmaker	Janty of Topaz
Vicmars Balnoble Royale Owned by Mrs. V. Marshall Bred by Mrs. A. Beswick	Springett Darken Democrat	Vicmars Legacy of a Legend
Vulcan Champagne Goldsmith Owned by Miss S. E. Walne and Miss A. E. Coppage Bred by Miss S. E. Walne and Miss A. E. Coppage	Ch. Golden Light	Vulcan Merry Sonatina
Vulcan Champagne He's a Hobo Owned by Misses S. E. Walne and A. C. Coppage Bred by Misses S. E. Walne and A. C. Coppage	Ch. Vulcan Pacemaker He's a Tramp	Ch. Vulcan Pysche of Gayshaws

	Sire	Dam
Greeksmith Aphrodite Owned by Mrs. N. Creed Bred by Mrs. D. Taylor	Ch. Playhouse the Undertaker	Greeksmith Melpomene
Greeksmith Playhouse Dear Miss Brown Owned by Mrs. Julia Taylor Bred by Mrs. J. Jobson	Ch. Frenches Rockaven	Ch. Nunsoe Black Mantilla
Josato Vicmars Top That Owned by Mrs. J. McDermott Bred by Mrs. V. Marshall	Ch. Josato Everglens Star and Garter	Pethmelys Bracken Brown
Pacemaker Snowflake Owned by Mrs. P. Ashwell Bred by Mrs. P. Ashwell	Ch. Bibelot's Polar de la Fontaine of Springett	Pacemaker Glyndale Maid o' the Lochs
Knotrom's Desdemona Owned by Mrs. O. Morton and Mrs. M. V. Ackers Bred by Miss M. P. Cox	Ch. Springett Darken Democrat	Vicmars Falling Leaves
Josato Georgie Best Owned by Miss Macdermott Bred by Miss R. Chapman	Ch. Josato Everglen Star and Garter	Chandford Robena
Man about Town of Topaz Owned by Mrs. P. Ashwell Bred by Mrs. P. Ashwell	Ch. Springett Darken Democrat	Ch. Vicmars Follow That

Name	Sire	Dam
Vicmars Topscore of Topaz Owned by Mrs. P. Ashwell Bred by Mrs. V. Marshall	Ch. Josato Everglen Star and Garter	Pethmelys Bracken Brown
Vicmars Bon Ami Owned by Mesdames R. Stone and V. Marshall Bred by Mrs. V. Marshall	Ch. Vicmars Balnoble Royale	Vicmars Estralita Royale
Vulcan Bedecked in White Owned by Misses Walne and Coppage Bred by Misses Walne and Coppage	Ch. Vulcan Goldsmith	Vulcan All in White
Topflite of Topaz Owned by Mrs. P. Ashwell Bred by Mrs. P. Ashwell	Pacemaker Black and Gold	Ch. Vicmars Topscore of Topaz
Beguinette Blue Balthazar Owned by Mrs. Iggulden Bred by Mrs. Iggulden	Ch. Vicmais Balnoble Royal	Beguinette Vixen
Abendan Captain Cuttle Owned by Mrs. B. Sillitoe Bred by Mrs. Bowden	Ch. Vicmais Balnoble Royal	Dawn of Olingbourne
Acadia Detonator of Leander Owned by Mrs. Streatfield Bred by Mrs. J. Tongue	Ch. Hans Bran Executive of Acadia	Acadia Priscilla
Murtravia Dark and Dreamy Owned by Mrs. P. Gibbs Bred by Miss S. Walne & Miss A Coppage	Ch. Vulcan Pacemaker He's a Tramp	Ch. Springett Dark 'n' endearing of Montravia

	Sire	Dam
Peramount Ebony Star Owned by Miss Langley Bred by Miss Langley	Ch. Springett Darken Democrat	Parkro Princess Caroline
Vulcan Crystal Clear Owned by Mrs. Cleaver Bred by Miss S. Walne and Miss A. Coppage	Ch. Vulcan Champagne Goldsmith	Vulcan Beguinette Crystal
Tragapanze By Chance Eroica Owned by Mrs. Flatt Bred by Messrs. Chandler and Mills	Ch. Sylphic Fiddler	Swiss Royal Big Deal by Chance
Vicmain The Ringmaster Owned by Mrs. V. Marshall Bred by Mrs. V. Marshall	Ch. Vicmain Balnoble Royale	Vicmain Estralita Royale
Parkro Cordroyal of Supernova Owned by Mrs Nathan Bred by Mrs. Hiddlestone	Ch. Jonbir Covidens of Orlingbourne	Ch. Parkro Playhouse Christmas Carol
Malibre Beachboy of Sracell Owned by Mrs. Ashwide Bred by Mrs. Sillitoe	Sarcell Pacemaker Romulus	Malibre Balnoble Grandpa's Legacy
Vulcan April Fancy Owned by Miss Coppage Bred by Miss S. Walne and Miss A. Coppage	Int. Ch. Vulcan Champagne Goldsmith	Vulcan Champagne April Love
Vulcan Champagne Setanta Owned by Mr. and Mrs. Gillies Bred by Miss S. Walne and Miss A. Coppage	Ch. Vicmain Balnoble Royale	Dunollie Fionna of Vulcan

Torpaz Eskimo Nell
Owned by Mrs. P. Ashwell
Bred by Mrs. P. Ashwell

Prioryparks Atlantic Surf

Ch. Pacemaker Snowflake

Josato Pink Gin of Kelramo
Owned by Mrs. Timson
Bred by Mrs. McDermott

Ch. Josato Georgie Best

Josato Cassandra

Vicmain Royale Havoc
Owned by Mrs. Fry
Bred by Mrs. Marshall

Ch. Vicman Balnoble Royale

Vicmain Estralita Royale

Springett Cambrai's Camille
Owned by Miss Coppage
Bred by Miss Willis

Ch. Bibelot Polar de la Fontaine
of Springett

Springett Park Quite the
Lady of Bibelot

1975

*Camelotian Lancelot of Supernova (D. Black.
Born 17.4.72)*
Owned by Mr. and Mrs. K. Nathan
Bred by Mrs. N. Creed

Ch. Parkro Court Royal of
Supernova

Ch. Greekmyth Aphrodite

*Am. Ch. Montravia Acadia Nevermore Neville
(D. Black. Born 10.7.66)*
Owned by Mrs. P. Gibbs
Bred by Mrs. J. Tongue

Am. Ch. Acadia Jubilee

Am. Ch. Bel Tor Caramel
Souffle

	Sire	Dam
Beguinette Bar Sinister of Syba (D. White. Born 31.8.72) Owned by Mrs. W. Hammel Bred by Mrs. M. Iggulden	Ch. Beguinette Blue Balthazar	Beguinette Sylphic London Pride
Am. Ch. Jaylee Banacek (D. Black. Born 4.9.72) Owned by Dr. and Mrs. Dazzio and Miss M. Willis Bred by Dr. and Mrs. Dazzio	Am. Ch. Wycliffe Hadrian	Molly Brown's Creme de Cacao
Vicmars Royale Opponent of Coelegant (B. Black. Born 1.10.72) Owned by Mrs. Falconer-Attlee Bred by Mr. and Mrs. Marshall	Ch. Vicmars Balnoble Royale	Vicmars Estralita Royale
Torpaz Shady Lady (B. Black. Born 10.9.72) Owned by Mrs. P. Ashwell Bred by Mrs. P. Ashwell	Ch. Man About Town of Torpaz	Ch. Vicmars Top Score of Torpaz
Captains Lady from Malibu (B. Black. Born 11.1.74) Owned by Mrs. and Miss Sillito Bred by Mrs. M. Cleaver	Ch. Abendow Captain Cuttle	Vulcan Wicked Lady

1976

	Sire	Dam
Tiopepi Baymer Golden Sunrise (D. Apricot. Born 11.8.70) Owned by Mrs. C. Coxall Bred by Miss M. Bayliss	Ch. Alpenden Golden Sand	Baymer Maidec Sun Goddess

	Sire	Dam
Roushka's Pacific (D. Black. Born 3.7.74) Owned by Messrs. R. Bayliss and D. Thomas Bred by Mr. D. Thomas	Ch. Malibu Beach Boy of Sarcell	Vicmars Look At Me Desilva
Acadia Stagedoor Johnny of Leander (D. White. Born 16.12.74) Owned by Mesdames W. Streatfield and J. Sering Bred by Mrs. J. Tongue	Am. Ch. Acadia Commander Performance	Am. Ch. Eaton Baladier
Balnoble Paly It Again Sam (D. Black. Born 12.10.73) Owned by Mrs. A. Beswick Bred by Mrs. A. Beswick	Ch. Vicmars Balnoble Royale	Bibelots Dreams Come True
Janavons Daughter of Blest (B. White. Born 27.4.73) Owned by Mrs. E. Geeson Bred by Mrs. E. Geeson	Ch. Beguinette Blue Balthazar	Janavons Vulcan Heaven Blest
Vicmars Royale Debutante (B. Black. Born 26.10.74) Owned by Mr. J. Marshall Bred by Mrs. V. Marshall	Ch. Vicmars Balnoble Royale	Vicmars Esralita Royale
Kelramo Lily The Pink (B. Black. Born 30.12.74) Owned by Mrs. A. Timson Bred by Mrs. A. Timson	Ch. Man About Town of Torpaz	Ch. Josato Pink Gin of Kelrarmo

	Sire	Dam
1977		
Josato Capability Brown of Tragapanz (D. Brown. Born 3.12.72) Owned by Mrs. C. Flatt Bred by Mrs. J. McDermott	Call Me After Dark of Springett	Ch. Josato Vicmars Top That
Lentella Son of a Gun (D. Black. Born 23.8.74) Owned by Messrs. P. Parkinson and Cox Bred by Messrs P. Parkinson and Cox	Ch. Acadia Detonator of Leander	Davlen Chemin der Mer
Leighbridge Catmint (D. Black. Born 1.12.72) Owned by Mrs. N. Sanders Bred by Mrs. N. Sanders	Eng. and Ir. Ch. Vulcan He's a Hobo	Leighbridge Saucy Puss
Vanitonia Prunella Prune (B. Black. Born 25.2.75) Owned by Messrs. R. Stone and G. Thompson Bred by Messrs. R. Stone and G. Thompson	Ch. Leighbridge Catmint	Vanitonia Victoria Plum
Larling Champers Galore (B. White. Born 31.5.73) Owned by Mrs. E. Gillam Bred by Mrs. E. Gillam	Ch. Josato Georgie Best	Beguinette Nadia
1978		
Kimanjoes Mr. Whippy (D. White Born 9.11.74) Owned by Mrs. J. Arthurton Bred by Mrs. J. Arthurton	Lanhill Laertes	Maggie May of Kimanjoes

	Sire	Dam
Lentella Stagestruck of Glyndale (D. White. Born 10.11.76) Owned by Messrs. Parkinson & Cox and Mrs. D. Poole Bred by Messrs. Parkinson & Cox	Ch. Acadia Stagedoor Johnny of Leander	Lentella Annie Get Your Gun
Torpaz Gambit (D. Black. Born 17.8.76) Owned by Mrs. P. Ashwell Bred by Mrs. P. Ashwell	Torpaz Shaft	Torpaz Jezabel
Midshipman at Kertellas Supernova (D. Black. Born 22.8.76) Owned by Mr. and Mrs. K. Nathan Bred by Mrs. P. Ashwell	Ch. Roushas Pacific	Torpaz Outrageous Annie
Warwells Song of Sweden (B. Black. Born 20.9.74) Owned by Mr. J. Coottrell Bred by Mr. J. Cottrell	Ch. Abendow Captain Cuttle	Malibu Song of Norway
Groomar Sea Breeze (B. Black. Born 26.3.75) Owned by Mrs. M. Cleaver Bred by Mrs. M. Cleaver	Ch. Abendow Captain Cuttle	Vulcan Wicked Lady
Vicmars in Demand (B. Black. Born 12.6.75) Owned by Mrs. I. Pine Bred by Mrs. V. Marshall	Ch. Vicmars Balnoble Royale	Vicmars Estralita Royale

	Sire	Dam
Vicmars Royale Garter (B. Black. Born 11.4.76) Owned by Mr. and Mrs. J. Hutton Bred by Mrs. V. Marshall	Ch. Vicmars Blanoble Royale	Mearnskirk As You Like It
Balnoble Golly Miss Molly (B. Black. *Born 1.11.75)* Owned by Mrs. A. Beswick Bred by Mrs. A. Beswick and Miss Shannon	Ch. Balnoble Play It Again Sam	Balnoble Misty Miss Christy
Martindell Carolina (B. White. Born 24.4.76) Owned by Miss H. Martin Bred by Miss H. Martin	Ch. Acadia Stagedoor Johnny of Leander	Martindell Maria

MINIATURE CHAMPIONS, 1966 to 1978

(From 1975 I have included the champions' sex (*D* or *B*), colour and date of birth—S.W.)

Beritas Bellissima
Owned by Mr. & Mrs. K. Bullock
Bred by Mrs. R. Gee
    Beritas Textet Tycoon   Blackwood Rose of Eldonwood

Beritas Bo'sun
Owned by Mrs. R. Gee
Bred by Mrs. R. Gee
    Ch. Montmartre Marco Polo   Ch. Beritas Holly of Eldonwood

Bidabo Bath Bun
Owned by Mr. & Mrs. A. L. Watson
Bred by Mr. & Mrs. A. L. Watson
    Ch. Bidabo Lemon Pip   Ch. Bidabo Burnt Almond

Bidabo Lemon Peel
Owned by Mr. & Mrs. A. L. Watson
Bred by Mr. & Mrs. A. L. Watson
    Ch. Bidabo Bath Bun   Ch. Bidabo Bitter Lemon

Black Magic of Idadoun
Owned by Mrs. M. Howarth
Bred by Mrs. M. Howarth
    Rum Punch of Idadoun   Toots of Idadoun

Black Shadow of Idadoun
Owned by Mrs. M. Howarth
Bred by Mrs. M. Howarth
    Ch. Bidabo Bath Bun   Toots of Idadoun

Darrendell Don Orlando
Owned by Mrs. M. Taylor
Bred by Mrs. M. Taylor
    Ch. Tranchant Montmartre Best Man   Beritas Bernadette

	Sire	Dam
Frenrise Prince Zaroe of Risette Owned by Mrs. D. E. Williamson Bred by Miss B. Williamson	Ch. Montmartie Marco Polo	Frenrise Princess Fazala of Chelmont
Frenrise Princess Dalzselle Owned by Miss B. Williamson Bred by Miss B. Williamson	Ch. Montmartre Marco Polo	Frenrise Princess Fazala of Chelmont
Helmsview Groomsman Owned by Mrs. M. Clarke & P. Howard Price Bred by Mrs. M. Clarke & P. Howard Price	Ch. Tranchant Montmartre Best Man	Helmsview Muffin of Montfleuri
Kewbar Sweet Talk Owned by Mrs. B. R. Kuhler Bred by Mrs. C. Rayner	Betsans Rocket	The Queen of Cralpath
Meliora Kimona of Iniskhelltr Owned by Miss B. Ward Bred by Mrs. Edge	Ch. Montmartre Marco Polo	Fiona of Iniskhelltr
Montfleuri Ursula of Burdiesel Owned by Mr. & Mrs. P. Howard Price Bred by Miss Sendall	Bearskin of Montfleuri	Tiderace Daphne of Montfleuri
Montmartre Beritas Belle of the Ball Owned by Mrs. E. Conn Bred by Mrs. R. Gee	Ch. Montmartre Bartat By Jingo	Ch. Beritas Holly of Eldonwood
Montmartre Michel-Andre Owned by Mrs. E. Conn Bred by Mrs. E. Conn	Ch. Montmartre Bartat By Jingo	Montmartre Maryce

	Sire	Dam
Patrick Casey of Montfleuri Owned by Mr. & Mrs. P. Howard Price Bred by Mr. & Mrs. P. Howard Price	Tricorne of Montfleuri	Ch. Rioletta of Montfleuri
Perrark Beritas Brigand Owned by Mrs. P. E. Hubbard Bred by R. Gee	Ch. Beritas Bonaparte	Beritas Broadway Star
Piccoli Peacock's Pride Owned by Mrs. M. Worth Bred S. Wootton	Piccoli Beau Brummel	Piccoli Donalyn Dorinda
Risette Frenrise Caramella Owned by Miss J. Williamson Bred by Mrs. D. E. Williamson	Ch. Montmartre Marco Polo	Frenrise Princess Fazala of Chelmont
Risette Princess Felicia Owned by Miss S. J. Williamson Bred by Mrs. D. E. Williamson	Ch. Montmartre Marco Polo	Frenrise Princess Fazala of Chelmont
Sherion Showgirl of Longnor Owned by Mrs. S. M. Wootton Bred by Mrs. E. Worrall	Ch. Beritas Bonaparte	Ch. Philippa of Longnor
Silverstorm Black Beppo Owned by Mrs. M. C. Curtis Bred by Mrs. M. C. Curtis	Si'Bon Skylark	Silverstorm Black Bridget
Showboy of Longnor Owned by Mrs. E. Worrall Bred by Mrs. E. Worrall	Ch. Beritas Bonaparte	Ch. Philippa of Longnor

	Sire	Dam
Springett Fine Fashion Owned by Miss M. Willis Bred by the Misses Mycock	Ch. Springett Rupert of Montfleuri	Jantar Black Bettina
Tophill Marco of Peroma Owned by Mrs. B. Strawson Bred by Mrs. P. Perez	Ch. Tophill Orsino	Montravia Marquita of Peroma
Wyburn Sea Shell Owned by Mr. C. Walley Bred by Mr C. Walley	Ch. Beritas Bonaparte	Myrtlebury Jantzen
Darrendel Don Orlando Owned by Mrs. M. Taylor Bred by Mrs. M. Taylor	Ch. Tranchant Montmartre Best Man	Beritas Bernadette
Fury of Montifleuri Owned by Mr. and Mrs. P. Howard Price Bred by Mr. and Mrs. P. Howard Price and Mrs. A. Dowding	Ch. Patrick Casey of Montfleuri	Vilmarie Beautiful Dreamer of Montfleuri
Nairda Elegance Owned by Mrs. P. Harwood Bred by Mrs. P. Harwood	Montravia Sorrento	Nairda Brown Beauty
Perarrk Beritas Brigand Owned by Mrs. P. E. Hubbard Bred by Mrs. R. Gee	Ch. Beritas Bonaparte	Beritas Broadway Star

	Sire	*Dam*
Playboy of Longnor Owned by Mrs. E. F. Worrall Bred by Mrs. E. F. Worrall	Ch. Show Boy of Longnor	Ch. Susan of Longnor
Tarka of Montfleuri Owned by Mr. and Mrs. P. Howard Price Bred by Mr. and Mrs. P. Howard Price	Ch. Patrick Casey of Montfleuri	Ch. Montfleuri Sarah of Longnor
Tophill Tobacco Owned by Mrs. B. Strawson Bred by Mrs. B. Strawson	Ch. Tophill Orsino	Tophill Jenny Wren
Tophill White Lord of Montfleuri Owned by Mr. and Mrs. P. Howard Price Bred by Mrs. B. Strawson	Tophill Shadow	Idajacks Silver Seal
Beritas Bellissima Owned by Mrs. O. Bullock Bred by Mrs. R. Gee	Beritas Texet Tycoon	Black Rose of Eldonwood
Bidabo Lilywhite Owned by Mr. and Mrs. A. L. Watson Bred by Mr. and Mrs. A. L. Watson	Ch. Piccoli Peacock's Pride	Bidabo Frenches Musical Girl
Kewbar Sweet Talk Owned by Mrs. B. R. Kuhler Bred by Mrs. C. Rayner	Betstans Rocket	Tar Queen of Cralpath
Lochranza Desdemona Owned by Misses Macmillan and Coull Bred by Misses Macmillan and Coull	Lochranza Piero	Lochranza Ramona

	Sire	Dam
Lucy Doone of Montfleuri Owned by Mr. and Mrs. P. Howard Price Bred by Mr. and Mrs. P. Howard Price	Tomboy of Burdiesel	Ch. Lorna Doone of Montfleuri
Montmartre Beritas Nadine Owned by Mrs. E. Conn Bred by Mrs. R. Gee	Ch. Nonmartre Marco Polo	Ch. Beritas Holly of Eldonwood
Tranchant Christabelle Owned by Mr. and Mrs M. Jennings Bred by Mrs. G. Edge	Ch. Montmartre Marco Polo	Tranchant Bridesmaid of Helmview
Wybun Sea Shell Owned by Mr. C. Walley Bred by Mr. C. Walley	Ch. Beritas Bonaparte	Myrtlebury Jantzen
Beritas Ronlyn Rockafella Owned by Mrs. R. Gee Bred by Mr. and Mrs. A. J. Kidd	Ch. Beritas Bosun	Ch. Ronlyn Miss Irresistible
Bidabo Chinawhite Owned by Mr. and Mrs. A. L. Watson Bred by Mr and Mrs A. L. Watson	Ch. Piccoli Peacock's Pride	Bidabo Frenches Musical Girl
Meliora Make Believe Owned by Mrs. B. Ward Bred by Mrs. B. Ward	Lochranza Small Talk	Meliora Constance
Pandella Pickled Tink Owned by Mr. and Mrs. W. Dickinson Bred by Mr. and Mrs W. Dickinson	Ch. Beritas Bosun	Pandella Pickled Pepper

208

	Sire	Dam
Rothydd Beritas Bliss Owned by Mrs. D. W. Kidd Bred by Mrs. Francombe	Ch. Beritas Bosun	Ronita Lochranza Bonita
Black Nonsense of Idadoun Owned by Mrs. L. M. Howarth Bred by Mrs. J. Lawrence	Ch. Black Shadow of Idadoun	Tophill Persiad Delight
Tranchant Statesman Owned by Mrs. G. Edge Bred by Mrs. G. Edge	Beritas Beware	Tranchant Bridesmaid of Helmview
Nairda Spring Rhapsody Owned by Mrs. P. Harwood Bred by Mrs. A. J. Curtis	Ch. Bidabo Lemon Pip	Silverstorm Black Babette
Frenrise Prince Zardin Owned by Misses B. Williamson and K. McCarthy	Ch. Beritas Bonaparte	Ch. Frenrise Princess Dalzelle
Ronlyn Miss Irrella Owned by Mr. and Mrs. A. J. Kidd Bred by Mr. and Mrs. A. J. Kidd	Ch. Beritas Bosun	Ronlyn Miss Irresistible
Florontie Black Tricel Owned by Mr. J. Outterside Bred by Mr. J. Outterside	Tricorne of Montfleuri	Ch. Florontie Black Tulle of Montfleuri
Beritas Buccaneer Owned by Mrs. M. Clarke Bred by Mrs. L. Austin	Ch. Montmartre Marco Polo	Beritas Cover Girl

	Sire	Dam
Montmartre Maton Owned by Mrs. E. Conn Bred by Mrs. C. Walley	Ch. Montmartre Marco Polo	Ch. Wybun Sea Shell
Risette Master Marcus Owned by Miss S. J. Williamson Bred by Miss S. J. Williamson	Ch. Tranchant Montmartre Best Man	Ch. Risette Frenrise Caramella
Belstar Blue Witch of Walditch Owned by Mrs. Gundry Bred by Mrs. Wallis	Montmartre Mark Twain	Belstar Boadicea
Beritas Suella Owned by Mrs. R. Gee Bred by Mrs R. Gee	Ch. Beritas Bonaparte	Beritas Babaloo
Blue Angel of Montfleuri Owned by Mr. and Mrs. P. Howard Price Bred by Mrs. A. Dowding	Ch. Fury of Montfleuri	Quivala Meryl of Montfleuri
Katrina from Conersk Owned by Miss K. W. Rees Bred by C. Peel	Gay Charmer of Ardian	Pelsinora Romance
Meliora Make Believe Owned by Mrs. B. Ward Bred by Mrs. B. Ward	Lochranza Small Talk	Meliora Constance
Pandella Pickled Tink Owned by Mr. and Mrs. W. Dickinson Bred by Mr. and Mrs W. Dickinson	Ch. Beritas Bosun	Pandella Pickled Pepper

	Sire	Dam
Rothydd Beritas Bliss Owned by Mrs. D. W. Kidd Bred by Mrs. Francombe	Ch. Beritas Bosun	Ronita Lochranza Bonita
Black Nonsense of Idadoun Owned by Mrs. L. M. Howarth Bred by Mrs. J. Lawrence	Ch. Black Shadow of Idadoun	Tophill Persiad Delight
Tranchant Statesman Owned by Mrs. G. Edge Bred by Mrs. G. Edge	Beritas Beware	Tranchant Bridesmaid of Helmview
Nairda Spring Rhapsody Owned by Mrs. P. Harwood Bred by Mrs. A. J. Curtis	Ch. Bidabo Lemon Pip	Silverstorm Black Babette
Frenrise Prince Zardin Owned by Misses B. Williamson and K. McCarthy	Ch. Beritas Bonaparte	Ch. Frenrise Princess Dalzelle
Ronlyn Miss Irrella Owned by Mr. and Mrs. A. J. Kidd Bred by Mr. and Mrs. A. J. Kidd	Ch. Beritas Bosun	Ronlyn Miss Irresistible
Stanlyn Cleopatra Owned by P. L. Rose Bred by Mrs. E. Humberstone	Stanlyn Lucky Dream	Stanlyn White Cloud
Wybun Carrie Anne Owned by Mr. C. Walley Bred by Mr. C. Walley	Ch. Montmartre Marco Polo	Ch. Wybun Sea Shell

	Sire	Dam
Montmartre Marstella Owned by Mrs. E. Conn Bred by Mrs. M. R. Sweeting	Ch. Montmartre Michel-Andre	Barace Dame Hannan
Camilla of Jolda Owned by Mr. and Mrs. J. A. MacDougall Bred by Mr. and Mrs. J. A. MacDougall	Cuckoo of Jolda	Jolda Claudia of Longnor
Aesthete Avalanche Owned by Mr. and Mrs. H. Heron Bred by Mrs. J. Heron	Aesthete Pablo	Lochranza Amelia
Dominique From Conersk Owned by Miss K. W. Rees Bred by Miss K. W. Rees	Ch. Beritas Bonaparte	Ch. Katrina from Conersk
Lochranza Hell For Leather Owned by Misses J. MacMillan and J. Coull Bred by Misses J. MacMillan and J. Coull	Lochranza Piero	Lochranza Kristina
Mickey Finn of Montfleuri Owned by Mrs. N. Howard Price Bred by Mrs. B. Kuhler	Ch. Tarka of Montfleuri	Ch. Kewbar Sweet Talk
Minarets Court Jester Mrs. M. Harwood Bred by Mrs. B. E. Haley	Minarets Merry Jester	Joanville Wynburgh White Mink
Bennetsmead Enchantress of Pandella Owned by Mr. and Mrs. W. Dickinson and Mrs. P. Gore Rees Bred by Mrs. P. Gore Rees	Ch. Playboy of Longnor	Bennetsmead Black Opal

	Sire	Dam
Clover of Burdiesel Owned by Miss C. Seidler Bred by Miss C. Seidler	Ch. Tophill Marco of Peroma	Ch. Black Tulip of Burdiesel
Texet Gaiety Girl Owned by Mrs. Alice Hatton Bred by Mr. R. Hubbard	Perarrk Warrior	Pararrk Intrique
Tophill Temptress of Idadoun Owned by Mrs. L. M. Howarth Bred by Mrs. V. Bayis	Ch. Tophill Marco of Peroma	Cavcot Bequinette Odile
Bidabo Cloverwhite Owned by Mr. and Mrs. A. L. Watson Bred by Mr. and Mrs. A. L. Watson	Frenches Kings Rhapsody	Ch. Bidabo Lilywhite
Tranchant Belle Sarah Owned by Mrs. G. Edge Bred by Mrs. G. Edge	Ch. Beritas Bosun	Tranchant Bridesmaid of Helmview
Cartford Bragwells Moon Magic Owned by Mrs. D. M. McNutt Bred by Miss P. Jarrett	Cartford Moon Rocket	Delightful of Cartford
Jolda Cinderella Owned by Mr. and Mrs. MacDougall Bred by Mr. and Mrs. MacDougall	Cuckoo of Jolda	Jolda Claudia of Longnor
Minarets Martinette Owned by Mrs. M. Harwood Bred by Mrs. M. Harwood	Pandella Paddywhack	Minarets Martine

	Sire	Dam
Frenches Golden Breese Owned by Mrs. R. E. Price-Jones Bred by Mrs. R. E. Price-Jones	Frenches Black Demon	Frenches Golden Lilly
Wynburgh Black Shadow Owned by Mrs. M. Machin Bred by Mrs. M. Machin	Lizzlan Satacko	Wynburgh Black Tricolette
Konelga Cinderella Owned by Mr. and Mrs. K. Bullock Bred by Mr. and Mrs. K. Bullock	Ch. Beritas Ronlyn Rockafella	Ch. Beritas Bellisima
Tranchant Philismar Pablo Owned by Mrs. G. Edge Bred by Mrs. M. S. Donaghy	Ch. Tranchant Montmartre Best Man	Philesmar Madam Pompadour
Aspen Arabella Owned by Mrs. Mackenzie Bred by Mrs. Mackenzie Spencer	Ch. Lochranza Hell for Leather	Aspen Con Amor
Florontie Black Odette Owned by Mr. J. Outterside Bred by Mr. J. Outterside	Florontie Black Brigand	Florontie Black Organza
Bidabo Lemon Pip Owned by Mr. and Mrs. A. L. Watson Bred by Mr. and Mrs. A. L. Watson	Ch. Bidabo Bitta Crumpet	Ch. Bidabo Bitta Lemon
Frederick of Rencroft Owned by Mr. E. Wheeler Bred by Mr. E. Wheeler	Alistair of Eldonwood	Ronlyn Cassandra of Rencroft

	Sire	Dam
Justin Black of Pequette Owned by Miss M. Willis Bred by Mr. and Mrs. Adams	Pacos of Montfleuri	Only Me of Pequette
Othello of Cartford Owned by Mrs. D. M. McNutt Bred by Mrs. D. M. McNutt	Ch. Betstans Tarquin	Cartford Ronlyn's Clarinda
Token of Montfleuri Owned by Mr. P. Howard Price Bred by Mrs. M. Turnbill	Attenclures Benedick of Montfleuri	Pride of Montfleuri
Bidabo Broken Date Owned by Mr. and Mrs. A. L. Watson Bred by Mrs. A. L. Watson	Frenches Above Suspicion	Ch. Bidabo Burnt Almond
Black Tulip of Burdiesel Owned by Miss C. Seidler Bred by Mrs B. Simpson.	Tomboy of Burdiesel	Magnolia of Sendora
Deodar Morzetta Owned by Mrs. R. Borthwick Bred by Mrs. R. Borthwick	Ch. Deodar Little White Rebel	Mexicalli Maid
Florontie Black Tulle of Montfleuri Owned by Mr. J. Outterside Bred by Mrs I. Hogg	Ch. Baroque of Montfleuri	Serita of Surreydown
Montravia Anna Marie Owned by Mrs. G. P. Gibbs Bred by Mrs. G. P. Gibbs	Noel of Eldonwood	Montravia Marcilla of Montfleuri

	Sire	Dam
Rarma's Gaytime Girl Owned by Mr. and Mrs. P. Tuckley Bred by Mr. and Mrs. P. Tuckley	Rarma's Earl of Charnwood	Princess Jenette
Susan of Longnor Owned by Mrs. E. F. Worrall Bred by Mrs. E. F. Worrall	Spencer of Longnor	Clara of Longnor
Bidabo Bath Bun Owned by Mr. and Mrs. A. L. Watson Bred by Mr. and Mrs. A. L. Watson	Ch. Bidabo Lemon Pip	Ch. Bidabo Burnt Almond
Bidabo Lemon Peel Owned by Mr. and Mrs. A. L. Watson Bred by Mrs. A. L. Watson	Ch. Bidabo Bath Bun	Ch. Bidabo Bitta Lemon
Frenrise Prince Zaroe of Risette Owned by Mrs. D. E. Williamson Bred by Miss B. Williamson	Ch. Montmartre Marco Polo	Frenrise's Princess Fazala of Chelmont
Montmartre Michel-Andre Owned by Mrs. E. Conn Bred by Mrs E. Conn	Ch. Montmartre Bartat By Jingo	Montmartre Maryce
Perrark Beritas Brigand Owned by Mrs. P. E. Hubbard Bred by Mrs. R. Gee	Ch. Beritas Bonaparte	Beritas Broadway Star
Piccoli Peacock's Pride Owned by Mrs. M. Worth Bred by S. Wooton	Piccoli Beau Brummel	Piccoli Donalyn Dorinda

	Sire	Dam
Silverstorm Black Beppo Owned by Mrs. M. J. Curtis Bred by Mrs. M. Curtis	Sibon Skylark	Silverstorm Black Bridget
Meliora Kimona of Iniskelltr Owned by Mrs. B. Ward Bred by Mrs. G. Edge	Ch. Montmartre Marco Polo	Thalia of Iniskhelltr
Montfleuri Ursual of Burdiesel Owned by Mr. and Mrs. P. Howard Price Bred by Mrs. Sendall	Bearskin of Montfleuri	Jasmine of Sendora
Montmartre Beritas Belle of the Ball Owned by Mrs. E. Conn Bred by Mrs. R. Gee	Ch. Montmartre Bartat By Jingo	Ch. Beritas Holly of Eldonwood
Risette Frenrise Caramella Owned by Miss S. J. Williamson Bred by Miss B. Williamson	Ch. Montmartre Marco Polo	Frenrise's Princess Fazala of Chelmont
Sherion Showgirl of Longnor Owned by Mrs. S. M. Wootton Bred by Mrs. E. F. Worrall	Ch. Beritas Bonaparte	Ch. Philippa of Longnor
Springett Fine Fashion Owned by Miss M. Willis Bred Misses I & L. Mycock	Ch. Springett Rupert of Montfleuri	Jantar Black Bettina
Beritas Bosun Owned by Mrs. R. Gee Bred by Mrs. R. Gee	Ch. Montmartre Marco Polo	Ch. Beritas Holly of Eldonwood

	Sire	Dam
Black Shadow of Idadoun Owned by Mrs. L. M. Howarth Bred by Mrs. L. M. Howarth	Ch. Bidabo Bath Bun	Toots of Idadoun
Helmview Groomsman Owned by Mrs. M. Clarke Bred by Mrs. M. Clarke and Mr. P. Howard Price	Ch. Tranchant Montmartre Best Man	Helmview Muffin of Montfleuri
Patrick Casey of Montfleuri Owned by Mr and Mrs P. Howard Price Bred by Mr. and Mrs. Howard Price	Tricorne of Montfleuri	Ch. Rioletta of Montfleuri
Show Boy of Longnor Owned by Mrs. E. F. Worrall Bred by Mrs. E. F. Worrall	Ch. Beritas Bonaparte	Ch. Philippa of Longnor
Sylaps The Most in Black Owned by Misses M. Willis and A. Love Bred by Miss A. Love	Ch. Montravia The Trojan	Springett Montravia Vanessa
Tophill Marco of Peroma Owned by Mrs. B. Strawson Bred by Mrs. O. Perez	Ch. Tophill Orsino	Montravia Marquita of Peroma
Frenrise Princess Dalzelle Owned by Miss B. Williamson Bred by Miss B. Williamson	Ch. Montmartre Marco Polo	Frenrise's Princess Fazala of Chelmont

	Sire	Dam
Risette Princess Felicia Owned by Miss S. J. Williamson Bred by Mrs. D. E. Williamson	Ch. Montmartre Marco Polo	Frenrise's Princess Fazala of Chelmont
Silcresta Sequin Silver Owned by Mrs. M. Gower Bred by Mrs. Gander	Silcresta Silver Smoke	Silcresta Charmalot Starlight
Tranchant Annabelle Owned by Mrs G. Edge Bred by Mrs. G. Edge	Ch. Montmartre Marco Polo	Tranchant Bridesmaid of Helmview
Darrendel Don Orlando Owned by Mrs. M. Taylor Bred by Mrs. M. Taylor	Ch. Tranchant Montmartre Best Man	Beritas Bernadette
Fury of Montfleuri Owned by Mr. and Mrs. P. Howard Price Bred by Mr. and Mrs. P. Howard Price and Mrs. A. Dowding	Ch. Patrick Casey of Montfleuri	Vilmarie Beautiful Dreamer of Montfleuri
Nairda Elegance Owned by Mrs. P. Harwood Bred by Mrs P. Harwood	Montravia Sorrento	Nairda Brown Beauty
Perarrk Beritas Brigand Owned by Mrs. P. E. Hubbard Bred by Mrs. R. Gee	Ch. Beritas Bonaparte	Beritas Broadway Star

	Sire	Dam
Playboy of Longnor Owned by Mrs. E. F. Worrall Bred by Mrs. E. F. Worrall	Ch. Show Boy of Longnor	Ch. Susan of Longnor
Tarka of Montfleuri Owned by Mr and Mrs. P. Howard Price Bred by Mr. and Mrs. P. Howard Price	Ch. Patrick Casey of Montfleuri	Ch. Montfleuri Sarah of Longnor
Tophill Tobacco Owned by Mrs. B. Strawson Bred by Mrs. B. Strawson	Ch. Tophill Orsino	Tophill Jenny Wren
Tophill White Lord of Montfleuri Owned by Mr. and Mrs. P. Howard Price Bred by Mrs. B. Strawson	Tophill Shadow	Idajacks Silver Seal
Beritas Bellissima Owned by Mrs. O. Bullock Bred by Mrs. R. Gee	Beritas Texet Tycoon	Black Rose of Eldonwood
Bidabo Lilywhite Owned by Mr. and Mrs. A. L. Watson Bred by Mr. and Mrs. A. L. Watson	Ch. Piccoli Peacock's Pride	Bidabo Frenches Musical Girl
Kewbar Sweet Talk Owned by Mrs. B. R. Kuhler Bred by Mrs. C. Rayner	Betstans Rocket	Tar Queen of Cralpath
Lochranza Desdemona Owned by Misses Macmillan and Coull	Lochranza Piero	Lochranza Ramona

	Sire	Dam
Lucy Doone of Montfleuri Owned by Mr. and Mrs. P. Howard Price Bred by Mr. and Mrs. P. Howard Price	Tomboy of Burdiesel	Ch. Beritas Holly of Eldonwood
Montmartre Beritas Nadine Owned by Mrs. E. Conn Bred by Mrs. R. Gee	Ch. Montmartre Marco Polo	Ch. Beritas Holly of Eldonwood
Tranchant Christabelle Owned by Mr. and Mrs. M. Jennings Bred by Mrs. G. Edge	Ch. Montmartre Marco Polo	Tranchant Bridesmaid of Helmview
Wybun Sea Shell Owned by C. Walley Bred by C. Walley	Ch. Beritas Bonaparte	Myrtlebury Jantzen
Beritas Ronlyn Rockafella Owned by Mrs. R. Gee Bred by Mr. and Mrs. A. J. Kidd	Ch. Beritas Bosun	Ch. Ronlyn Miss Irresistible
Bidabo Chinawhite Owned by Mr. and Mrs. A. L. Watson Bred by Mr. and Mrs. A. L. Watson	Ch. Piccoli Peacock's Pride	Bidabo Frenches Musical Girl
Florontie Black Tricel Owned by Mr. J. Outterside Bred by Mr. J. Outterside	Tricorne of Montfleuri	Ch. Florontie Black Tulle of Montfleuri
Beritas Buccaneer Owned by Mrs. M. Clarke Bred by Mrs. L. Austin	Ch. Montmartre Marco Polo	Beritas Cover Girl

	Sire	Dam
Montmartre Maton Owned by Mrs. E. Conn Bred by Mrs. C. Walley	Ch. Montmartre Marco Polo	Ch. Wybun Sea Shell
Risette Master Marcus Owned by Miss S. J. Williamson Bred by Miss S. J. Williamson	Ch. Tranchant Montmartre Best Man	Ch. Risette Frenrise Caramella
Belstar Blue Witch of Walditch Owned by Mrs. Gundry Bred by Mrs. A. Wallis	Montmartre Mark Twain	Belstar Boadicea
Beritas Suella Owned by Mrs. R. Gee Bred by Mrs. R. Gee	Ch. Beritas Bonaparte	Beritas Babaloo
Blue Angel of Montfleuri Owned by Mr. and Mrs. P. Howard Price Bred by Mrs. A. Dowding	Ch. Fury of Montfleuri	Quivala Meryl of Montfleuri
Katrina from Conersk Owned by Miss K. W. Rees Bred by Mrs. C. Peel	Gay Charmer of Ardian	Pelsinora Romance
Meliora Make Believe Owned by Mrs. B. Ward Bred by Mrs. B. Ward	Lochranza Small Talk	Meliora Constance
Pandella Pickled Tink Owned by Mr. and Mrs. W. Dickinson Bred by Mr. and Mrs. W. Dickinson	Ch. Beritas Bosun	Pandella Pickled Pepper

	Sire	Dam
Rothydd Beritas Bliss Owned by Mrs. D. W. Kidd Bred by Mrs. Francombe	Ch. Beritas Bosun	Ronita Lochranza Bonita
Black Nonsense of Idahoun Owned by Mrs. L. M. Howarth Bred by Mrs. J. Lawrence	Ch. Black Shadow of Idadoun	Tophill Persian Delight
Tranchant Statesman Owned by Mrs. G. Edge Bred by Mrs. G. Edge	Beritas Beware	Tranchant Bridesmaid of Helmview
Nairda Spring Rhapsody Owned by Mrs. P. Harwood Bred by Mrs. A. J. Curtis	Ch. Bidabo Lemon Pip	Silver storm Black Babette
Frenrise Prince Zardin Owned by Misses B. Williamson and K. McCarthy Bred by Miss B. Williamson	Ch. Beritas Bonaparte	Ch. Frenrise Princess Dalzelle
Ronlyn Miss Irrella Owned by Mr. and Mrs. A. J. Kidd Bred by Mr. and Mrs. A. J. Kidd	Ch. Beritas Bosun	Ronlyn Miss Irresistible
Stanlyn Cleopatra Owned by Mrs. P. L. Rose Bred by Mrs. E. Humberstone	Stanlyn Lucky Dream	Stanlyn White Cloud

	Sire	Dam
Wybun Carrie Anne Owned by C. Walley Bred by C. Walley	Ch. Montmartre Marco Polo	Ch. Wybun Sea Shell
Montmartre Marstella Owned by Mrs. E. Conn Bred by Mrs. M. R. Sweeting	Ch. Montmartre Michel-Andre	Barace Dame Hannan
Camilla of Jolda Owned by Mr. and Mrs. J. A. MacDougall Bred by Mr. and Mrs. J. A. MacDougall	Cuckoo of Jolda	Jolda Claudia of Longnor
Aesthete Avalance Owned by Mr. and Mrs. H. Heron Bred by Mrs. J. Jeron	Aesthete Pablo	Lochranza Amelia
Dominique from Conersk Owned by Miss K. W. Rees Bred by Miss K. W. Rees	Ch. Beritas Bonaparte	Ch. Katrina from Conersk
Lochranza Hell for Leather Owned by Misses J. Macmillan and J. Coull Bred by Misses J. Macmillan and J. Coull	Lochranza Piero	Lochranza Kristina
Mickey Finn of Montfleuri Owned by Mrs. N. Howard Price Bred by Mrs. B. Kuhler	Ch. Tarka of Montfleuri	Ch. Kewbar Sweet Talk
Minarets Court Jester Owned by Mrs. M. Harwood Bred by Mrs. B. E. Haley	Minarets Merry Jester	Joanville Wynburgh White Mink

	Sire	Dam
Bennetsmead Enchantress of Pandella Owned by Mr. and Mrs. W. Dickinson and Mrs. P. Gore Rees Bred by Mrs. P. Gore Rees	Ch. Playboy of Longnor	Bennetsmead Black Opan
Clover of Burdiesel Owned by Miss C. Seidler Bred by Miss C. Seidler	Ch. Tophill Marco of Peroma	Ch. Black Tulip of Burdiesel
Textet Gaiety Girl Owned by Mrs. Alice Hatton Bred by Mr. R. Hubbard	Perarrk Warrior	Pararrk Intrique
Tophill Temptress of Idadoun Owned by Mrs. L. M. Howarth Bred by Mrs V. Bayis	Ch. Tophill Marco of Peroma	Cavcot Bequinette Odile
Aspen Alika Owned by Mrs. Mackenzie Spencer Bred by Mrs. Mackenzie Spencer	Aspen Argos	Aspen Aliza
Aspen Arabella Owned by Mrs. Mackenzie Spencer Bred by Mrs. Mackenzie Spencer	Ch. Lochranza Hell for Leather	Aspen Conamor
Bidabo Clover White Owned by Mr. and Mrs. Watson Bred by Mr. and Mrs. Watson	Frenches King's Rhapsody	Bidabo Lilywhite

	Sire	Dam
Cartford Bragwells Moon Magic Owned by Miss P. Jarrett Bred by Miss P. Jarrett	Cartford Moon Rocket	Delightful of Cartford
Lochranza Hell's Fire Owned by Mrs. Macmillan and Mrs. Gillespie Bred by Mrs. Macmillan and Mrs. Gillespie	Lochranza Hell for Leather	Lochranza Desdemona
Jolda Cinderella Owned by Mrs MacDougall Bred by Mrs. MacDougall	Cuckoo of Jolda	Jolda Claudia
Konelga Cinderella Owned by Mr. Bullock Bred by Mr. Bullock	Beritas Ronlyn Rockafella.	Beritas Bellisima
Lorahpats Ronata of Romar Owned by Mrs. Yates Bred by Mrs. Boulton	Roderique of Roman	Roxanne of Roman
Michandy Beritas Barbarian Owned by Mr. Kitchener Bred by Mrs. Hubbard	Beritas Bugle Boy	Perarak Miss Sheba
Minarets Martinette Owned by Mrs. Harwood Bred by Mrs. Harwood	Pandella Paddy Whack	Minarets Martine
Montmartre Superlad Owned by Mrs. Conn Bred by Mrs. Sweeting	Ch. Montmartre Maton	Teckle Topknot

	Sire	Dam
Nairda Carmoquist Lottie Louise Owned by Mrs. P. Harwood Bred by Miss M. Espley	Ch. Mickey Finn of Montfleuri	Carmoquist Cranberry Sauce
Roundtable Brandy Sniff of Frenches (American Champion) Owned by Mrs Price Jones Bred by Mr. T. Gesullo	Roundtable Cognac (American Champion)	Roundtable Cookie
Sancere Dark 'N' Dainty Owned by Mrs. P. L. Gee Bred by Mrs. P. L. Gee	Ch. Black Nonsense of Idadoun	Aesthete Dark Fashion
Tiopepi Puckshill Amber-Night-Life Owned by Mrs. Coxall Bred by Mrs. Dobson	Puckshill Ambersunrock	Puckshill Amersunquest
Tophill Topgrade of Idadoun Owned by Mrs. L. M. Howarth Bred by Mrs. B. Strawson	Ch. Black Nonsense of Idadoun	Tophill Trinka
Pearrk Purdie Owned by Mrs. E. S. Hubbard Bred by Mrs. E. S. Hubbard	Playboy of Longnor	Perarrk Miss Sheba
Tranchant Belle Sarah Owned by Mrs. G. Edge Bred by Mrs. G. Edge	Ch. Beritas Bosun	Tranchant Bridesmaid of Helmview

	Sire	Dam
Tranchant Philesmar Pablo Owned by Mrs. G. Edge Bred by Mrs. M. Donaghy	Ch. Tranchant Montmartre Best Man	Philesmar Madame Pompadour
Valetta Tranchant Man Appeal Owned by Miss U. M. Dunn Bred by Mrs. Gray	Ch. Tranchant Statesman	Tranchant Cleopatra
Vasahope Court Vogue of Minarets Owned by Mrs. M. Harwood Bred by Mrs. E. H. Jenkins	Minarets Court Jester	Vasahope Myrtlebury Maria Maid
Wharfholm Lizzlan White Bride Owned by Mrs B. S. Holmes Bred by D. Lane	Berengreave Bambi	Lizzlan Berengreave Bernadine
Wynburgh Black Shadow Owned by Mrs. M. Machin Bred by Mrs. M. Machin	Lizzlan Satacko	Wynburgh Black Tricolette
Jason of Montfleuri Owned by Miss Stott Bred by Mr. and Mrs. Heron	Aesthete Pablo	Aesthete Shady Lady of Montfleuri
Tragapanz Seychelle Owned by Mrs. H. Ridley Bred by Miss A. Flatt	Lighterman of Kelgram	Montmartre Monetta
Jacksville Alycidon of Kasado Owned by Mr. and Mrs. Dixon Bred by Mrs. V. Rivkin	Ch. Tranchant Philismar Pablo	Bareza My Sweetie Pie

	Sire	*Dam*
Jaytor Mista Softee Owned by Miss J. M. Coram Bred by Miss J. M. Coram	Drumaids Freebooter of Jaytor	Jaytor Patrioona Meri Elsa
Vorton Slick Chic of Jolanta Owned by Miss J. Hargreaves Bred by Mr. and Mrs. Jennings	Texet Tennessee	Vorton Mona Lisa
Conersk Marianna Owned by Miss K. W. Rees Bred by Miss K. W. Rees	Perarrk Monolito	Delilah From Conersk
Black Delinquent of Idadoun Owned by Mrs. L. M. Howarth Bred by Mrs. L. M. Howarth	Ch. Dominique from Conersk	Black Amusement of Idadoun
Aesthete Hell's Bells Owned by Mr. J. Currie Bred by Mr. and Mrs. Heron	Aesthete Pablo	Aesthete Hellfire
Foreman of Tranchant Owned by Mrs. G. Edge Bred by Mrs. Jennings	Ch. Tranchant Philesmar Pablo	Ch. Vorton Tranchant Christabelle
Beritas Bo-Jo of Wyburn Owned by Mr. C. Walley and Mrs R. Gee Bred by Mrs. R. Gee	Ch. Beritas Bonaparte	Beritas Bula
Bennetsmead Exquisite Elf Owned by Mr. and Mrs. Briggs Bred by Mrs. Gore-Rees and Dickenson	Pandella Paddy Whack	Bennetsmead Black Opal

	Sire	Dam

Vernlil Angela from Conersk
Owned by Mrs. Coxall
Bred by Miss K. Rees

Ch. Beritas Bonaparte   Ch. Katrina from Conersk

Gosmore Beritas Talked About
Owned by Mrs. Gee
Bred by Mrs. D. Kidd

Ch. Beritas Ronlyn Rockafella   Ch. Rothydd Beritas Bliss

Trespetite Wicked Wings of Vernlil
Owned by Miss H. Weinert
Bred by Mrs. Bentley

Ch. Trespetite Jansteen   Trespetite Dream Girl
Black Wings

Gillian of Montfleuri
Owned by Mrs. Howard Price
Bred by Mrs. Howard Price

Ch. Mickey Finn of Montfleuri   Fiona of Montfleuri

1975

Jaytor Mista Softee (D. White. Born 19.9.69)
Owned by Miss J. Coram
Bred by Miss J. Coram

Drumaids Freebooter of Jaytor   Jaytor Patrioona Meri
    Elsa

Jason of Montfleuri (D. Black. Born 25.5.71)
Owned by Mr. and Mrs. Heron
Bred by Mr. and Mrs. Heron

Aesthete Pablo   Aesthete Shady Lady of
    Montfleuri

Gillian of Montfleuri (B. Black. Born 16.9.72)
Owned by Mr. and Mrs. P. Howard-Price
Bred by Mr. and Mrs. P. Howard-Price

Ch. Mickey Finn of Montfleuri   Fiona of Montfleuri

	Sire	Dam
Foreman of Tranchant (D. Black. Born 19.12.72) Owned by Mrs. Edge, Bred by Mrs. Jennings	Ch. Tranchant Philesmar Pablo	Ch. Vorton Tranchant Christabelle
Vorton Slick Chick of Jolanta (B. Black. Born 16.12.72) Owned by Mrs. J. Porter, Bred by Mrs. Jennings	Textet Tennessee	Vorton Mona Lisa
Vernlil Angela from Conersk (B. Black. Born 5.10.69) Owned by Mrs. C. Coxall, Bred by Miss K. Rees	Ch. Beritas Bonaparte	Ch. Katrina from Conersk
Jacksville Alycidon of Kasado (D. Black. Born 7.7.72) Owned by Mr. and Mrs. Dixon, Bred by Mrs. V. Rivkin	Ch. Tranchant Philesmar Pablo	Bareza My Sweetie Pie
Bennetsmead Exquisite Elf (B. Black. Born 12.11.71) Owned by Miss Briggs, Bred by Mrs. P. Gore Rees	Pandella Paddywhack	Bennetsmead Black Opal
Black Delinquent of Idadoun (B. Black. Born 28.4.73) Owned by Mrs. M. Howarth, Bred by Mrs. M. Howarth	Ch. Dominique from Conersk	Black Amusement of Idadoun

	Sire	Dam
Conersk Marianne (B. Black. Born 22.12.71) Owned by Miss K. Rees Bred by Miss K. Rees	Parrark Monolito	Delilah from Conersk
Aesthete Hells Bells (B. Black. Born 9.3.72) Owned by Mr. J. Currie Bred by Mr. and Mrs. Heron	Aesthete Pablo	Aesthetet Hell Fire
Walditch Larling Silver Overture (D. Silver. Born 10.3.69) Owned by Mrs. B. Gundy Bred by Mrs. E. Gillam	Ch. Walditch Silver Cavalier	Larling Losvale Silver Louise
Aesthete What the Hell of Tiopepi (D. Black. Born 11.12.72) Owned by Mrs. C. Coxall Bred by Mr. and Mrs. Heron	Ch. Lochranza Hell for Leather	Aesthete Quality Fair of Tiopepi
Florontie Black Onyx of Navarre (D. Black. Born 25.7.71) Owned by Miss E. Holmes Bred by Mr. J. Outterside	Ch. Beritas Ronlyn Rockafella	Florontie Black Organza
Florontie Black Orchid (B. Black. Born 18.5.72) Owned by Mr. J. Outterside Bred by Mr. J. Outterside	Beritas Brando	Florontie Black Organza

	Sire	Dam
Florontie Blue Peter (D. Black. Born 27.5.71) Owned by Mr. J. Outterside Bred by Mr. J. Outterside	Ch. Beritas Ronlyn Rockafella	Florontie Black Organza
Renwin Wot a Boy (D. Black. Born 8.3.73) Owned by Mrs. R. Smith Bred by Mrs. R. Smith	Ch. Tranchant Philesmar Pablo	Winnicot Boedicia of Renwin
Gosmore Beritas Talked About (D. Black. Born 21.4.70) Owned by Mrs. R. Gee Bred by Mrs. D. Kidd	Ch. Beritas Ronlyn Rockafella	Rothydd Beritas Bliss
Tragapanz Seychelle (B. Black. Born 14.3.71) Owned by Mrs. H. Ridley Bred by Miss A. Flatt	Lighterman of Kelgram	Montmartre Monetta
Beritas Bo-Jo of Wybun (D. Black. Born 13.8.72) Owned by Mrs. R. Gee and Mr. C. Whalley Bred by Mrs. R. Gee	Ch. Beritas Bonaparte	Beritas Bula
Beritas Banacheke (D. Black. Born 25.4.73) Owned by Mrs. R. Gee Bred by Mrs. R. Gee	Beritas Bonaparte	Beritas Bula
Chiltern Magic Moments (B. Black. Born 17.10.70) Owned by Mrs. Heron and Miss Sprake Bred by Mr. and Mrs. Heron	Ch. Beritas Bonaparte	Gt. Westwood Montmarte Dainty Maid

	Sire	Dam
Blackbird of Bennetsmead from Garbosa (B. Black. Born 24.4.73) Owned by Miss L. Briggs Bred by Mrs. Gore-Rees and Mr. and Mrs. Dickinson	Ch. Beritas Bonaparte	Pandella Bennetsmead Minx
Eyecote Enigma (B. Black. Born 24.5.73) Owned by Mrs. A. Holland-Bignell Bred by Mrs. A. Holland-Bignell	Ch. Lochranza Hell for Leather	Vorton Mona Lisa
Vorton Fabrique (B. Black. Born 7.11.73) Owned by Mr. and Mrs. M. Jennings Bred by Mr. and Mrs. M. Jennings	Vorton Special Agent	Vorton Mona Lisa
1976–77		
Minarets Dancing Jester (D. White. Born 24.7.73) Owned by Mrs. M. Harwood Bred by Mrs. M. Harwood	Int. Ch. Roundtable Brandy Sniff of Frenches	Ch. Vasahope Court Vogue of Minarets
Bronshaws Miranda (B. Black. Born 23.8.72) Owned by Mrs. R. Taylor Bred by Mrs. R. Taylor	Ch. Lochranza Hell for Leather	Russallan Baccarat of Bronshaws
Rogersmead Tolly Cobbald (B. Black. Born 24.10.72) Owned by Mrs. H. Reynolds Bred by Mrs. H. Reynolds	Tranchant Helmsman	Stanshaw Woodlark of Rogersmead

	Sire	Dam
Tranchant Mantoman (D. Black. Born 25.8.74) Owned by Mrs. G. Edge Bred by Mrs. G. Edge	Ch. Foreman of Tranchant	Ch. Tranchant Belle Sarah
Am. Ch. Tiopepi Amber Tanya (B. Apricot. Born 3.3.74) Owned by Mrs. C. Coxall Bred by Mrs. C. Coxall	Eng & Aust Ch. Tiopepi Puckshill Amber Nightfall	Tiopepi Amber Tizz Wizz
Tiopepi Typhoon (D. Black. Born 9.12.73) Owned by Mrs. C. Coxall Bred by Mrs. C. Coxall	Eng & Aust Ch. Lochranza Hells Fire	Ch. Vernlil Angela from Conersk
Mirandel Cleo (B. White. Born 1.6.71) Owned by Mrs. P. Rose Bred by Mrs. P. Rose	Ch. Aesthete Avalanche	Ch. Stanlyn Cleopatra
Florontie Black Oberon (D. Black. Born 9.5.70) Owned by Mr. J. Outterside Bred by Mr. J. Outterside	Penthouse Trouper	Florontie Black Organza
Rangabee Black Lace (B. Black. Born 28.10.71) Owned by Mrs. M. Smith Bred by Mrs. M. Smith	Ch. Black Nonsense of Idadoun	Rangabee Polly Flinders
Merit Monogram (D. Black. Born 28.10.73) Owned by Mrs. J. Merritt Bred by Mrs. J. Merritt	Merit Mancub	Merit Pararrk Sorona

217

	Sire	Dam
Virnelle Stylistic (B. Black. Born 24.8.75) Owned by Miss H. Weinert Bred by Miss H. Weinert	Ch. Mickey Finn of Montfleur	Ch. Vernlil Angela from Conersk
Maralph Debutante (B. Black. Born 1.9.73) Owned by Miss Sillito and Mrs. Milner Bred by Mrs. M. Milner	Ch. Tranchant Philesmar Pablo	Maralph Royale Madonna
Tiopepi Tornado (D. Black. Born 20.12.75) Owned by Mrs. C. Coxall Bred by Mrs. C. Coxall	Eng & Am Ch. Tiopepi Typhoon	Aesthete Quality Fair of Tiopepi
Vorton Chantal (B. Black. Born 4.10.74) Owned by Mrs. H. Jennings Bred by Mrs. H. Jennings	Ch. Beritas Banacheke	Vorton Mona Lisa
Vasahope Lucille (B. White. Born 22.10.74) Owned by Mrs. R. Price-Jones	Int Ch. Roundtable Brandy Sniff of Frenches	Vasahope Myrtlebury Maria Maid
Carmoquist Campbell of Persan (D. Black. Born 25.10.74) Owned by Mr. and Mrs. Perry Bred by Miss M. Espley	Ch. Jason of Montfleuri	Ch. Nairda Carmoquist Lottie Louise
Trueman of Tranchant (D. Black. Born 11.9.74) Owned by Mrs. M. Howarth and Mr. D. Gilles Bred by Mrs. M. Milner	Ch. Foreman of Tranchant	Tranchant Darabelle

1978

	Sire	Dam
Minarets the Maverick (D. Black. Born 9.9.75) Owned by Mrs. M. Harwood Bred by Mrs. M. Harwood	Ch. Minartes Court Jester	Ch. Minarets Martinette
Black Fascination of Idadoun (B. Black. Born 16.9.75) Owned by Mrs. M. Howarth Bred by Miss J. Slee	Ch. Black Nonsense of Idadoun	Jolda Claudella
Son of My Father of Navaree (D. Black. Born 3.8.75) Owned by Miss E. Holmes Bred by Miss E. Holmes	Ch. Florontie Black Onyx of Navarre	Ch. Wharfholm Lizzlan White Bride
Orlaine Fonteyn (B. Black. Born 14.11.75) Owned by Mrs. V. Witham Bred by Mrs. V. Witham	Longnor Oh Johnny	Vorton Sweet Charity
Brenard Tudor Classic (B. Black. Born 28.5.76) Owned by Miss Holmes and Mrs. Anderson Bred by Mr .and Mrs. Anderson	Longnor Oh Johnny	Martinella Gemini
Jolanta By Jove (D. Black. Born 7.10.76) Owned by Mrs. J. Porter Bred by Mrs. J. Porter	Ch. Tranchant Philesmar Pablo	Ch. Vorton Slick Chick of Jolanta

	Sire	Dam
Jolda Cincinnatus (D. Black. Born 17.11.75) Owned by Mr. and Mrs. J. A. MacDougall Bred by Mr. and Mrs. J. A. MacDougall	Jolda Chough	Ch. Jolda Cinderella
Jolda Joceline (B. Black. Born 5.10.76) Owned by Mr. and Mrs. J. A. MacDougall Bred by Mr. and Mrs. J. A. MacDougall	Jolda Chough	Jolda Cincilla
Knotroms Mistress Matilda (B. Black. Born 22.12.73) Owned by Mrs. O. Morton and Miss V. Ackers Bred by Miss J. Royle	Mr. Maclusky of Knotrom	Knotroms Lucy Locket
Lochranza Ailsa (B. Black. Born 20.5.77) Owned by Mrs. H. Lunnun-Turner Bred by Macmillan and Gillespie	Lochranza Benedict	Lochranza Priscilla
Merit Michelle (B. Black. Born 10.8.76) Owned by Mrs. J. Merritt Bred by Mrs. J. Merritt	Ch. Merit Monogram	Minarets Mariette of Merit
Mista Mutiny of Knotrom (D. Black. Born 2.10.76) Owned by Mrs. V. Ackers Bred by Miss J. Royle	Mista Per-C-Veer	Vorton Perdita

	Sire	Dam
Montravia Laviness Snow Blanche (B. White. Born 23.7.76) Owned by Mrs. P. Gibbs Bred by Mrs. P. G. Charter	Miradel Courtney of Montravia	Shoremel Snow Blanche
Pasire Ebony Emperor of Florontie (D. Black. Born 14.11.75) Owned by Mr. J. Outterside and English and Hammel Bred by Mrs. A. English	Ch. Florontie Black Tricel	Pasire Mountbernard Belrose
Tiopepi Take by Storm (D. Black. Born 15.5.75) Owned by Mrs. Grice Bred by Mrs. C. Coxall	Eng & Am Ch. Tiopepi Typhoon	Aesthete Quality Fair of Tiopepi

APPENDIX C

TOY CHAMPIONS, 1966 to 1978

(From 1975 I have included the champions' sex (*D* or *B*), colour and date of birth—S.W.)

	Sire	Dam
Barsbrae Branslake Harriet Owned by Mrs. F. M. Barlow Bred by Mrs. Beach	Ch. Wemrose Newsboy	Branslake Wee Mite
Bbormot Hot-Ice Owned by Mr. Wm. Robb Bred by Mr. Wm. Robb	Ch. Bbormot Willing of Catalpa	Bbormot Teazie Weazie
Bbormot Montmartre Marchon Owned by Mr. Wm. Robb bred by Mrs. P. Buffaline	Ch. Montmartre Master Singer	Belle of Greatcoats
Bbormot Willing of Catalpa Owned by Mr. Wm. Robb Bred by Mrs. S. Thoy	Armagnac Joint Surprise of Catalpa	Jane of Catalpa
Capilon Dreamboat of Dovevalley Owned by Mr. J. Walkden Bred by Miss D. Williamson	Montmartre Spellbinder of Dovevalley	Snow White of Dovevalley
Capilon Graywood Pedlar's Chick Owned by Mr. J. Walkden Bred by G. Gray	Ch. Capilon Toy Pedlar	Graywood Pom Pom

Sire	*Dam*
Deregis Silver Diamante Owned by Mr. R. Masters Bred by Mr. R. Masters Capilon Silver Chime	Ch. Deregis Silver Diana
Deodar Showdown Owned by Mrs. Borthwick Bred by Mrs. Borthwick Ch. Pixiecroft Capilon Toytime	Deodar Showtime
Great Westwood Chaman Be Damned Owned by Mrs. S. Barratt Bred by Mrs. M. Sharpe Chaman Benito	Chaman Lindy Lou
Great Westwood Montmartre Marcia Owned by M. S. Barratt Bred by Mrs. D. Lane Montmartre Million Dollars	Parkro Poppet
Great Westwood Montmartre Maria Owned by Mrs. S. Barratt Bred by Mrs. M. Clarke Montmartre Ring Master	Helmview Mona Lisa
Great Westwood Montmartre Marla Owned by Mrs. S. Barratt Bred by Mrs. M. Clarke Montmartre Ring Master	Helmview Mona Lisa
Linora Mr. Somebody Owned by Mrs. A. Hills Bred by Mrs. A. Hills Ch. Sudbrook Sunday Special	Lindy Lou of Poughan
Merrymorn Morning Sun Owned by Mrs. L. E. Ellis Bred by Mrs. L. E. Ellis Merrymorn Golden Apollo	Merrymorn Golden Angel

223

	Sire	Dam
Montmatre Beritas Miss Dior Owned by Mr. W. Robb Bred by Mrs. R. Gee	Ch. Montmartre Ringmaster	Beritas Bizzilli
Montmatre Carmen Miranda Owned by Mrs. E. Conn Bred by Mrs. E. Conn	Montmartre Minute Man	Montmartre Madame Pompadour
Oakington Puckshill Sunblush Owned by Mrs. C. Perry Bred by Mrs. M. Dobson	Puckshill Amber Suncrush	Puckshill Amber Sunsprite
Panavon Little Snow-Berry Owned by Miss J. Pantlin Bred by Miss J. Pantlin	Panavon Little Perry	Panavon Princess Serenity
Si Bon Suco Suco Owned by Mrs. M. Binder Bred by Mrs. M. Binder	Braebeck Achievement	Si Bon Ooh La La of Jallahali
Silcresta Silver Sprat Owned by Mr. D. Wickens Bred by Mrs. L. Emery	Trespetite Gilsland Silver Toni	Silcresta Lucroy's Silver Charm
Strawcot Mona Lisa Owned by Mrs. I. Riley Bred by Mrs. Davies	Strawcot the Toff	Duchess of Shard
Sudbrook Very Best of Moonland Owned by Mrs. S. Cox Bred by Miss Lomax	Ch. Sudbrook Sunday Best	Spring Song of Moonland

	Sire	Dam
Tiopepi Firegoldie Owned by Mrs. C. Perry Bred by Mrs. C. East	Tiopepi Firecracker	Yaverland Lady in Gold
Tophill Tuttlebees Timothy Owned by Mrs. B. Strawson Bred by Mr. N. Butcher	Midula Beat Time	Tuttlebees Winter Morn
Toy Topic from Conersk Owned by Miss K. Rees Bred by Miss K. Rees	Braebeck Achievement	Princess Tina from Conersk
Trespetite Gorgeous Owned by Mrs. J. Phillips Bentley Bred by Mrs. J. Phillips Bentley	Braechievement Achievement	Trespetite Kinky
Tuttlebees Winter Nite Owned by Mr. N. Butcher Bred by Mr. N. Butcher	Ch. Tuttlebees Winter Starturn	Tuttlebees Winterstar
Tuttlebees Morningstar Owned by Mrs. Ridehalgh Bred by Mr. N. Butcher	Ch. Sudbrook Sunday Special	Drumaids Morning Light
Barsbrae Branslake Darty Owned by Mrs. M. Barlow Bred by Mrs. S. J. Beech	Barsbrae Mr. Solo	Branslake Gypsy
Bbormot Bit O'Bother Owned by Mr. W. Robb Bred by Mrs. S. Borthwick	Ch. Sudbrook Sunday Xpress	Atir Deodar Toy Show

	Sire	Dam
Bbormot Hot Ice Owned by Mr. W. Robb Bred by Mr. W. Robb	Ch. Bbormot Willing of Catalpa	Bbormot Teazie Weazie
Sibon Seabird Owned by Mrs. M. Binder Bred by Mrs. M. Binder	Ch. Sibon Circus Dancer	Sibon Tiny Sherry
Tiopepe Fire Goldie Owned by Mrs. C. Coxall Bred by Miss C. East	Tiopepe Fire Cracker	Yaverland Lady in Gold
Aesthete Hot Secret Owned by Mrs. J. Heron Bred by Mrs. M. Brown	Lochranza Titbits	Tolbarend Golliwog
Great Westwood Montmartre Marcia Owned by Mrs. S. Barratt Bred by Mr. S. Lane	Montmartre Million Dollar	Lizzlan Parkro Poppet
Sudbrook Very Best of Moonland Owned by Mrs. S. Cox Bred by Miss H. Lomas	Ch. Sudbrook Sunday Best	Spring Song of Moonland
Tea Tray of Petitbrun Owned by Mrs. M. V. Kempson Bred by Mr. and Mrs. A. L. Watson	Ch. Petitbrun Screwball	Snippet of Petitbrun
Capilon Penthouse Pipparoo Owned by Mr. J. Walkden Bred by Mrs. J. Harris-Morgan	Penthouse Capilon Toy Tattoo	Penthouse Sweet Talk

	Sire	Dam
Deregis Silver Carnival Owned by Mr. R. E. Masters Bred by Mr. R. E. Masters	Deregris Silver Simon	Deregris Toy Crown
Linora Penny Stamp Owned by Mrs. A. Hills Bred by Mrs. A. Hills	Ch. Wemrose Newsboy	Strawcot Penny Black
Merrypoo See Mee Owned by Mrs. F. Nicholson Bred by Mrs. J. Webber	Merrypoo This Is It	Jo Jo Rum Punch
Sheepcote Leander Lancelot Owned by Mrs. I. Turner Bred by Mr. and Mrs T. Eves-Thorpe	Leander Lover Boy	Leander Melanie
Tallassee Snuff Box Owned by Mrs. S. M. Squire Bred by Mrs S. M. Squire	Ch. Montmartre Madcap	Sharnette Bubaloo of Tallassee
Tresilva Sirius Owned by Mrs. J. Ransom Bred by Mrs. Johnson	Fremar Silver Thimble of Sandoval	Sandoval Tresilva Starshine
Tuttlebees Donalyn Discussion Owned by Mr. N. E. Butcher Bred by Mrs. I. Ridehalgh	Montmartre Million Dollar	Tuttlebees Right Royal
Apposyte Thursday Owned by Mrs. M. Welch Bred by Mrs. M. Welch	Montravia Capilon Circus Boy	Apposyte Sole Mio

227

	Sire	Dam
Chanticleer Ardynas Brandy Nan Owned by Mr. and Mrs. S. Moseley Bred by Mr. and Mrs. G. Wright	Ardynas Tophill Benedictine	Ardynas Trespetite Delilah
Contecrest Crescot Contessa Owned by Miss V. Fergusson Bred by Mrs. Goodchild	Ch. Tuttlebees Winter Starturn	Snowy Ice of Harlow
Great Westwood Aesthete Secret Treasure Owned by Mrs. S. Barratt Bred by Mrs. J. Heron	Montmartre Mozart	Ch. Aesthete Hot Secret
Linora New Penny Owned by Mrs. A. Hills Bred by Mrs. A. Hills	Ch. Wemrose Newsboy	Strawcot Penny Black
Maribrens Miss Delightful Owned by Miss B. Hudson and Mrs. M. Pickup Bred by Miss B. Hudson	Starwood Summer Bounty	Carousel Charcoal Candy
Petitbrun Tea Rose Owned by Mr. and Mrs. A. L. Watson Bred by Mr. and Mrs. A. L. Watson	Ch. Petitbrun Screwball	Ch. Petitbrun Tea Leaf
Phantasie Tiopepe Golden Peach Owned by Mrs. M. Lynch Bred by Mrs. C. Coxall	Ch. Tiopepe Fire Goldie	D'Orcote Tiopepe Red Belle
Bbormot Barrow Boy Owned by Mr. W. Robb Bred by Mr. W. Robb	Ch. Bbormot Montmartre Marchon	Bbormot Anna Marie

	Sire	Dam
Braeval Bit of Glamour Owned by Mrs. P. Austin Smith Bred by Mrs. P. Austin Smith	Braeval Starturn of Topaz	Braeval Clarabelle of Topaz
Branslake Becky Owned by Mrs. S. J. Beech Bred by Mrs. S. J. Beech	Branslake Diabolo	Branslake Wee Topsy
Devadale Petitbrun Tea Chest Owned by Mrs. M. V. Kempson Bred by Mr. and Mrs. A. L. Watson	Ch. Teapot of Petitbrun	Ch. Petitbrun Little Plum
Frenches Montmartre Silver Wings Owned by Mrs. R. E. Price Jones Bred by Mrs. Edge	Montmartre Merrylegs	Tranchant Dolly Silver
Karronbre Black Mystic Owned by Mr. R. Dutton Bred by Mr. R. Dutton	Ch. Montmartre Madcap	Karronbre Black Magic
Sunspark of Knotrom Owned by Mrs. O. Morton Bred by Mrs. O. Morton	Suntan of Knotrom	Victoria of Knotrom
Sudbrook Sunday Billing Owned by Mrs. S. Cox Bred by Mrs. S. Cox	Sudbrook Sunday Surprise	Sudbrook Tophill Sundancer
Tiopepe Gee Tee Owned by Mrs. C. Coxall Bred by Mrs. M. Butler	Jagerwald Mighty Mandarin	Honeyrose of Yenaled

	Sire	Dam
Tresilva Successor Owned by Mrs. J. Ransom Bred by Mrs. J. Ransom	Tresilva Success	Tresilva Starlight
Winnicott Prince Rupert Owned by Miss J. Edmonds Bred by Miss J. Edmonds	Winnicott Son of David	Winnicott Simonette
Wemrose Krismick Newsgirl Owned by Miss K. R. Machon Bred by Mrs. C. Hultman	Ch. Wemrose Newsboy	Krisnick Chorus Girl
Bbormot Bartat Beano Owned by Mrs. S. Barratt Bred by Mrs. A. Tomkin	Bartat Busy Bee	Bartat Barrasca
Bbormot Para Handy Owned by Mr. W. Robb Bred by Mr. W. Robb	Bbormot Peter Pan	Bbormot Anna-Marie
Fremar Fernando Owned by Mrs. M. Pride Bred by Mrs. M. Pride	Ch. Ardynas Gay Scandal	Fremar Better Sweet
Great Westwood Sibon Circus Jester Owned by Mrs. S. Barratt Bred by Mrs. Binder	Ch. Sibon Circus Dancer	Sibon Jalahalli Halo
Pixiecroft Plutocrat Owned by Mrs. E. Davis Bred by Miss E. Turier	Pixiecroft President	LittleRaven of Weewonder

	Sire	Dam
Silcresta Silver Spruce Owned by Mr. D. Wickens Bred by Mrs. J. Reeves	Fremar Silver Thimble of Sandoval	Joycrest Silver Peach
St. Aubrey Phantasie Flatterer Owned by Messrs. N. Aubrey-Jones and R. W. Taylor Bred by Mrs. M. Lynch	Ch. Fremar Fernando	Phantasie Frederica
Aesthete Branslake Black Magic Owned by Mrs. S. Barratt Bred by Mrs. S. J. Beech	Branslake Diabolo	Sandale Storson Brown Magic
Aesthete Miss Demena Owned by Mr. and Mrs. Heron Bred by Mr. and Mrs. Heron	Aesthete Mr. Scrooge	Aesthete Little Mo
Attocyl Major Barbara Owned by Mrs. M. E. Kaye Bred by Mrs. M. E. Kaye	Attocyl The Little General	Attocyl Fortune
Barsbrae Fleur Owned by Mrs. F. M. Barlow Bred by Mrs. F. M. Barlow	Ch. Barsbrae Branslake Darty	Ch. Barsbrae Branslake Harriet
Krisnick Clever Girl Owned by Mrs. C. Hultman Bred by Mrs. C. Hultman	Ch. Wemrose Newsboy	Krisnick Chorus Girl

	Sire	Dam
	Branslake Diabolo	Sandale Storson Brown Magic
	Ardynas Crackerjack	Ardynas Trespetite Delilah
	Ch. Montmartre Mastersinger	Belle of Greatcoats
	Armagnac Joint Surprise of Catalpa	Jane of Catalpa
	Capilon Toy Vagabond	Capilon Toy Gigolette
	Capilon Toy Piper	Julie of Tonryl
	Lochleal Phoebus	Pleiades Halfpenny
	Lochranza Small Talk	Lochranza Mantilla

Aesthete Branslake Black Magic
Owned by Mrs. S. Barratt
Bred by Mrs. S. J. Beech

Ardynas Gay Whisper
Owned by Mr. and Mrs. G. Wright
Bred by Mr. and Mrs. G. Wright

Bbormot Montmartre Marchon
Owned by Mr. W. Robb
Bred by Mrs. P. Buffaline

Bbormot Willing of Catalpa
Owned by Mr. W. Robb
Bred by Mrs. S. Thoy

Capilon Toy Toddy
Owned by Mr. J. Walkden
Bred by Mr. J. Walkden

Pixicroft Capilon Toytime
Owned by Mrs. E. Davis
Bred by Mrs. B. Lawton

Pleiades Wonderviews Smart Boy
Owned by Lady Tennell
Bred by Mr. A. C. Shorten

Lochranza Suzuki
Owned by Misses J. Macmillan and J. Coull
Bred by Misses J. Macmillan and J. Coull

	Sire	Dam
Montmartre Minouche Owned by Mrs. E. Conn Bred by Mrs. E. Conn	Montmartre Ringmaster	Montmartre Madame Pompadour
Montravia Tuttlebees Winter Moonglow Owned by Mrs. P. Gibbs Bred by Mrs. M. Butcher	Ch. Sudbrook Sunday Suit	Drumaids Dancing Light
Sibon Circus Dancer Owned by Mrs. M. Binder Bred by Mrs. M. Binder	Montravia Capilon Circus Boy	Sibon Ooh La La of Jalahalli
Sudbrook Sunday Excursion Owned by Mrs. S. Cox Bred by Mrs. S. Cox	Ch. Sudbrook Sunday Special	Sudbrook Sunshine
Pleiades Primavera Owned by Lady Rennell Bred by Miss P. Green	Pleiades Le Dauphin Pagageno	Pleiades Mignonette
Sharnette Lesave Her Glory Owned by Mr. T. Bailey Bred by Mrs. A. Aston	Lesave Black Soloist	Jewel Song of Lesave
Sibon Suco Suco Owned by Mrs. M. Binder Bred by Mrs. M. Binder	Braebeck Achievement	Sibon Ooh La La of Jallahalli
Starwood Summer Gem Owned by Mr. T. Harwood Bred by Mr. T. Harwood	Starwood Summer Bounty	Sh. Starwood Summer Surprise

233

	Sire	Dam
Teacup of Petitbrun Owned by Mr. and Mrs. A. L. Watson Bred by Mr. and Mrs. A. L. Watson	Ch. Petitbrun Screwball	Snippet of Petitbrun
Viewpark Jennifer Owned by Mr. A. MacLaren Bred by Mrs. J. Lurie	Glendoune Pepe	Charme of Whitecraigs
Viewpark Lolita Owned by Mr. A. MacLaren Bred by Mr. A. MacLaren	Ch. Janmark Gay Spark	Ch. Viewpark Jennifer
Capilon Dreamboat of Dovevalley Owned by Mr. J. Walkden Bred by Miss D. Williamson	Montmartre Spellbinder of Dovevalley	Snow White of Dovevalley
Merrymorn Morning Sun Owned by Mrs. L. E. Ellis Bred by Mrs. L. E. Ellis	Merrymorn Golden Apollo	Merrymorn Golden Angel
Panavon Little Snowberry Owned by Miss I. Pantlin Bred by Miss I. Pantlin	Panavon Little Perry	Panavon Princess Serenity
Silcresta Silver Sprat Owned by Mr. D. Wickens Bred by Mrs. L. Emery	Trespetite Gilsland Silver Toni	Silcresta Lucroy's Silver Charm
Tuttlebees Winter Nite Owned by Mr. N. E. Butcher Bred by Mr. N. E. Butcher	Ch. Tuttlebees Winter Starturn	Tuttlebees Winterstar

	Sire	Dam
Barsbrae Branslake Harriet Owned by Mrs. M. Barlow Bred by Mrs. S. J. Beech	Ch. Wemrose Newsboy	Branslake Wee Mite
Great Westwood Bbormot Blossom Owned by Mrs. S. Barratt Bred by Mr. W. Robb	Ch. Sudbrook Sunday Xpress	Sudbrook Sunnyday
Great Westwood Montmartre Marla Owned by Mrs. S. Barratt Bred by Mrs. M. Clarke	Montmartre Ringmaster	Helmview Mona Lisa
Montmartre Beritas Miss Dior Owned by Mr. W. Robb Bred by Mrs. R. Gee	Montmartre Ringmaster	Beritas Bizilizi
Montmartre Carmen Miranda Owned by Mrs. E. Conn Bred by Mrs. E. Conn	Montmartre Minuteman	Montmartre Madame Pompadour
Oakington Puckshill Ambersunblush Owned by Mrs. C. Coxall Bred by Mrs. Myles Dobson	Puckshill Ambersuncrush	Puckshill Ambersunsprite
Tuttlebees Morning Star Owned by Mrs. I. Ridehalgh Bred by Mr. N. E. Butcher	Ch. Sudbrook Sunday Special	Drumaids Dancing Light
Ardynas Gay Scandal Owned by Mr. and Mrs. G. Wright Bred by Mrs. D. E. Kemp	Ch. Ardynas Gay Whisper	Parisian Sue

	Sire	Dam
Capilon Graywood Pedlars Chick Owned by Mr. J. Walkden Bred by Mrs. G. Gray	Ch. Capilon Toy Pedlar	Graywood Pompom
Deodar Showdown Owned by Mrs. R. Borthwick Bred by Mrs. R. Borthwick	Ch. Pixiecroft Capilon Toytime	Deodar Showtime
Linora Mr. Somebody Owned by Mrs. A Hills Bred by Mrs. A. Hills	Ch. Sudbrook Sunday Special	Lindy Lou of Pooghan
Montmartre Mintmaster Owned by Mrs. E. Conn Bred by Mrs. V. Penrose	Montmartre Minuteman	Montmartre My Beauty
Teapot of Petitbrun Owned by Mr. and Mrs. A. L. Watson Bred by Mrs. Riordan	Ch. Petitbrun Screwball	Lady Cinderella of Pressway
Tophill Tuttlebees Timothy Owned by Mrs. B. Strawson Bred by Mr. N. E. Butcher	Misula Beat Time	Tuttlebees Winter Morn
Toy Topic from Conersk Miss K. W. Rees Bred by Miss K. W. Rees	Braebeck Achievement	Princess Tina from Conersk
Deregis Silver Diamite Owned by Mr. R. E. Masters Bred by Mr. R. E. Masters	Capilon Silver Chime	Ch. Deregis Silver Diana

	Sire	Dam
Great Westwood Montmartre Maria Owned by Mrs. S. Barratt Bred by Mrs. M. Clarke	Montmartre Ringmaster	Helmview Mona Lisa
Lochranza Sugar 'n' Spice Owned by Miss Macmillan and Coull Bred by Miss Macmillan and Coull	Ch. Sudbrook Sunday Special	Lochranza Hot Diggotty
Sibon Circus Spangle Owned by Mrs. M. Binder Bred by Mrs. M. Binder	Montravia Capilon Circus Boy	Sibon Ooh La La of Jalahalli
Trespetite Gorgeous Owned by Mrs. J. Bentley Bred by Mrs. J. Bentley	Braebeck Achievement	Trespetite Kinky
Larling Warrenrise Wrinkle Owned by Mrs. E. Gillam Bred by Miss V. Warren-Wise	Branslake Diabolo	Warrenrise Puffin
Montravia Dream Time Owned by Mrs. P. Gibbs Bred by Mrs. P. Gibbs	Ch. Capilon Dreamboat of Dovevalley	Ch. Montravia Tuttlebees Winter Moonglow
Pixiecroft Lis; Owned by Mrs. D. Davis Bred by Mrs. D. Davis	Pixiecroft President	Pixiecroft Tiny Mite
Prudent of Knotrom Owned by Mrs. O. Morton Bred by Mrs. O. Morton	Suntan of Knotrom	Glorianna of Knotrom

	Sire	Dam
Aesthete Secret Question Owned by Mr. and Mrs. Heron Bred by Mr. and Mrs. Heron	Aesthete Dark Secret	Aesthete Question in Brown
Benidorm Daisy's Image of Great Westwood Owned by Mrs. G. Barratt Bred by Mrs. Austin	Branslake Diabolo	Mayday of Benidorm
Contecrest D'Orcote Saffron Owned by Miss V. Fergusson Bred by Mr. and Mrs. C. Hartley	D'Orcote Honey Dandy	D'Orcote Tiopepi Red Belle
Embercourt Step-in-Time Owned by Miss S. Sheard Bred by Mr. E. Turier	Pixiecroft President	Oldtimbers Trudi
Lochranza Fun 'in' Games Owned by Mrs. B. E. Bond Bred by Misses J. Macmillan and J. Coull	Silver Starlight of Longnor	Lochranza Nice 'n' Naughty
Maribrens Marty Owned by Miss B. Hudson and Mrs. W. Pickup	Maribrens Monty	Maribrens Victoria
Montmartre Master Spy Owned by Mrs. E. Conn Bred by Mrs. E. Conn	Montmartre Miniscule	Montmartre Carmen Mirand
Stonesby Black Saphire Owned by Mrs. B. M. Francks Bred by Mrs. M. Henery	Branslake Diabolo	Stonesbydale Rona

	Sire	Dam
Sudbrook Spring Sunday Owned by Mrs. H. Cox Bred by Miss Wright	Sudbrook Sunday Billing	Aesthete Weeping Willc
Tiopepi Golden Trinxie Owned by Mrs. C. L. Coxall Bred by Mrs. C. L. Coxall	Tiopepi Golden Flash	Tiopepi Golden Trinke
Warrenrise Dollybird Owned by Miss V. Warren-Wisc Bred by Miss V. Warren-Wise	Branslake Diabolo	Warrenrise Freckle
Warrenrise Maximilian Owned by Miss V. Warren-Wise Bred by Miss V. Warren-Wise	Branslake Diabolo	Warrenrise Puffin
Watwood Jackson of Rehsif Owned by Mrs. L. Fisher Bred by Mrs. M. Huckle	Rysenshyne Tiptoe Taffy	Watwood Rebecca
Risette Country Hostess Owned by Mrs. Williamson Bred by Mrs. Williamson	Ch. Trespetite Jansteen Black Wings	Risette Country Delight
Conersk Campari Owned by Miss K. Rees Bred by Miss K. Rees	Ch. Barsbrae Branslake Darty	Conersk Smallfry
Montravia Spring Flamenco Owned by Miss M. Gibbs Bred by Mrs. S. Chamberlaine	Montravia Spring Fanfare	Amberflake Montravia Spring Love

239

	Sire	Dam
Grayco Black Onyx of Stonesby Owned by Mrs. M. Francks Bred by Mrs. L. Howard	Trespetite Classic	Grayco Glamour
Rhosbridge Golden Corn of Bbormot Owned by Mr. W. Robb Bred by Miss A. Moody	Rhosbridge Golden Bobbin	Rhosbridge Golden Halo
Falbala Flirtinuity Owned by Mrs. P. J. McGarrity Bred by Mrs. P. J. McGarrity	Ch. Warrenrise Maximilian	Falbala Warrenrise Fliptacious
Springett Ere I Be Owned by Miss M. Willis Bred by Miss M. Willis	Leander Lawrance	Springett Ca Sera Sera
Aromaric Sundance Kid of Seabrook Owned by Mrs. I. Brough Bred by Mrs. Terry	Aromaric Gold Shot	Aromaric Sunny Girl
Panavon Little Snow Puff Owned by Miss I. Pantlin Bred by Miss I. Pantlin	Panavon Little White Picot	Panavon Little Snow Sharone
Fremar Velucia's Merriment Owned by Mrs. Pride Bred by Mrs. Barratt	Fremar Fernando	Warrenrise Hilarious
Busby of Silcresta Owned by Mr. D. Wickens Bred by Mr. F. Henderson	Eng. Am & Nordic Ch. Stortuuans Silver Figaro	Cavania Silver Desire

Great Westwood Halloween of Bendidorm Owned by Mrs. G. Barratt Bred by Mrs. Austin	Braslake Diabolo	Mayday of Benidorm
Helmview Candida Owned by Mrs. M. Clarke Bred by Mrs. M. Clarke	Helmview Charlie Boy	Helmview Hiedi
Ardynas Gay Goblin Owned by Mr. and Mrs. Wright Bred by Mr. and Mrs. Wright	Ardynas Sergei	Wanderwood Colleen
Warrenrise Liver Bird Owned by Miss Warren-Wise Bred by Miss Warren-Wise	Bartat Bonanza	Ch. Warrenrise Dollybird

1975

Busby of Silcresta (D. Silver. Born 12.11.73) Owned by Mr. D. Wickens Bred by Mr. F. Henderson	Eng. Am. & Nordic Ch. Stortuvans Silver Figaroa	Cavania Silver Desiree
Warrenwise Ladybird (B. Brown. Born 25.12.72) Owned by Miss Warren Wise Bred by Miss Warren Wise	Ch. Trespetite Jansteen Black Wings	Ch. Warrenwise Dollybird
Ardynas Gay Goblin (D. Black. Born 6.6.73) Owned by Mr. and Mrs. Wright Bred by Mr. and Mrs. Wright	Ardynas Sergei	Ardynas Whispered Words

241

Warrenwise Scatterbrain (B. Black. Born 30.5.72) Owned by Miss Warren Wise Bred by Miss Warren Wise	Branslake Diabolo	Warrenwise Puffin
Montmartre Marmion of Montflair (D. Brown. Born 31.1.74) Owned by Mr. W. M. Akers Bred by Mrs. Conn	Sunnitoun Black Barnard of Jansteen	Bronte Saga Rosamond of Montmartre
Sunnitoun Black Everard of Branslake (D. Black. Born 29.10.72) Owned by Mrs. Beech Bred by Mrs. Pugh	Ch. Montmartre Master Spy	Jansteen Ruth
Bartat Burnt Almond of Grayco (B. Brown. Born 29.10.72) Owned by Mrs. Howard Bred by Mrs. Tomkin	Trespetite Classic	Bartat Donalyn Desire
Snowstar Sarachi (B. Black. Born 11.2.73) Owned by Mr. and Mrs. Gregory Bred by Mr. and Mrs. Gregory	Snowstar Black Ice	Snowstar Black Wichita
Karronbre To Be or Not To Be (D. Black. Born 14.5.72) Owned by Mr. R. H. Dutton Bred by Mrs. M. M. Hughs	Karronbre Kommander	Karronbre Kismet

242

Falbala Flirtinuity (B. Black. Born 4.12.71) Owned by Mrs. McGarrity Bred by Mrs. McGarrity	Warrenwise Maximilian	Falbala Warrenwise
		Flirtacious
Sudbrook Sunday Gladrags (D. White. *Born 20.7.72)* Owned by Mrs. H. Cox Bred by Mrs. H. Cox	Sudbrook Spring Sunday	Sudbrook Happy Sunday
Clopton Tiger Bay (B. Brown. Born 25.2.74) Owned by Mrs. S. P. Jones Bred by Mrs. S. P. Jones	Sunnitoun Black Barnard of Jansteen	Clopton Devil Woman
Patida Chocolate Charmer (B. Brown. *Born 22.11.73)* Owned by Mrs. I. Birch and Miss E. Holmes Bred by Mrs. I. Birch	Chocolate Cracknel of Patida	Chocolate Charm of Patida
Capilon Back in Town At Lotsmoor (B. Black. *Born 1.9.73)* Owned by Mr. P. Young Bred by Mr. J. Walkden	Capilon Toy Gambler	Capilon Toy Folly
Knotrom's Golden Partidge (D. Apricot. *Born 2.10.72)* Owned by Mrs. Oliver Morton Bred by Mrs. Oliver Morton	Knotrom's Golden Pheasant	Greatcoats Della

Karronbre Cover Girl of Montmartre (B. Black. Born 9.2.74)
Owned by Mrs. E. Conn
Bred by Mr. R. Dutton

Ch. Montmartre Masterspy

Karronbre Che Sara Sara

Trespetite Classic (D. Black. Born 26.7.71)
Owned by Mrs. L. Howard
Bred by Mrs. J. Bentley

Ch. Trespetite Jansteen Black Wings

Trespetite Fancy

Langstrath Lorenzo of Merrypoo (D. Black. Born 3.1.75)
Owned by Mrs. F. Nicholson
Bred by Mrs. A. Murphy

Ch. Sunnitoun Black Everard of Branslake

Fantabulous of Warrenwise

Kivox Golden Nymph (B. Apricot. Born 8.7.73)
Owned by Miss I. Cox
Bred by Miss I. Cox

Kivox Rhosbridge Gold Harvester

Daphene Golden Mandy

Holyport Man Friday of Montmartre (D. Black. Born 9.4.74)
Owned by Mrs. E. Conn
Bred by Miss M. Dayer Smith

Sunnitoun Black Barnard of Jansteen

Holyport Capilon Toy Cantata

Branslake Bit'O'Black at Falbala (D. Black. Born 22.1.74)
Owned by Mrs. P. J. McGarrity
Bred by Mrs. J. Beech

Ch. Sunnitoun Black Everard of Branslake

Sandale Storson Brown Majic

Leander Lullababy (B. Black. Born 31.3.73) Owned by Miss D. Buck Bred by Mrs. W. Streatfield	Ch. Barsbarae Branslake Darty	Montravia Hot Summer
Bartat Boy'Oh'Boy (D. Black. Born 31.5.74) Owned by Mr. and Mrs. W. Harry Bred by Mrs. Tomkin	Grayco Gravy Gourmet	Bartat Bunny Hug
Romar Jodie at Malibu (B. Brown. Born 29.11.74) Owned by Miss and Mrs. Sillito Bred by Mrs. M. Boulton	Grayco Gravy Gourmet	Olbarr Burnt Amber of Romar
Persan Bistokid (D. Brown. Born 16.11.74) Owned by Mr. and Mrs. P. Perry Bred by Mr. and Mrs. P. Perry	Trespetite Superwings of Persan	Kaolic Fantasy Fleur
Nailditch Silver Cassius (D. Silver. Born 3.12.74) Owned by Mrs. B. Gundry Bred by Mrs. B. Gundry	Ch. Lochranza Fun 'N' Games Of Manapouri	Walditch Silver Festivity
Extra Special of Clopton at Cransville (B. Black. Born 23.7.75) Owned by Mrs. B. Morgan Bred by Mrs. L. Hayward	Ch. Montmartre Masterspy	Clopton Twice as Nice
Merit Marvellous (D. Black. Born 28.12.75) Owned by Mrs. J. Merritt Bred by Mrs. J. Merritt	Bareza Bonaparte	Merit Bareza Bardot

Tiopepi True Temptress (B. Apricot. Born 10.8.75)
Owned by Mrs. C. Coxall
Bred by Mrs. C. Coxall

Tiopepi Golden Genius

Tiopepi Amber Twinkie

Stonesby Obsidian (D. Black. Born 29.6.75)
Owned by Mrs. K. Francks
Bred by Mrs. M. Francks

Ch. Sunnitoun Black Everard of Branslake

Stonesby Black Opal

Tickertape of Petitbrun (D. White. Born 30.1.74)
Owned by Mr. and Mrs. L. Watson
Bred by Mr. and Mrs. L. Watson

Piccoli Pocket Money

Cigarette of Petitbrun

Seabrook Silk 'N' Honey (B. Apricot. Born 30.7.74)
Owned by Mrs. I. Brough
Bred by Mrs. I. Brough

Ch. Aromatic Sundance Kid Of Seabrook

Orange Flare of Tuttlebees and Seabrook

Aspen Arethusa (B. Black. Born 14.12.75)
Owned by Mrs. S. Mackenzie-Spencer
Bred by Mrs. S. Mackenzie-Spencer

Tuttlebees Rather Royal

Aspen Amazing Grace

Aesthete Secret Issue (D. Black. Born 10.2.76)
Owned by Mr. and Mrs. Heron
Bred by Mr. and Mrs. Heron

Aesthete Secret Edition

Aesthete Branslake Black Magic

Tudor Ebony Treasure of Kivox (B. Black. Born 17.6.74)
Owned by Mr. I. Cox
Bred by Mrs. I. Westcott

Kivox Capilon Toy Rebel

Sheba Baroness of Tudor

	Sire	Dam
Sumbuddy of Silcresta (D. Silver. Born 24.5.74) Owned by Mrs. D. Wickens Bred by Mrs. L. Emery	Int. Ch. Busby of Silcresta	Lucrays Silver Babe
Leander Spring Fever (D. Black. Born 5.4.74) Owned by Mrs. W. Streatfield Bred by Mrs. W. Streatfield	Ch. Leander Lawrence	Leander Spring 'N' Summer
Winnicott Honey Princess (B. White. Born 31.7.74) Owned by Miss J. Edmonds Bred by Miss J. Edmonds	Winniciott Beloved Prince	Winnciott Bronze Princess
1978		
Bareza Bonaparte (D. Black. Born 7.6.74) Owned by Mrs. S. Breeze Bred by Mrs. S. Breeze	Ch. Sunnitoun Black Everard of Branslake	Ch. Bareza by Gibby
Clopton Marron Glace of Kinwood (B. Brown. Born 8.5.76) Owned by Mrs. J. Wood Bred by Mrs. S. P. Jones	Ch. Montmartre Marmion of Montflair	Clopton Turkish Delight
Dourada Dashing of Roseala (D. Black. Born 31.10.74) Owned by Mr. and Mrs. Mott Bred by Mrs. D. A. Lilley	Ch. Leander Lawrence	Dourada My Dream

247

	Sire	Dam
Lotsmoor Honky Tonk (D. Brown. Born 2.6.77) Owned by Mr. P. Young Bred by Mr. P. Young	Grayco Talk About Lotsmoor	Ch. Capilon Back in Town at Lotsmoor
Merrymorn Hot Rod (D. Apricot. Born 17.2.75) Owned by Mrs. L. E. Ellis Bred by Mrs. L. E. Ellis	Knotroms Jaffatam of Merrymorn	Merrymorn Mai Gold
Ranjis C'Est La Vie (D. Black. Born 18.10.76) Owned by Mr. E. Helm Bred by Mr. E. Helm	Capilon Toy Gambler	Mahneldene Top Model
Rehsif Kingsley (D. Apricot. Born 15.6.75) Owned by Mrs. L. Fisher Bred by Mrs. L. Fisher	Emmrill Golden Cornet	Forever Amber of Rehsif
Ridingleaze Dainty Toes of Valette (B. White. Born 8.3.76) Owned by Miss U. M. Dunn Bred by Mrs. M. Irwin	Ch. Sudbrook Sunday Glad Rags	Ridingleaze Merry Twinkle Toes
Starwood Milday of Persan (B. Black. Born 4.4.76) Owned by Mr. and Mrs. Perry Bred by Mr. D. Barker	Ch. Capilon Graywood Pedlars Chick	Roxy Toy Frolic
Valencia Short 'N' Sweet (B. Brown. Born 25.4.75) Owned by Miss A. Hyland Bred by Miss A. Hyland	Ch. Maribens Marty	Vallencia Twiggy

APPENDIX D

SALIENT POINTS FROM THE FRENCH STANDARD, 1951

This Standard was proposed by the Comité d'Entente des Clubs du Caniche en France and has been approved by the Commission des Standards de la Société Centrale Canine de France and recognized in 1936 by the Fédération Cynologique Internationale, as being the *only* Official Standard on the Continent.

GENERAL APPEARANCE AND CLASSIFICATION

Classification : Useful.

The Poodle has the appearance of a very intelligent animal, always on the alert, and giving an impression of elegance and pride. He has a light dancing action and must never move smoothly or "all in one piece".

He is renowned for his fidelity and because of his aptitude for learning he is easily trained and consequently makes an agreeable companion.

HEAD: Distinguished and well carried. The length should be a little more than two-fifths of the height of the dog from the ground to the withers.

NOSE: Very defined and developed in straight line with muzzle —nostrils open. The nose must be black in blacks and whites, brown in browns.

MUZZLE: The top of the muzzle must be straight and about nine-tenths of the length of the skull. The upper and lower jaws must be parallel and must be solid and elegant but not pointed.

LIPS: Tight, dry, not thick, the upper coming over the lower lip. No lippiness. Blacks and whites should have black lips, and browns, brown lips.

JAWS: Normal, with strong teeth.

CHEEKS: Flat.

STOP: Slight.

SKULL: Well modelled, the width to be a little more than half the length of the head.

R

EYES: Very soft in expression. Placed level with the stop, flat and almond shaped. Black or dark brown in blacks and whites; they may be dark amber in browns.

EARS: Very long, falling flat against the cheeks, set low, must be broad and thick in substance. They must be covered with very curly hair. Very long.

NECK: Well proportioned, arched, with the head carried proudly and high. No loose skin allowed—length should be less than that of the head.

SHOULDERS: Shoulders well laid back, the shoulder-blade making an angle of 90 to 100 with the foreleg. Length of foreleg should be equal to that of the shoulder-blade.

FEET: Rather small, compact and oval in shape. Toes well arched, pads hard and thick. Toe-nails must be black in blacks— black or brown in browns. In whites they must be black.

BODY: General appearance of the Poodle is well proportioned, the length of the body being roughly the length of the foreleg to the withers.

LOINS: Strong and well muscled.

QUARTERS: Well rounded and not straight.

TAIL: Well set in angle to the quarters. Should be about one-third of the natural length in Curly Poodles and left full length in Corded Poodles. The tail must be carried at an oblique angle when in movement.

LEGS: Hind feet seen from the back must be parallel, well muscled hocks, well angulated.

COAT: The Poodle coat, corded or curly, must be black, white or brown. Browns must be deep in colour and even all over. No colours other than these are permitted in the ring.

PRESENTATION: The Poodle, whether corded or curly, must be shaved from the hocks to the ribs. No hair is allowed on the quarters. Feet shaved close, also the forelegs. The muzzle and the whole of the face to be shaved and between the eyes up to the stop. Hair is permitted on the hocks and bracelets of the forelegs. Moustaches are permitted for all sizes.

HAIR: The Curly Poodle must have a thick coat of fine texture, woolly, curly, springy. It must be dense and of a uniform length and well combed. The Corded Poodle must have an abundant coat, very woolly and hard, the cords being well defined and of even length. This must be at least 20 centimetres (8 inches).

SKIN: Supple with softness. For white Poodles the skin should be silver. The blacks and browns should have pigmentation in accordance with the colour of the coat.

HEIGHT: (1) The medium Poodle, 35 cms. to 45 cms. (14 inches to 17¾ inches). (2) Big Poodles, 45 cms. to 55 cms. (17¾ inches to 21¾ inches). (3) Miniature Poodles, up to 35 cms. (13¾ inches).

FAULTS: Snipy jaw. Ear leathers short or narrow.

Anatomical: Undershot jaw. A dog with overshot jaw cannot win a first prize. Yellow teeth caused by illness are not a fault, provided they are correctly placed. Badly placed, or missing teeth, are faults.

Of Type: Light eyes, or showing red. Nose lacking pigment. Nose speckled. Sparse coat. A few white hairs on the chest are tolerated. White hairs on feet are a bad fault and dogs with these cannot be placed. Tail carried over the back.

Unplaceable: All dogs with white patches. All coats that are not even in colour. Dew claws or traces of dew claws on the back legs. Monorchids, Cryptorchids and tailless dogs cannot be shown.

POODLES NOT PRESENTED IN THE STYLE LAID DOWN IN THE STANDARD are not allowed to be judged for prizes at any Show (even though they may have been admitted), but they are not disqualified from being used for breeding.

APPENDIX E

Poodle Clubs

British Toy Poodle Club
Eastern Counties Poodle Club
International Poodle Club
London & Home Counties Toy Poodle Club
Mercia Toy Poodle Association
Midland Counties Poodle Club
Miniature Poodle Club
Nothern Toy Poodle Club
Northern Ireland Poodle Club
Northumbria Poodle Club
North Western Poodle Club
Poodle Club
Poodle Club of Scotland
Poodle Club of Wales
South Western Poodle Club
Standard Poodle Club
Trent to Tweed Poodle Club

The names and addresses of secretaries can be obtained on application to the Kennel Club, 1–4 Clarges Street, London W1Y 8AB.

INDEX